Property Investment
and the Capital Markets

Property Investment and the Capital Markets

GERALD R. BROWN
Professor of Property, University of Auckland, New Zealand

E & FN SPON
An Imprint of Chapman & Hall
London · New York · Tokyo · Melbourne · Madras

Published by E & FN Spon, an imprint of Chapman & Hall, 2–6 Boundary Row, London SE1 8HN

Chapman & Hall, 2–6 Boundary Row, London SE1 8HN

Van Nostrand Reinhold Inc., 115 5th Avenue, New York NY10003, USA

Chapman & Hall Japan, Thomson Publishing Japan, Hirakawacho Nemoto Building, 7F, 1-7-11 Hirakawa-cho, Chiyoda-ku, Tokyo 102, Japan

Chapman & Hall Australia, Thomas Nelson Australia, 102 Dodds Street, South Melbourne, Victoria 3205, Australia

Chapman & Hall India, R. Seshadri, 32 Second Main Road, CIT East, Madras 600 035, India

First edition 1991
© 1991 Gerald R. Brown

Typeset in $10\frac{1}{2}/12\frac{1}{2}$pt Sabon by
KEYTEC, Bridport, Dorset

Printed in Great Britain by
St. Edmundsbury Press, Bury St. Edmunds, Suffolk

ISBN 0 419 15530 9   0 442 31346 2 (USA)

A catalogue record for this book is available from the British Library

Library of Congress Cataloging-in-Publication data
Brown, Gerald R. (Gerald Roderick), 1944–
  Property investment and the capital markets/Gerald R. Brown. – 1st ed.
    p. cm.
  Includes bibliographical references and index.
  ISBN 0–442–31346–2
    1. Real estate investment. 2. Real property–Finance. 3. Capital market. I. Title.
HD1382.5.B77 1991
332.63′24–dc20   91–13210
                                                                                CIP

Printed on permanent acid-free text paper, manufactured in accordance with the proposed ANSI/NISO Z 39.48–199X and ANSI Z 39.48–1984

Contents

Acknowledgements

Most of the material used in this book is based on the lectures I have given on the MBA and MSc courses in property investment held at the City University Business School and the Centre for Studies in Property Valuation and Management. I am indebted to both departments for giving me the opportunity to develop these ideas, and to the many students who have provided a useful sounding board.

I am grateful to Richard Ellis for the use of the data on which the original research for my PhD was based. I should also like to thank Colin Barber for providing the monthly total returns series used in Chapter 6 and for his permission to use this information. My thanks also go to Jones Lang Wooton for the use of their property index.

The performance analysis undertaken in Chapter 6 was based on data supplied by the Investment Property Databank. My thanks go to Rupert Nabarro and Jean Anderson of IPD for providing information on their monthly property index together with the property details used in the analysis.

I should also like to thank Madeleine Metcalfe of E. & F. N. Spon for providing guidance and encouragement during the time it took to complete the manuscript.

I have tried to be as accurate as possible in the presentation of the material and in the calculations and analyses. Any errors which remain are my own.

Finally, I wish to thank my wife Janet and my children Jacqueline and David for their patience and understanding during the long hours when it seemed that the end would never be in sight.

Gerald R. Brown

Preface

Most of the background work for this book is derived from my PhD research and was developed during my time with Richard Ellis. The approach I adopted was to undertake empirical research on a database of property derived from the portfolios under management at Richard Ellis. Other parts of the research have been based on publicly available information. The findings are however of a general nature and are not intended to be a reflection of the performance of any portfolio.

Some of the empirical findings are based on data which are now historic. I make no apologies for this. The database on which the original analyses were undertaken proved difficult and time-consuming to put together and would be difficult to update. Although the period over which the database was collected was short, it did have the virtue of having verified information and at the time was probably the best that could be achieved. It remains for others to extend this work to much larger databases.

It is inevitable that some of the ideas presented in this book are controversial as it is very much a personal view based on observation of the market. I have, however, tried to justify the approach with relevant evidence and an understanding of the underlying economics. To this extent it is believed the approach is valid and worthy of further research.

Introduction

Over the last few years there has been a significant shift towards the use of quantitative techniques in property analysis. The logic for this development is understandable and derives from the growing application of quantitative analysis in the capital markets and acceptance of the view that property is just part of a much wider collection of investment assets.

The change has been gradual but has gained momentum as the more progressive firms of chartered surveyors have embraced a wider range of property and financially related services. Although these changes are still in their infancy they could well lead in the future to the development of a range of property-based investment products which could significantly enhance the performance of traditional investment portfolios.

The shift in emphasis has manifested itself in the market-place through the growing importance of research departments in the larger firms of chartered surveyors and financial institutions together with the emergence of independent property information services. It is the desire to capitalize on information that has given rise to organizations which provide details on individual property transactions as well as market trends and performance measurement of property portfolios.

The need for careful and meaningful research is now recognized as a precondition for improved investment advice. Chartered surveying firms no longer destroy valuable data but recognize that it forms the basis for valuable empirical research. It is anticipated that this approach will grow and develop as financial institutions find it increasingly important to justify their decisions through good analysis.

Professional advisers can no longer hide behind the view that property is a long-term investment when restructuring decisions are being made over shorter time periods. As major investors in property, acting on behalf of shareholders, they are being placed under increasing scrutiny to justify their actions in terms of investment performance. This of course is very much a reflection of the view that investment is risky and that decisions must be taken in full knowledge of the risks incurred. Although there is greater awareness that there is risk in property investment, understanding of the subject is still in its infancy.

The principal questions which need to be asked are how should property be viewed in a mixed asset context and are the techniques currently being developed adequate to cope with complex investment decisions? This raises a number of issues relating to valuation, inflation hedging, asset allocation, market efficiency, investment strategy and performance measurement. This book attempts to look at these aspects within the economic and investment framework which has developed over the last thirty years.

It is also significant to note that in the United States there is now a growing body of research in these areas and finance academics are beginning to make a contribution to the development of new techniques. This type of research is beginning to have an influence on the way investors look at property and to question many traditional beliefs and attitudes.

Against these new developments must be viewed the natural reluctance of surveyors to become involved in quantitative techniques. Although this is understandable, investment surveyors will find that it will gradually be forced upon them by fund managers responsible for global asset allocation, whose background is not in property but who nevertheless require justification of investment decisions.

In addressing these issues this book attempts to bridge the gap between contemporary developments in modern finance and current property research, and to cover the technical aspects of investment which have proved to be important. The emphasis has been to place property in an economic context and to show how this approach has an impact on the way investments should be valued and analysed. Perhaps that the most significant advances in property research will come about only through adopting an approach which has a sound economic basis. In view of the growing body of research which is now developing it seems it is only the foolhardy who would pursue the view that property is totally different from all other investment assets and that it warrants the development of a separate theory.

Although data on property has been collected by firms of surveyors it is often in a form which is not amenable to analysis without considerable manipulation. Coupled with this is the problem of confidentiality which surrounds many figures relating to property valuations and transactions. Despite there being considerable interest in those matters which could result in a better understanding of the property market there remains a great reluctance to release data. The climate is changing however and it is likely that in time our understanding of the property market will significantly improve.

It must be borne in mind that the amount of information available for analysis is relatively sparse. For example the publication of regular property indexes based upon valid data has only been established since the late seventies. Index figures are now regularly published on an annual and quarterly basis for varying sample sizes intending to represent the market. Contrast this with the stock market where index figures are available back to the early part of the century on a daily basis. It is only recently that the market has recognised that monthly index figures would provide a valuable indicator of market movements.

In addressing the issues of property investment in an economic framework there is bound to be a reasonable amount of mathematics involved. The intention has been to keep the majority of this to appendices so that the reader can gain an understanding of the main concepts through the text and illustrations. Fortunately many of the ideas developed in modern finance are easy to grasp through simple examples which provide a conceptual framework for understanding the main principles. For those who find the subject matter difficult I can only recommend perseverance.

The investment market is becoming more sophisticated and property is an important part of that sophistication. The aim of this book is to provide an introduction to the techniques and empirical research which hopefully will form the basis for understanding property within a capital market framework.

1
Decision making under certainty and uncertainty

In a world of complete certainty we know in advance the outcome of each investment proposition and are able to make decisions in a rational manner by comparing returns with comparable investments. In reality, however, the world is uncertain and it is that uncertainty which makes the investment decision challenging.

This chapter examines the principles of decision making which should be followed in a world of certainty and extends this to a world of uncertainty. It is this approach which has dominated financial theory for the last thirty years and is the foundation on which the whole area of valuation and pricing is based. Although the principles involved are of a general nature they will, wherever possible, be applied to property to show their relevance.

1.1 The importance of present value

Property investment is concerned with acquiring real assets which are worth more than their cost. In developing a valid economic framework within which the decision process can take place it is necessary to understand the basics of valuation and the need for well-functioning markets.

Unlike stock market investments, property is not frequently traded in an open market and access to information is often limited. Although this may appear to be a problem it should be recognized that one of the rôles of the professional valuer is to fill the information gap by developing comprehensive knowledge of individual properties and transactions. This need for information has led to the emergence of independent property information services and assuming that the acquired knowledge is efficiently circulated to interested parties, there should be no need for a formal theory of valuation. The valuer should process relevant information concerning a property and arrive at a value which should be within a few per cent of the true value. In a well-functioning market we can take the market view as representing the true value. Whether this is the case or not is examined empirically in Appendix 2A to Chapter 2.

A formal theory of value is only necessary therefore to understand why a property is worth what it is. Only with an assessment of true economic value is it possible to tell whether a property is under- or over-priced. This is a matter for economics and an understanding of the way capital markets function and affect value. For example, a property may well be worth more to one person than to another purely because of the way the information content is viewed. These aspects will be examined in a later chapter.

Returning to the principal problem of choice it is essential to have an intuitive grasp of how investment decisions should be made and the criteria that should be used to aid that process. This can best be illustrated using a simple example.

Let us assume that an investor is interested in buying a small office building. A suitable proposal is found and, after having taken advice from a professional valuer, the investor is informed that because of a known increase in demand for offices the building will be worth £1 300 000 in twelve months' time. In order to proceed with the purchase the investor needs to know what to offer in order to induce the vendor to part with the property. In other words, what is the present value of the £1 300 000 which the property will be worth in twelve months' time?

The **present value rule** states that a pound today is worth more than a pound tomorrow. This is because it is possible to invest today's pound so that it will start earning interest immediately. If there is a delayed pay-off it must be compared with what could have been earned by investing today. To make an assessment of the office investment the pay-off value must be discounted back to its present value at some rate of interest.

So far we are dealing with a world of complete certainty. We know exactly what the value of the office building will be in twelve months' time because there is no risk attached to the investment. Under these conditions the appropriate rate of return to use can be derived from the return on government securities which have a one-year guaranteed pay-off. Assuming that this is 12%, the present value of the office building can be calculated from the following:

$$PV = \frac{\text{pay-off}}{(1 + r)} = \frac{£1\,300\,000}{(1 + 0.12)} = £1\,160\,714.$$

The present value of £1 160 714 represents the price at which the office building could be sold in the market in order to earn £1 300 000 in twelve months' time. This is exactly the same cost that would be incurred to make £1 300 000 in one year's time by investing in government securities. Because it is the only reasonable price in an open market that would satisfy both the buyer and the seller the present value is therefore its market price. The discount rate used is known as the **opportunity cost of capital** because it represents the return foregone by investing in the project rather than government securities.

Our investor can therefore offer £1 160 174 for the building and be assured that it represents a fair price. Whether he is better off depends on the final price he pays, and the amount by which he is better off can be determined by calculating the net present value.

Net present value is simply the difference between the pay-off and the investment. If we assume that our investor has no reason to offer other than the market price the net present value (NPV) can be determined as follows:

$$\text{NPV} = \frac{£1\,300\,000}{(1 + 0.12)} - £1\,160\,174 = 0.$$

The fact that the net present value is zero merely means that the property is correctly priced and that the investor is earning a return of 12% on his money.

Let us assume now that our investor knows that the seller is desperate to sell the property because he is in financial difficulty and needs to realize his assets quickly. This is additional information which is outside the open market situation described above. Our investor decides to offer £1 000 000 and finds that it is accepted. The final pay-off is still the same but the net present value under this deal is:

$$\text{NPV} = \frac{£1\,300\,000}{(1 + 0.12)} - £1\,000\,000 = £160\,714.$$

There is a net contribution in value to the investor of £160 714 and of course a net loss to the seller of the same amount. Because the net present value is positive the office building is worth buying. Even with a zero net present value it would still be worth buying because the investment will achieve a return equal to the opportunity cost of capital.

Another way of looking at this problem is in terms of rates of return. The investment criterion is to accept those projects which have an internal rate of return in excess of the opportunity cost of capital.

This can be calculated from the present value expression by solving for the rate of return. If we assume the cost of the office is accepted at £1 000 000 then the internal rate of return can be calculated as

$$£1\,000\,000 = \frac{£1\,300\,000}{(1 + r)}$$

$$r = 30\%.$$

As this exceeds our opportunity cost of capital of 12% the office building is worth buying. To our investor the property is under-priced. If, however, he had offered £1 160 714 the internal rate of return would be given by

$$£1\,160\,714 = \frac{£1\,300\,000}{(1 + r)}$$

$$r = 12\%.$$

This merely confirms the present value calculation above.

1.2 The effect of risk on present value

The assumption of a guaranteed pay-off is clearly unrealistic. The valuer cannot be certain about the future value of the property, he can only put forward his best forecast based on the information he has today. We must therefore talk in terms of expected returns over the holding period of the investment. To this extent, expected return has meaning only at the beginning of the holding period. At the end of the period the outcome may be completely different and it is this difference which creates the uncertainty in the return. Appendix 1A discusses methods of quantifying this uncertainty.

Because of the uncertainty concerning the outcome our investor is no longer prepared to offer as much to secure the office building. As most investors try to avoid risk without losing return, the concept of opportunity cost of capital and net present value is still valid for risky investments. It therefore remains sensible to discount our investment at a rate which is comparable to investments of equivalent risk. How this rate is chosen has yet to be discussed but it is a common belief that the risk premium to be offered for investing in property should be close to 2% over the riskless rate of return. For the purposes of illustration it is assumed this is valid and so the opportunity cost of capital is now 14%. On this basis the property has an expected present value of

$$E(PV) = \frac{\text{expected pay-off}}{(1 + r)} = \frac{£1\,300\,000}{(1 + 0.14)} = £1\,140\,351.$$

If the offer of £1 000 000 was accepted then the expected net present value of the investment would be

$$E(NPV) = \frac{£1\,300\,000}{(1 + 0.14)} - £1\,000\,000 = £140\,351.$$

The property is worth buying still because it represents a net contribution to value for our investor. The internal rate of return is still 30% but is now drafted in terms of expectations. As it exceeds the opportunity cost of finance of 14% this indicates the property is a worthwhile purchase.

1.3 Principal issues

This simple illustration raises a number of fundamental issues which are central to the theme of this book. The principal points are listed below.

1. In a well-functioning market, present value is equal to market price.
2. Positive net present values represent a net contribution to value.
3. The opportunity cost of capital for a property is determined by reference to other investments of equivalent risk.
4. Under conditions of risk, property valuations are drafted in terms of expectations.
5. The expected value of a property depends upon the quality of information available.

   The sensible investment criterion to pursue is one which increases the net contribution to value of an investor's wealth. Property investors therefore should aim to maximize net present value. Although this is a sound economic objective it is based on three assumptions.

1. There are no barriers which prevent investors gaining access to the capital markets and no single investor is sufficiently large to have a significant effect on price.
2. There are no costs involved in accessing the capital markets and there are no taxes.
3. All relevant information is widely available.

   These are the conditions of a perfect capital market which in reality cannot be met. This aspect will be discussed in Chapter 3; for the present suffice it to say that this does not significantly affect the net present value rule. The reason for this is that where investment is undertaken on behalf of others, such as a financial institution acting on behalf of its shareholders, the only action which will satisfy the objectives of the shareholders is the maximization of net present value. As long as the firm pursues this objective, individual shareholders are free to construct their own portfolios in whatever manner they wish to suit their own tastes. It is therefore possible to separate the functions of management from ownership insofar as the firm is concerned which leaves the maximization of net present value as the main criterion.

Pursuing this aim means that investors should try to acquire those properties which are under-priced relative to some agreed economic standard. To do this requires a better understanding of **capital market theory** and how it affects our understanding of valuation models and performance measurement.

The starting point for this is understanding the development of **portfolio theory** and investment risk.

1.4 Diversification and portfolio theory

The development of portfolio theory is based on the premise that an individual, by investing, can maximize his expected return for a given level of risk or minimize his risk for a given level of expected return. Most of the work in this area and its subsequent development into capital market theory and the **capital asset pricing model** have related to the market for equity shares. It is evident, however, that the market for real property, at both personal and institutional levels, is such that it consumes a major proportion of available investment funds. For many people, the commitment of funds to house purchase far outweighs that which would be allocated to equities. The risk return profile of their total assets will, therefore, be heavily dependent on their property holdings. The same is of course true of financial institutions and given this scenario it is appropriate to consider property in a portfolio context.

The pioneering work of Markowitz (1959) resulted in a radical reappraisal of the way in which investors behaved and laid the way for the development of capital market theory.

Markowitz's contribution was to see portfolio selection as a problem of maximizing the utility of an investor's wealth under conditions of uncertainty. By recognizing that each investment could be defined in terms of its risk and return, he developed a means of efficiently diversifying portfolios in order to give the maximum expected return for any given level of risk or the minimum level of risk for a given rate of return. Appendix 1A presents a simple example related to a two-asset portfolio.

Portfolio risk can be reduced only by investing in the minimum of two assets where the cyclical patterns of their rates of return do not move in perfect lockstep. Figure 1.1 shows two assets, A and B, which have the same expected rate of return. However, when the expected return on asset A is high it is counterbalanced by a low return on asset B. Combining A and B into a portfolio has the effect of eliminating much of the risk of holding each on an individual basis without sacrificing the expected return.

Figure 1.2 shows the same idea applied to a time series of monthly property returns together with the resulting portfolio. The measure of risk used in portfolio analysis is the standard deviation of returns. Squaring the standard deviation gives the variance, and although it is not the only measure of risk which could be used it has a number of desirable properties which favour its use. These are considered in Appendix 1A.

From these simple examples it will be evident that in order to assess the risk of the portfolio, not only is it necessary to know the expected return for each asset together with a measure of its risk but it is important also to know how the returns move in relation to each other. Altering the proportion of funds invested in each asset could produce a portfolio of zero risk depending on how the returns co-vary. This is shown in Figure 1.1. However a portfolio which has assets with returns moving together cannot eliminate risk.

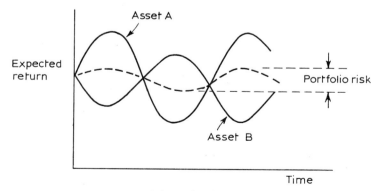

Figure 1.1 The principle of diversification.

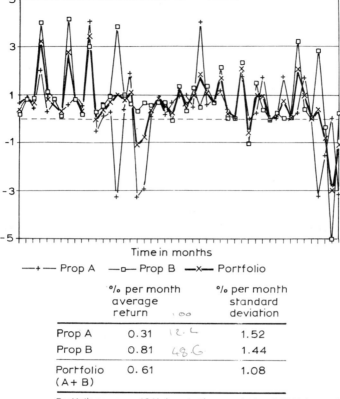

	% per month average return		% per month standard deviation
Prop A	0.31	12.4	1.52
Prop B	0.81	48.6	1.44
Portfolio (A + B)	0.61		1.08

Portfolio assumes 40 % invested in property A and 60 % in prop. B
Coefficient of correlation between A and B is 0.056

Figure 1.2 Combining property returns.

For a full Markowitz portfolio analysis, the movement of returns is described by a single measure, usually referred to as the covariance. As its name implies it describes how a number of rates of return are related or co-vary.

For the risk in a portfolio to be eliminated it is necessary for the rates of return to exhibit negative covariance. By analysing historical data concerning rates of return for a large number of assets it is possible to quantify their covariance for use in a portfolio analysis. Generally speaking, rates of return for most groups of assets tend to exhibit some degree of positive covariance so that it is almost impossible to construct a portfolio which completely eliminates risk. The main objective of a portfolio analysis is, therefore, to locate and combine those securities which exhibit less than perfect positive covariance in order to establish minimum risk.

Figure 1.3 illustrates how the rate of return and risk can change as the proportion of funds invested in two assets alters. It is assumed that the rates of returns on both assets exhibit some degree of positive covariance.

If the proportion of funds available for investment is split between X and Y the resulting portfolio will plot at some point along the arc XPQY. It will be seen that the portfolio lies on a curve, the curvature of which depends on the covariance between X and Y. If, for example, they exhibited perfect positive covariance, the resulting portfolio would lie at some point along a straight line joining X and Y. Conversely if they exhibited perfect negative covariance the curve would touch the rate of return axis indicating that under these conditions the proportion of funds could be selected which would produce a portfolio with zero risk.

It will be seen then that once the covariance term is known the risk/return characteristics of the portfolios can be adjusted by altering the proportion of funds available for investment. This does however raise important questions concerning the efficiency of the resulting portfolio. In Figure 1.3 for example not all the points along XPQY represent efficient portfolios in terms of risk and return. Portfolio P, for example, is inefficient because it is possible to obtain a higher return for the same level of risk merely by altering the proportion of funds invested in X and Y to produce portfolio Q. Examination of Figure 1.3 reveals that all portfolios lying between X and R are inefficient because it is possible to achieve a higher rate of return for

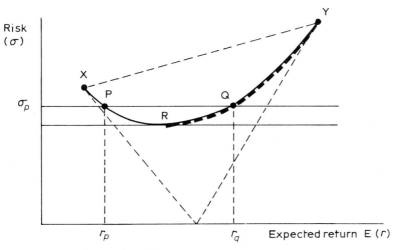

Figure 1.3 Portfolio risk and covariance.

the same risk level with a portfolio which lies along the line RY. It follows, therefore that a portfolio can be considered efficient only if it achieves the maximum rate of return for a given level of risk. Therefore only portfolios lying along the line RY can be considered to be efficient.

This represents a simple two-asset case. Generally speaking an individual has the opportunity to invest in a large number of assets and can vary the proportion he wishes to invest in any single asset. As the proportion of funds alters the position of the resulting portfolio in risk-return space alters. Plotting all possible combinations onto a graph will give rise to an area of portfolios as opposed to a line, as shown in Figure 1.4.

The enclosed area in this graph is referred to as the **opportunity set of portfolios**. Points such as A, B, C and D represent total investment in a single security. Comparing this illustration with Figure 1.3 it will be seen that only those portfolios which lie along the line RY are efficient as there is no other portfolio within the opportunity set which will give a higher rate of return for the same level of risk or lower risk for the same rate of return. The line RY is referred to as the **efficient frontier** of the opportunity set.

An investor should aim to choose a portfolio lying on the line RY which suits his own preferences towards risk. Choosing a single portfolio can be solved by constructing a series of risk-indifference

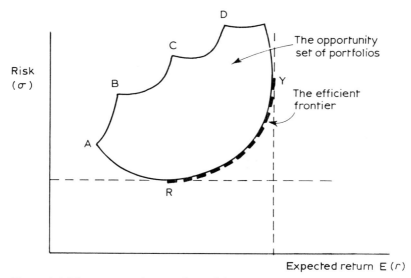

Figure 1.4 The opportunity set of portfolios.

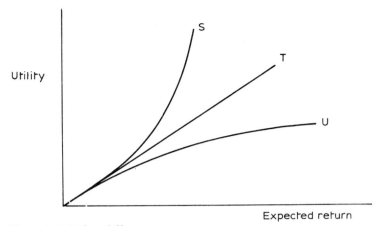

Figure 1.5 Risk-indifference curves.

curves for an individual investor. Figure 1.5 shows a range of possible alternatives.

Investor S is a risk lover as he is willing to take on more risk on the promise of higher expected return. His risk-indifference curve is concave. Investor T is indifferent to risk and expected return. His risk-indifference curve is a straight line. Investor U wishes to avoid risk preferring less risk to more risk so that his indifference curve is convex. Generally speaking most investors tend to be risk-averse, preferring less risk to more risk. There is now a considerable amount of evidence to support the view that almost all investors are risk-averse when making important decisions.

Once a family of risk-indifference curves has been established for a particular individual they can be plotted onto a graph of the opportunity set of portfolios. The point where the appropriate risk-indifference curve touches the efficient frontier establishes the optimal efficient portfolio for the investor. This condition is shown in Figure 1.6.

The assumptions on which this analysis are based are as follows.

1. Investors aim to maximize the single-period expected utility of their terminal wealth and choose among alternative portfolios on the basis of the mean and variance of return.
2. Investors' risk estimates are proportional to the variability of the returns they visualize.
3. All assets are perfectly divisible and marketable and there are no transactions costs.
4. There are no taxes.
5. For any given risk class, investors prefer a higher to a lower return.

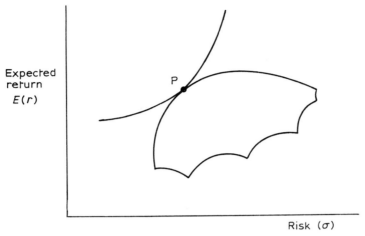

Figure 1.6 Establishing an optimal efficiently diversified portfolio.

Given the above it can be shown that the expected return and variance of returns on a portfolio can be expressed as follows.

$$E(r_p) = \sum_{i=1}^{n} x_i E(r_i) \tag{1.1}$$

$$\text{Var}(r_p) = \sum_{i=1}^{n} \sum_{j=1}^{n} x_i x_j \sigma_{ij} \tag{1.2}$$

where

$E(r_p)$ = expected return of portfolio P;
$\text{Var}(r_p)$ = variance of returns of portfolio P;
x_i = proportion of funds invested in ith asset;
σ_{ij} = covariance of returns between the ith and jth asset.

The standard portfolio problem is therefore to select all values of x which minimize the portfolio variance subject to two constraints. The first is that the expected return on the portfolio be achieved and the second is that the total proportion of funds invested should not exceed 100%.

By selecting an expected return the optimal weights of each investment are calculated in order to minimize the portfolio variance. Successive repetitions of this procedure produce the efficient frontier which identifies the maximum level of risk for a given rate of return.

Although this process plots out the efficient frontier it does not identify which portfolio would be most suitable for an individual investor. As described above the final choice depends on the particular preferences of the individual as defined by his utility function.

In practice the mean-variance approach described above requires a significant amount of input data relating to the covariance between each pair of returns. Computationally the process can be reduced by recognizing that it is possible for the expected returns and covariances to be described by reference to some common index. This was the approach adopted by William Sharpe (1963) in the development of the **diagonal portfolio model**.

Although the mean-variance approach to portfolio construction has received much coverage in the literature in relation to equities and mixed-asset portfolios there are few examples which have extended it to property. Of those which have, two deserve to be mentioned.

The first was by Harris C. Friedman (1970) who constructed portfolios based on a sample of fifty shares and fifty properties using data over the period 1963–8. He attempted to delineate the efficient frontier for separate portfolios of property and stocks and for the mixed-asset portfolio. In examining the property portfolio Friedman was faced with two problems.

The first problem was calculating the rate of return and standard deviation of returns of individual properties. Given that transaction prices were not available Friedman interpolated all intermediate figures from the values of the individual properties in 1963 and 1968, on the assumption that the growth between these two dates was a constant compound rate. Unfortunately this process causes the variance of returns for individual properties to be reduced to zero.

The second problem related to the indivisible nature of property. The portfolio model presented above assumes that every asset is perfectly divisible and this of course creates a major computational problem as far as property is concerned. Friedman overcame this problem by adopting an approach which simulated a true integer solution. Briefly the method assumed that in identifying the efficient frontier any property which has a non-zero weight would be purchased. Revised weights were then recalculated based on the value of each property and the total proportion of property in the portfolio assuming a mixed-asset portfolio. Thus having calculated the desired weights for each of the properties ignoring the integer constraint, the weights were recalculated taking the integer constraint into consideration.

In computing the efficient frontier, Friedman made use of a simplified approach developed by Sharpe (1963) for relating the returns on an asset to some index of economic activity. This approach considerably reduced the input data required for the analysis. Single-index models were used to compute the efficient frontier for both property and stocks. From this early analysis Friedman concluded that property portfolios can give greater returns and less risk than portfolios of common stock. When combined the resulting portfolios are dominated by those portfolios which include property assets.

These results, however, appear to be largely a product of the data and methodology used and his analysis has subsequently been criticized on these points. He was aware of the shortcomings in his paper and tried to guard against them by utilizing the same methodology in constructing stock portfolios. He also compensated for thin markets by decreasing the sale value of the properties by 15%. Even with these adjustments, however, the property portfolios still appeared to be the most efficient.

Although subject to major criticisms, Friedman's paper focused attention on the use of mean-variance analysis in the construction of property portfolios. Its principal contribution was therefore to draw attention to the need to cope with the integer constraint and also the calculation of the risk and return associated with investment in property.

A more extensive example of mean-variance analysis applied to property was undertaken by Findlay, Hamilton, Messner and Yormark (Findlay *et al*, 1979). They rejected the use of the index models identified by Friedman as being poorly specified. This resulted in low covariance between the returns on the index and the property, giving the impression that most of the risk associated with property could be diversified away. They argued that as most property portfolios tend to be reasonably small there is no reason to use an index model particularly when there are no good indices available. As a result they considered that a full Markowitz analysis becomes a feasible proposition because the increased computational efficiency outweighs the need for additional data.

In addressing themselves to the problem of risk and return they employed a Monte Carlo simulation model to calculate the variance of returns using the **financial management rate of return** (FMRR). This is in effect a geometric mean rate of return calculated from the start and terminal wealth positions for the projected cash flow of the property. By using repeated sampling they generated a frequency distribution of the FMRR enabling expected returns, variances and covariances to be estimated. They then made use of recent advances in discrete optimization which they had developed to handle the problem of non-divisible assets. The methodology employed is similar to the standard portfolio model but ensures that any unallocated funds which arise because of the discrete nature of property are invested at the risk-free rate of return.

Their analysis was undertaken using a portfolio of fifteen properties and produced the efficient frontier shown in Figure 1.7. The discrete nature of investing in property can be clearly seen as the efficient frontier is not continuous. Considerable gaps occur so it is not clear which portfolio an investor should choose in order that it lies on his highest risk-indifference curve. This problem seems as yet unresolved.

The choice of an appropriate indifference curve is in a sense arbitrary as the maximization of net present value is wholly consistent with the desire of investors to maximize the utility of their terminal wealth. This criterion will be satisfied as long as investors are able to identify and select those properties which are under-priced in an economic sense.

Although these approaches are interesting, it is doubtful whether they have much application in terms of constructing efficient property portfolios. Institutions, for example, are never in a situation where they can choose amongst a number of candidate properties subject to some budget constraint. Properties are generally acquired sequentially. The choice is rarely between several opportunities – it is usually an accept or reject situation. Portfolio revision is also unlikely to benefit from the Markowitz approach as this presupposes the possibility of complete liquidation in order to readjust the relative weights of each property in

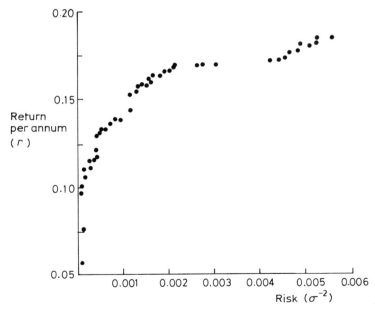

Figure 1.7 Efficient frontier for a property portfolio (after Findlay *et al.*).

the portfolio. Such a course of action would have severe consequences on the market and would be impossible to implement.

Assuming that the efficient frontier could be found, the choice of optimal portfolio still remains. As institutions tend to be the major force in property investment this presupposes that it is possible to establish a family of indifference curves which are applicable to a particular institution. As they are difficult enough to determine for individuals it is unlikely that they could be estimated for something as nebulous as a financial institution. The choice of optimal portfolio in the Markowitz sense is, therefore, difficult to ascertain. In fact there appears to be no evidence to support the view that institutions should be risk-averse in the same sense as individual investors or that they should hold efficient portfolios. As it is possible to separate the function of management from ownership, institutions can satisfy the needs of their shareholders merely by pursuing the simple criterion of maximizing net present value. In pursuing this objective alternative decision-making procedures must be employed which rely heavily on the development of a general capital market theory and the pricing of capital assets.

1.5 The development of capital market theory

Following the development of portfolio theory, a number of researchers began to examine the implications of all investors adopting the rationale of Markowitz portfolio diversification techniques. The results of this research has given rise to what has become known as **capital market theory**. This represented a major leap forward in the understanding of investment and had a significant impact on the theory and practice of investment appraisal and valuation.

The way in which capital market theory evolved from portfolio theory can be described as follows. It has been shown above that those portfolios which lie on the efficient frontier dominate all other portfolios within the opportunity set. It has also been shown that an optimal portfolio can be constructed for any investor once his particular risk-indifference curve has been established. This implies that it is not possible to achieve a portfolio which is more efficient that one which lies on the efficient frontier. This was assumed to be the case until it was realized that an investor could construct a portfolio which would lie outside the opportunity set if he invested in a risk-free asset such as government securities in addition to a risky portfolio lying on the efficient frontier, as illustrated in Figure 1.8.

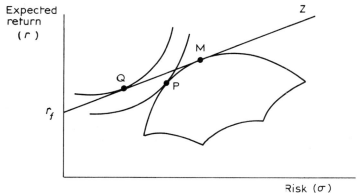

Figure 1.8 The capital market line.

By investing in a risk-free asset (r_f) in addition to a risky portfolio M it is possible to create a new portfolio Q which lies on a higher risk-indifference curve than portfolio P. By altering the proportion of funds available for investment between r_f and M it is possible to create a portfolio lying at any point along the line r_fQM. Similarly by borrowing at the risk-free (r_f) rate and investing in M, portfolios can be created lying along the line MZ. As it is possible to create portfolios which lie outside the opportunity set it will be evident that r_fQMZ must represent the true efficient frontier; this is the **capital market line**. It consists only of efficient portfolios which have been created through the process of diversification. Each portfolio has the minimum level of risk which cannot be diversified away. Inefficient portfolios will lie below this line.

Proponents of this model argue that portfolio M will, in equilibrium, contain every risky asset in proportion to its share of the total value of all assets in the market. If this were not the case then investors would adjust their portfolio holdings in order to attain the efficient combination. Changes in price would occur such that when the market reached equilibrium the above conditions would hold again.

The capital market line relates only to portfolios. However, it has been developed into a general model of capital asset pricing by Sharpe (1964), Lintner (1965) and Mossin (1966). Because the capital market line consists only of efficient portfolios this implies that total risk is made up of two components. One part reflects the level of risk which through diversification can be eliminated and the other reflects the level of risk which cannot be diversified away. In capital market theory these are referred to as the **specific** and **systematic** risk components.

The total risk of any portfolio or for that matter any asset will be the sum of these two components such that

$$\text{Total risk} = \text{systematic risk} + \text{specific risk}.$$

Systematic risk is characterized by economic and market changes which affect all assets. Because the effect is market-wide this type of risk cannot be eliminated.

Specific risk on the other hand can be diversified away and is usually characterized by factors specific to an individual asset. If a property-company undertakes a series of uneconomic developments, an individual can eliminate the riskiness of investing in the company by diversifying into other sectors of the market which are not affected by the poor quality of decision-making.

As specific risk can be eliminated by diversification it will be seen that it is the systematic or market-risk component which assumes major importance. Much of the current work on capital market theory is focused on the way the systematic component can be measured. In essence systematic risk is a measure of volatility. It was first evolved in relation to the performance of company shares but is equally applicable to the performance of real assets such as property. The measure of risk used is expressed in terms of a coefficient which is related to the performance of some index of market movements, and is known as the **beta coefficient**. A company or asset which has the same volatility as the market will therefore have a beta coefficient of 1.0. A risk-free asset will, if held to maturity, be non-volatile and will have a beta coefficient of zero. Similarly a company or asset with a beta coefficient greater or less than 1.0 will be more or less risky than the market.

Plotting rates of return which are in equilibrium against their respective levels of systematic risk will give rise to a linear relationship known as the **security market line**, shown in Figure 1.9.

The application of risk-indifference curves shown in Figure 1.8 can also be applied to the security market line. Investors can maximize their utility by moving onto the highest risk-indifference curve. If an asset or portfolio is correctly priced in relation to the market then it will lie on the security market line. The expected return derived from this line will give a net present value of zero when used to discount the asset's cash flows. If however the asset or portfolio is under-priced it will lie above the security market line. An investor holding such an asset or portfolio will be able to move onto a higher risk-indifference curve and thus maximize his utility. What is equally important is that the portfolio or asset will generate a positive net present value.

It should be evident from this that selecting portfolios or assets with

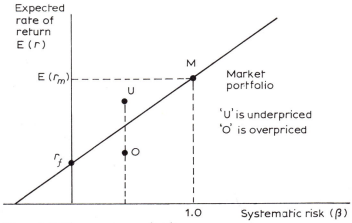

Figure 1.9 The security market line.

positive net present values is entirely consistent with maximizing utility. The earlier proposition that investors should aim to follow a strategy which maximizes net present value therefore remains valid within the risk-return framework outlined above. Hence a knowledge of systematic risk in this context is important in terms of understanding the valuation process and subsequently, developing performance measurement systems.

Relating the concept of systematic and specific risk to property it will be evident that the factors affecting these aspects can be split up in the following manner.

Systematic risk
  general economic factors
  finance changes
  taxation

Specific risk
  tenant effects
  location effects
  structural effects
  building quality
  legal effects
  depreciation

It will be seen that there are more specific factors than systematic factors and by building portfolios of property the influence of specific factors can be diversified away. As investors will only expect to be compensated for those factors which cannot be diversified away systematic risk assumes greater importance in explaining how valuations should be determined.

Systematic risk is the appropriate measure to use for diversified portfolios. However, even if investors are unable to hold diversified portfolios systematic risk is still important for the simple reason that investors are not compensated for all the risk that they take on, only that which cannot be eliminated through diversification. This proposition is extremely important because it indicates that it is systematic risk which determines the correct opportunity cost of finance to use in assessing an investment project. This will apply irrespective of the diversification policy being pursued.

Although a property may be extremely risky in total risk terms, its contribution to the risk of a mixed-asset portfolio may well mean that it can be considered to be of low systematic risk. It is for this reason that when analysing property the premium added to the rate of return on riskless securities is frequently taken as approximately 2%.

1.6 The capital asset pricing model

The understanding of risk and return outlined above has led to the development of asset pricing models as a means of developing equilibrium values. An **equilibrium value** is one in which the market will clear and represents the correct trade-off between risk and expected return. This has naturally led on to the development of the security market line which relates expected return to systematic risk. It is a completely different relationship from the capital market line although the two illustrations are similar. The fundamental difference, as indicated above, is that in equilibrium every asset will lie on the security market line while under- or over-priced assets will lie above or below the line. The security market line also refers to individual assets as well as portfolios. The capital market line refers only to efficient portfolios.

The relevant risk in the security market line is systematic risk. Appendix 1B develops the mathematical basis for the security market line together with the **capital asset pricing model**. The beta coefficient (β) is related to the returns on the market portfolio and acts as a proxy for the covariance of returns. An asset which has the same volatility as the market will have a beta coefficient of 1.0 whereas a riskless asset held to maturity with a guaranteed pay-off will have a beta coefficient of zero.

The security market line and the theory of the capital asset pricing are drafted in terms of expectations and are based on the following assumptions.

1. All investors are risk-averse and choose portfolios on the basis of maximizing the expected utility of their terminal wealth.

2. Single-period portfolio returns can be described in advance in terms of the mean and variance (or standard deviation).
3. All investors have similar views concerning means, variances and covariances of all assets within the opportunity set.
4. All assets are perfectly divisible and there are no transactions costs.
5. There are no restrictions to short sales and no taxes.
6. The riskless rate at which money can be borrowed and lent is the same.
7. All investments have the same time-horizon which coincides with an identical time-horizon for investors.

Under these assumptions it is possible to show that the expected return on any asset for a single period can be given by

$$E(r_j) = r_f + \beta_j[E(r_m) - r_f] \qquad (1.3)$$

where

$$
\begin{aligned}
E(r_j) &= \text{expected return on asset } j \text{ for the period under} \\
&\quad \text{consideration;} \\
r_f &= \text{riskless rate of return for period under} \\
&\quad \text{consideration;} \\
E(r_m) &= \text{expected return on the market portfolio;} \\
\beta_j &= \text{systematic risk of the asset } j.
\end{aligned}
$$

Althouth the assumptions from which this model has been derived may seem extremely restrictive they are merely a framework for deriving the basic relationship. The model provides a very powerful and yet simple explanation of the economic process which generates returns and much research has been undertaken to investigate the effect of relaxing many of the assumptions. Note however that it is drafted in terms of expectations although estimates of the beta coefficient are generally derived from historic data on the assumption that over reasonably long periods expectations concerning asset returns are more likely to be realized.

A further point to bear in mind is that the beta coefficient was first devised as a means of simplifying the input data for a portfolio analysis. It was calculated by reference to some index of market movements. It later took on a more important meaning under the form of the capital asset pricing model which defined a special class of equilibrium model by measuring the beta coefficient relative to a theoretical market portfolio. This distinction is important otherwise it can lead to confusion in the understanding and application of measures of systematic risk.

In the later case the definition of the market portfolio is critical. It should contain every risky asset in the market place if the capital asset pricing model is to be used for estimating expected returns in a capital market framework. In terms of performance measurement, however, the beta coefficient may well be measured relative to some other index of market movements. In both cases the mathematical derivation of the beta coefficient is exactly the same, it is only the definition of the reference portfolio which differs.

1.7 Relaxing the assumptions

The assumptions on which the capital asset pricing model is based are of course very restrictive and when property is taken within the framework, many of these assumptions are violated. The principal constraints which have a bearing on property are considered as follows.

Distribution of returns

Portfolio theory is based on the assumption that the probability distribution of returns is Normal. Although the returns on individual assets may not be Normal, the Central Limit Theorem suggests that if the returns can be regarded as a random variable then as the number of assets combined in a portfolio increases the distribution of returns for the portfolio should approach Normality. In addition there is more likelihood of the portfolio returns being Normally distributed the more diversified it is, because more assets will be included which have less than perfect positive correlation.

Two points are of interest here. Firstly there is little evidence in the UK concerning the distribution of returns from direct investment in property. What evidence there is suggests that as the holding period increases (i.e. beyond six months) returns tend to be Normally distributed. In fact if returns are computed in continuous time, the effect of taking natural logs will tend to pull in the high returns causing the distribution to approach Normality.

Secondly, there is little evidence concerning the correlation structure of property returns. What research has been carried out (Brown, 1985) however, does suggest that the correlation of returns between individual properties is extremely low and in many cases negative. This characteristic is largely a result of specific factors relating to individual properties such as location, type and quality of building, tenant, lease structure and so on.

Perfectly divisible assets

The problem of perfectly divisible assets is rarely found in stock portfolios. It is, however, a major problem as far as property is concerned as each newly-acquired investment will represent a discrete percentage of the total assets. The net effect is that at any point in time investors will be holding portfolios which will be sub-optimal. Size is important here because in the larger portfolios each new property will represent a smaller percentage of the total holdings.

In terms of the capital asset pricing model this lack of liquidity could be crucial. It does not apply however, solely to property. Human capital also can be regarded as a non-marketable claim on the probability distribution of future income. It is important to know whether the results of the capital asset pricing model would be violated by the presence of non-liquid assets.

This problem has been addressed by Mayers (1972) who has shown that if assets are considered to be either perfectly liquid or perfectly non-liquid the capital asset pricing model can be redrafted to incorporate the covariance of returns on the non-marketable assets with all other assets. His examination of this problem shows that the basic results of the theory are not weakened in any major respect by the presence of non-marketable assets. In fact he demonstrates that even with homogeneous expectations the portfolios of marketable assets held by investors will be widely different because the probability distributions of their non-marketable assets differ. This is a useful insight because the conventional view of the capital asset pricing model is that investors tend to hold identical portfolios each having the same composition as the market, the only difference being in the way they are financed.

Unequal lending and borrowing rates

Capital market theory has been developed on the assumption that investors can borrow or lend at the risk-free rate. The capital market line however, will be linear only if both lending and borrowing rates are the same. When this condition is not met, the line will no longer be straight, with the result that there is no longer a single optimal

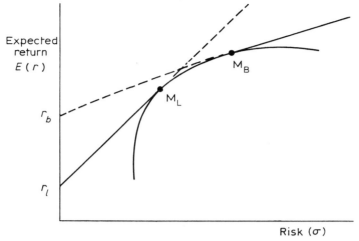

Figure 1.10 Unequal borrowing and lending rates.

combination of risky assets. This is of course important because financial leverage is a major characteristic of property investment. The position is illustrated in Figure 1.10.

Although this would seem to indicate a possible breakdown in the theory, Brennan (1971) has shown that in equilibrium the return on any asset is a linear function of the covariance of its return with the market portfolio, and that all efficient portfolios are linear combinations of any two efficient portfolios, namely the least variance risky asset portfolio and the optimal risky asset portfolio for all investors if borrowing and lending rates were both zero. Where divergent borrowing and lending rates exist, the intercept of the capital market line shifts to a point where it represents the return on the asset which has zero covariance with the market portfolio.

Multi-period investment

The assumption that all investments are single-period and coincide with the time-horizons of all investors has been chosen for analytical simplicity. It enables the difficulties encountered in comparison of investments of unequal duration and the problems of multiple rates of return to be avoided.

Although investors are generally faced with a multi-period problem Fama (1970) has shown that under very general conditions they will behave as though they were maximizing single-period utility. Within the context of a lifetime consumption pattern investors will choose those portfolios which are efficient in terms of single-period parameters.

Even when the assumptions on which the capital asset pricing model is based are relaxed it will be seen that the model still remains robust. In fact this is one of its attractions. It provides an intuitive way of looking at the performance of investments in a simple and direct manner.

1.8 Tests of the capital asset pricing model

The capital asset pricing model is a theoretical construct and to have validity in the real world it must be capable of being tested empirically.

Examination of equation (1.3) reveals that it is drafted in terms of expectations. A true test therefore would need to be based on ex-ante relationships. Such data however, are not available and the usual assumption made is that by using ex-post data investors' expectations have been realized on average. The difference between actual and expected returns therefore is not expected to differ statistically from zero. In an efficient market this assumption is considered reasonable, because the presence of any systematic bias over long periods would enable investors to develop trading strategies in order to earn abnormal returns. The evidence to date on the effectiveness of trading rules in the stock market seems to indicate this is likely to be very difficult.

Empirical tests of the model therefore have relied on two basic methodologies; cross-sectional and time series. **Cross-sectional tests** examine a single period and from previously estimated beta coefficients try to estimate the risk-free rate of return from a regression of β against holding-period returns. **Time series tests** have examined the problem in risk premium form and have analysed the asset premium against the market premium to see if the regression intercept is zero.

There are considerable statistical and methodological problems involved in testing the capital asset pricing model. Although many tests support the general notion that by taking on more risk investors are rewarded by higher returns, none of them provide overwhelming evidence either in support or in rejection of the basic model. For example there remains the problem of reconciling the use of ex-post data within a model which is drafted in ex-ante terms. Although all tests to date confirm a positive relationship between systematic risk and return, many of them give rise to an intercept term which either exceeds the risk-free rate of return or, as in the case of the time series tests, is significantly different from zero. This departure from the model has led to alternative versions of the capital asset pricing model in an attempt to reconcile the discrepancies.

Roll (1977) has shown that the market portfolio used in the tests does not in fact include all risky assets. As a result the slope of the regression line will be biased. Generally speaking the market portfolio is usually based on the returns calculated from an index of stock market returns. The assumption underlying this surrogate portfolio is that all omitted risky assets are perfectly positively correlated with the returns on the index. This however is clearly incorrect. Real property for example is a major investment medium which is not included in the index. In addition far from being perfectly positively correlated with the returns on the index, property exhibits very low correlation with the index. Thus in the absence of a suitable market index, tests of the capital asset pricing model must be considered with caution. Having said this, the empirical tests do seem to offer considerable support for the basic implications of the capital asset pricing model. Despite its shortcomings in terms of empirical testing the model has considerable intuitive appeal which encourages its use in many areas of investment analysis.

1.9 Property and the market portfolio

The problem of incorporating property into a market index has received little coverage although two attempts are worthy of consideration.

Miles and Rice (1978) in examining the problem from the individual investor's point of view constructed an index consisting of human capital, real property and common stock. Data for the index was taken from the *United States Statistical Abstract* which included the value of personal assets in addition to common stock and real estate. The weightings used in the index were heavily biased in favour of human capital. It covered a twenty-year period from 1955 to 1975 and had the following average weightings:

Human capital	62%
Real property	24%
Common stock	14%.

By contrast Ward (1979) examined the problem from the point of view of the institutional investor and suggested that in order to overcome the criticisms raised by Roll, the market portfolio should be defined to include the widest range of assets possible which have an influence on investment decisions. He argued against the incorporation of human capital since the pricing of all risky assets was increasingly being influenced by the demand of institutional investors. Using data from *Financial Statistics* and the 1976 *Guide to Property Bonds and Managed Funds* he assessed the weights for common stock, property, long- and short-term fixed interest securities relating to insurance companies, pension funds, investment trusts, unit trusts and managed funds. These were then combined to form a market portfolio. He recognized that there were inadequacies in the data making it difficult to be confident that the resulting index formed a good proxy for the true market portfolio.

Any attempt to construct an index which is intended to represent a composite market portfolio inevitably runs into difficulties when it comes to incorporating property because of the lack of reliable time-series data on a sufficiently frequent basis. Although the availability and quality of data are improving there are still a number of problems which have yet to be addressed.

1.10 Portfolio expansion and revision

Arising out of the foregoing discussion it will be evident that financial institutions can face a problem in terms of portfolio expansion and revision and in accurately monitoring performance.

Institutions continuously face a portfolio problem although the need to hold an efficient portfolio is not as critical as for an individual. In fact the indivisible nature of property is such that it is unlikely that an institution would be in a position to hold an efficient property portfolio.

In addition the sequential nature of property purchases will tend to rule out the mechanics of constructing efficient portfolios. Since individuals can easily eliminate diversifiable risk present in a firm's investment portfolio it follows that an institution building up its property portfolio need not diversify for the individual. This is true only where the individual has free access to the market. Where, however, a group of individuals take out insurance policies which are linked to the performance of a property portfolio the attitude of those individuals in terms of risk aversion may be such that they would expect the fund's management to pursue a policy of efficient diversification in order to maximize long-term return. This will be true particularly where those individuals have to pay a penalty if an insurance policy is surrendered before its term expires.

A universal policy concerning diversification for a property fund therefore is not obvious and it may well be that the attitude to diversification will depend on where property fits into a fund's total investment portfolio of risky assets and how this is perceived by the individual. For example it would be reasonable to assume that in a portfolio consisting largely of common stock, but with a significant proportion of property, the choice of properties should be such that they achieve maximum growth. As property returns have low covariance with common stock, the choice of suitable properties for inclusion in a portfolio is more likely to be motivated by tax reasons. For example, low- or zero-rated tax payers are likely to have a preference for properties with a high beta coefficient which exhibit high growth whereas investors within a high tax bracket are more likely to prefer properties with low beta coefficient which have a high income element.

Continued acquisition should be made therefore against some risk-return criterion. In terms of the capital asset pricing model framework properties should be included within a portfolio only if for a given level of systematic risk they lie above the security market line. Using this criterion for acceptance will ensure that the value of the portfolio increases since it complies with the net present value rule discussed earlier.

1.11 Criticisms of risk return measures used in property investment analysis

Although the techniques described above form the basis from which modern financial theory has developed, and there is nothing to suggest that they are exclusive to stock market investments, it is nevertheless worth evaluating their applicability to property investment analysis.

Baum (1989) has identified the principal criticisms and has argued that use of the standard deviation of returns, which is central to the development of mean-variance analysis and the capital asset pricing model, has been uncritically accepted as being appropriate to the analysis of UK property investments. He further argues that such an approach is incorrectly founded because volatility as measured by the historic variance or standard deviation of returns is an inappropriate measure of risk for UK property and is impossible to measure accurately.

In developing this argument he identifies five areas which give rise to the main problems. These are availability of data, prices and valuations, sample and index errors, illiquidity, and efficient pricing. Clearly these are significant areas of debate and need to be addressed in a positive manner if our understanding of property in a capital market framework is to develop. The points he raises are therefore considered as follows.

Availability of data

This is a major problem as is the confidentiality which surrounds much of the data. Baum argues that in comparison with equities the volume of time-series data for property is insufficient to derive reliable measures of risk using either the standard deviation of returns or the beta coefficient. Although this is true it should be borne in mind that portfolio theory and the capital asset pricing model is drafted in terms of expectations, not in terms of historic returns. What is needed therefore is a measure of expected risk, not historic risk. To this extent historic data provides a starting point for estimating future risk.

The commercially available systems for measuring the beta coefficient of stocks tend to use five years of monthly historic data to estimate β by regression analysis and then to make a statistical adjustment to the figures to take out any historical bias. An alternative approach is to use cross-sectional information based on fundamental data concerning an asset which can then be used to predict future βs. It is also possible to combine historic data with fundamental data in order to improve the estimates of future βs.

Data in the property market is improving all the time and it is now possible to obtain a monthly-returns series of market movements. Although these are useful developments and in time will be helpful in verifying risk measures they do not overcome the need for expected risk measures. Appendix 2F presents one approach to this problem. As the quality of data improves it is likely that the fundamental approach developed by Rosenberg and Marathe (1973) will also lead to some useful insights.

In essence, the paucity of data should not be a constricting influence on the development of expected risk measures based on standard deviation or β.

Prices and valuations

The question of whether valuations can be used as a proxy for prices is examined in detail in Appendix 2A. The important issue here is whether the information set used for determining prices is the same as that used for valuations. If they are the same and the price achieved for a property is randomly drawn from that distribution then there should be no fundamental objection to using valuations as a proxy for prices. The problem however would be serious if there were significant bias between valuations and prices as this would imply that prices are formed from a completely different probability distribution to that of valuations. Suffice it to say that the empirical evidence does not support this viewpoint.

Baum also argues that valuations are influenced by previous valuations because the basis of the standard comparative method is the slow adjustment of prices based on accumulated historic evidence. On this basis he has suggested that valuations are erroneous and serially correlated. If however valuations are present values then historic evidence should have no bearing on a current valuation. The valuation of a property from one period to the next will not alter therefore, unless there is new information which will bring about a change. If valuations are properly discounted present values then, as Paul Samuelson (1965) has shown, changes in valuation should be random and so there should be little evidence of serial correlation. This aspect is also examined in Chapter 2.

Sample and index errors

As Baum quite rightly points out there are considerable problems associated with the construction of property indices. No two indices appear to behave exactly the same and it is probably impossible for an investor to track the returns of an index. There are of course other problems associated with smoothing which compound the difficulties so that the returns calculated from an index behave like a moving average.

To a large degree these are statistical problems which can be overcome (see for example Appendix 5A) and it may well be a matter of personal preference as to which index be used for performance measurement purposes. As long as the index is not unduly biased in the selection of properties the average return measured over a given period should be the same as any other index sampled from the same population. The principal difference is likely to occur in the measurement of the standard deviation of returns which will of course be greater for the index based on the smaller sample size. It is however possible to make corrections for this. The fact that individual property portfolios carry more specific risk than the index merely means that they stand a better chance of out-performing the index.

Illiquidity

The problem of liquidity has already been considered under section 1.7 where it was shown that incorporating non-marketable assets into the market model framework does not weaken the theory.

Efficient pricing

This aspect will also be dealt with in Chapter 2. The question of whether the property market is efficient can be determined only by empirical tests. Baum refers to the findings of Locke (1987) who argues that the real-estate market does not appear to satisfy the basic weak-form test of the efficient market hypothesis. This finding throws serious doubt on the potential for applying performance measures derived from the market model. The results offered by Locke however cannot be regarded as conclusive because little information was provided concerning the property samples used, although the tests were carried out mostly using property indices or portfolios. In both cases it would not be unusual to find evidence to support this view because the returns series is almost certain to be smoothed even though the underlying property returns may be independent of each other.

As mentioned earlier a distinction must also be drawn between the use of the beta coefficient within a capital asset pricing framework and a similar measure made relative to some market index. The former case requires the market portfolio to be specified to include all risky assets in order to arrive at a general pricing framework. As this does not exist in practice it is difficult to provide empirical evidence which either confirms or rejects the capital asset pricing model. The latter case is more appropriate for performance measurement purposes where risk is being measured against some agreed standard.

The paper by Baum has raised a number of issues which are of considerable concern to those undertaking research in this area. As shown here however the problems identified are capable of being overcome and should not restrict the development of property within a portfolio framework.

1.12 Conclusion

This chapter has attempted to establish a basic economic framework for looking at property within the capital markets, and has inevitably raised a number of issues. For example, how is systematic risk to be measured? Is the property market efficient in processing information? Are valuation models economically valid? How valid are performance measurement systems? These issues will be addressed in the following chapters, although it cannot be guaranteed that definitive answers will be provided. All that can be achieved is a better understanding of some of the issues involved.

As much of modern finance has a strong mathematical and statistical base the following Appendices are included to cover some of the basic quantitative techniques needed to develop these areas.

Appendix 1A: Statistical techniques, risk measures and portfolio analysis

Summation signs

The Greek symbol $\sum$ is a shorthand way of expressing the sum of a series of numbers. For example,

$$S = 1 + 2 + 3 + 4 + 5$$

can be written in a more compact form as

$$S = \sum_{x=1}^{5} x.$$

Moments of a probability distribution

The returns from any asset can be described in terms of four moments. These are the mean, variance, skewness and kurtosis. Each of these can be related to both future and historic returns and are described below.

First moment: M1 (mean)

The first moment is generally measured relative to the origin of a distribution and is indicative of location or central tendency.

Using future returns data the expected return is given as

$$E(r) = \sum_{i=1}^{n} p_i r_i. \tag{1A.1}$$

Alternatively using historic data it takes on the following form

$$\bar{r} = \frac{1}{n} \sum_{i=1}^{n} r_i. \tag{1A.2}$$

Note that the expected value makes use of probabilities such that $\sum p = 1$ whereas the mean return assumes a relative frequency equal to $1/n$.

When analyzing returns data it is more usual to estimate the moments about the mean of the distribution. The first moment (M1) will therefore be zero for both future and historic returns: using future returns,

$$M1 = \sum_{i=1}^{n} p_i[r_i - E(r_i)] = 0; \tag{1A.3}$$

and using historic returns,

$$M1 = \frac{1}{n} \sum_{i=1}^{n} (r_i - \bar{r}) = 0. \qquad (1A.4)$$

Second moment: M2 (variance)

The variance is a measure of dispersion about the mean or expected value. It can be estimated using future returns, where

$$M2 = \sigma^2 = \sum_{i=1}^{n} p_i[r_i - E(r)]^2, \qquad (1A.5)$$

or using historic returns, where

$$M2 = \sigma^2 = \frac{1}{n} \sum_{i=1}^{n} (r_i - \bar{r})^2. \qquad (1A.6)$$

Taking the square root of M2 gives a measure of the standard deviation.

Third moment: M3 (skewness)

Skewness measures how lop-sided is the distribution, and would occur

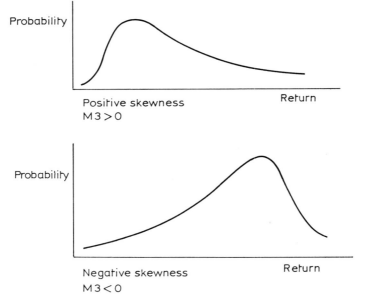

Figure 1A.1 Skewness.

if a returns series had a tendency to have a large number of high or low returns. Using future returns,

$$M3 = \sum_{i=1}^{n} p_i [r_i - E(r)]^3 \qquad (1A.7)$$

and using historic returns,

$$M3 = \frac{1}{n} \sum_{i=1}^{n} [r_i - \bar{r}]^3. \qquad (1A.8)$$

Because these expressions both involve cubed powers it will be evident that they can take on either positive or negative values. It is usual however to normalize the skewness by dividing M3 by the cube of the standard deviation ($M3/\sigma^3$), this transformation ensuring that the Normal distribution has a skewness of zero. Positive or negative skewness will be either greater or less than zero, and is illustrated in Figure 1A.1.

Fourth moment: M4 (kurtosis)

Kurtosis is a measure of how peaked or flat is a distribution, and is calculated in a similar manner to skewness. Using future returns,

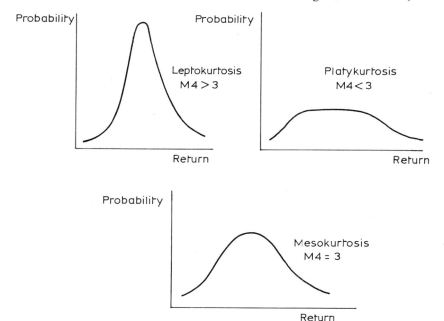

Figure 1A.2 Kurtosis.

$$M4 = \sum_{i=1}^{n} p_i[r_i - E(r)]^4 \qquad (1A.9)$$

and using historic returns,

$$M4 = \frac{1}{n} \sum_{i=1}^{n} (r_i - \bar{r})^4. \qquad (1A.10)$$

As with skewness these figures can be normalized by dividing by σ^4, and the revised measure, $M4/\sigma^4$, will have a value of 3.0 if the underlying distribution is Normal. Different examples of kurtosis are shown in Figure 1A.2.

Given a returns series and information about skewness and kurtosis it is possible to establish whether the underlying series is Normally distributed.

The studentized range (SR)

A further measure which can be used to examine the characteristics of a distribution is the studentized range. This is a useful measure capable of taking account of extreme observations in a returns series. It is computed from the following:

$$SR = \frac{\text{Max}(r) - \text{Min}(r)}{\sigma_r}. \qquad (1A.11)$$

The calculated studentized range needs to be compared with figures obtained from tables computed for the studentized range in order to establish whether the sample is derived from a Normal distribution (David *et al.*, 1954).

Covariance (Cov)

An important statistic which is central to the development of portfolio theory is the covariance which describes how asset returns move relative to each other. It can be estimated from the following:

$$\text{Cov}(a, b) = \frac{1}{n - 1} \sum (a - \bar{a})(b - \bar{b}). \qquad (1A.12)$$

Coefficient of correlation (ρ)

The covariance is measured in units related to the values of the variables, which in some cases makes it difficult to interpret. The problem of scale can be overcome by dividing by the standard deviation of each variable, thus:

$$\rho_{ab} = \frac{1}{n-1} \frac{\sum (a - \bar{a})(b - \bar{b})}{\sigma_a \sigma_b}. \qquad (1A.13)$$

The covariance is now in the form of a coefficient which lies within the range -1 to $+1$ depending on whether the variables being analysed are negatively or positively correlated. This is shown in Figure 1A.3.

The coefficient of correlation is often used in time-series analysis of investments. Where the return series from two or more assets are being examined, each having data in the same period, the cross correlation between the assets is known as the zero-order correlation coefficient.

If however we are interested in knowing how a time series of returns from an asset is related to returns in an earlier period, it is possible to use data from a single series to create a second series by lagging the returns. The correlation between the two sets of data is known as the serial-order correlation coefficient. The order of serial correlation depends on the lags involved. A lag of one period is first-order, two periods is second-order and so on.

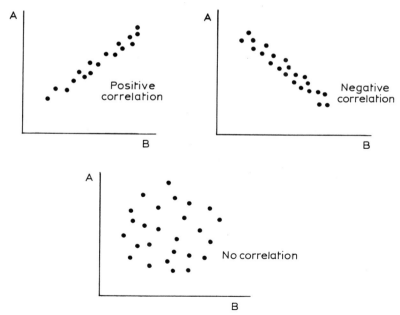

Figure 1A.3 Correlation.

Other risk measures

The standard deviation and variance are not the only measures of risk that have been suggested. The following can be used but have shortcomings which tend to limit their use.

Coefficient of variation (CV)

This is a measure of relative variability and is found by dividing the standard deviation by the expected value. In returns form,

$$CV = \frac{\sigma_r}{E(r)}. \tag{1A.14}$$

The coefficient of variation is a means of taking out scale differences when measuring risk. It is therefore more applicable to those situations where risk is measured in absolute rather than relative values. The following example illustrates the use of the coefficient of variation.

Project	Expected value £	Standard deviation £	CV
A	100 000	300 000	3.00
B	1 000 000	2 500 000	2.50

Although project A has a smaller standard deviation it is a more risky investment than project B. The coefficient of variation has made an adjustment for differences in scale between the projects.

The measure is less useful however when applied to rates of return. Because the standard deviation of rates of return is already in a standardized form it is directly comparable with other standard deviations and therefore it is not necessary to make a further transformation. If used without care it can produce odd results. For example:

Project	$E(r)$	σ_r	CV
X	3%	2%	0.67
Y	30%	20%	0.67

The coefficients of variation for X and Y are identical even though project Y is ten times as risky as project X. A further problem can arise when the expected return is equal to zero as this would imply a coefficient of variation which is infinitely large.

The semi-variance (SV)

Markowitz (1959) suggested that below-average returns (b_r) are risky and therefore suggested the use of the semi-variance, with

$$SV = E[b_r - E(r)]^2 \qquad (1A.15)$$

where

$$b_r < E(r).$$

Although intuitively appealing it can be shown that the ranking of returns by semi-variance is identical to that produced using the standard deviation. In addition the semi-variance is difficult to handle mathematically when used within a portfolio framework.

Mean absolute deviation (MAD)

This ignores sign differences when computing the deviation and can be calculated from the following:

$$MAD = \sum_{i=1}^{n} p_i |r_i - E(r)|. \qquad (1A.16)$$

This measure has the advantage of overcoming a problem with the variance whereby squaring the deviations can cause erratic changes in the variance due to large observed deviations. The MAD is more stable and is generally less than or equal to the standard deviation. However like the semi-variance it is difficult to handle mathematically which restricts its use in portfolio work.

Normal distributions

If asset returns are Normal they can be described in terms of two parameters, the mean and standard deviation. Higher order parameters such as skewness and kurtosis can be ignored. It is therefore advantageous to use the properties of the Normal distribution because they have finite variance, the statistics are dependable and the mathematics well understood.

Often however a returns series may have outliers which can invalidate the Normality assumption. This is not uncommon with returns from securities and also occurs with property. Under these circumstances the standard deviation becomes erratic and does not approach the true value for the population. It has also been suggested that securities' returns may be generated from a stable symmetric distribution which has a theoretically infinite variance.

Mandelbrot (1963) and Fama (1965) suggested that the frequency distribution of security returns were derived from a non-Normal stable Paretian distribution with the Normal distribution being a special case. Fama has also shown however that even operating with Paretian distributions the Markowitz model is still valid.

In addition if returns are measured in continuous time by taking natural logs this has the tendency to pull in the large positive returns and to ensure that the underlying series is Normally distributed.

There are therefore a number of alternatives for measuring risk. The principal problem however is in dealing with future risk as both capital market theory and portfolio theory are drafted in terms of expectations. Measures of expected risk are impossible to test and irrespective of which measure is used they are all amenable to the general Markowitz approach although each would produce a different efficient set.

Portfolio analysis with two assets

Although a full Markowitz analysis is extremely complex the basic mathematical procedures can be grasped by analysing a simple two-asset portfolio. Consider two assets A and B which have returns and standard deviations as shown below.

Asset	Rate of return	Standard deviation
A	6%	3%
B	8%	4%

Assume that the amount of funds invested in asset A varies between 0% and 100% and that the coefficient of correlation is either -1, 0 or $+1$. From this information it is possible to estimate the expected return and standard deviation of the portfolio from the following equations:

$$E(r_p) = w_a(r_a) + (1 - w_a)(r_b). \tag{1A.17}$$

$$\sigma_p^2 = w_a^2\sigma_a^2 + (1 - w_a)^2\sigma_b^2 + 2w_a(1 - w_a)\rho_{ab}\sigma_a\sigma_b. \tag{1A.18}$$

Using these equations it is possible to estimate the expected return and standard deviation for different proportions of funds invested in asset A. The results are given below.

Amount invested in A (%)	Expected rate of return (%)	Standard deviation (%)		
		Case 1 $\rho_{ab} = -1$	Case 2 $\rho_{ab} = 0$	Case 3 $\rho_{ab} = +1$
100	6.00	3.00	3.00	3.00
75	6.50	1.25	2.46	3.25
50	7.00	0.50	2.50	3.50
25	7.50	2.25	3.09	3.75
0	8.00	4.00	4.00	4.00

The effect of changes in the degree of correlation between the two assets can be illustrated by plotting each of the portfolios in risk-return space as shown in Figure 1A.4.

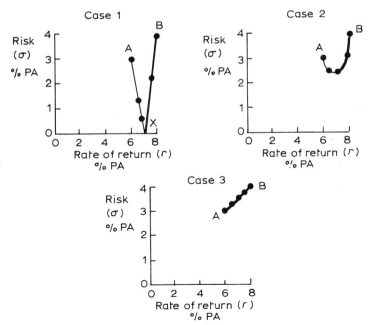

Figure 1A.4 Two-asset portfolio plotted in risk return space.

These illustrations have shown that the coefficient of correlation between assets is an important factor when constructing a portfolio to give the maximum return within a given risk class. Each part of the graph represents an attainable set of portfolios. However not every point is efficient in the sense that the highest return can be achieved for a given level of risk. In cases 1 and 2 the efficient set of portfolios is represented by the heavy line and occurs between points X and B. All portfolios between X and A are inefficient as it is possible to construct a portfolio with a higher return whilst remaining within the same risk class. In case 3 all points along the line are efficient although it is not possible to produce a portfolio which has a standard deviation which is lower than asset A.

Appendix 1B: The capital asset pricing model, the capital market line and index models

This appendix provides a mathematical derivation of the capital asset pricing model and shows that the capital market line is linear. It also shows how index models can be used to simplify the basic input information for a portfolio analysis.

The capital asset pricing model

Only portfolios which are efficient will lie on the capital market line. All other portfolios will lie below the line. By investing funds in both an inefficient portfolio (J) and the market portfolio (M) it is possible to construct another portfolio represented by Q in Figure 1B.1.

Assuming that a proportion x of available funds is invested in asset J the expected return and standard deviation of portfolio Q can be expressed as:

$$E(r_q) = xE(r_j) + (1 - x)E(r_m) \qquad (1B.1)$$

and

$$\sigma_q{}^2 = x^2\sigma_j{}^2 + (1 - x)^2\sigma_m{}^2 + 2x(1 - x)\rho_{jm}\sigma_j\sigma_m. \qquad (1B.2)$$

The shape of the curve JQM will depend on the degree of correlation that exists between portfolios J and M. The slope will change depending on the proportion of funds invested in J and M. At point M it will be equal to the slope of the capital market line as the curves are tangential. The slope at this point is important because it implies that

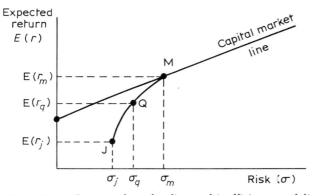

Figure 1B.1 The capital market line and inefficient portfolios.

all the systematic risk in the portfolio has been diversified away leaving only the systematic component.

From equation (1B.2), letting $w = \sigma_q{}^2$ and $\mathrm{Cov}(j, m)$ equal the covariance term gives

$$w = x^2\sigma_j{}^2 + (1 - x)^2\sigma_m{}^2 + 2x(1 - x)\mathrm{Cov}(j, m). \qquad (1B.3)$$

Differentiating with respect to x gives

$$\frac{\mathrm{d}w}{\mathrm{d}x} = 2x\sigma_j{}^2 + 2(1 - x)\sigma_m{}^2 + 2(1 - 2x)\mathrm{Cov}(j, m). \qquad (1B.4)$$

As $w = \sigma_q{}^2$ it is possible to differentiate σ_q with respect to w to give

$$\frac{\mathrm{d}\sigma_q}{\mathrm{d}w} = \tfrac{1}{2}w^{-1/2} \qquad (1B.5)$$

Substituting for w gives

$$\frac{\mathrm{d}\sigma_q}{\mathrm{d}w} = \frac{1}{2\sigma_q}. \qquad (1B.6)$$

The change in σ_q with respect to x is given by

$$\frac{\mathrm{d}\sigma_q}{\mathrm{d}x} = \frac{\mathrm{d}\sigma_q}{\mathrm{d}w}\frac{\mathrm{d}w}{\mathrm{d}x} = \frac{x\sigma_j{}^2 + (x - 1)\sigma_m{}^2 + (1 - 2x)\mathrm{Cov}(j, m)}{\sigma_q}. \qquad (1B.7)$$

The change in $\mathrm{E}(r_q)$ with respect to x is given by differentiating equation (1B.1), thus

$$\frac{\mathrm{d}\mathrm{E}(r_q)}{\mathrm{d}x} = \mathrm{E}(r_j) - \mathrm{E}(r_m). \qquad (1B.8)$$

The slope of the curve JQM can be defined as the change in $\mathrm{E}(r_q)$ with respect to σ_q, and can be derived from equations (1B.7) and (1B.8).

$$\frac{\mathrm{d}\mathrm{E}(r_q)}{\mathrm{d}\sigma_q} = \frac{\mathrm{d}\mathrm{E}(r_q)}{\mathrm{d}x}\frac{\mathrm{d}x}{\mathrm{d}\sigma_q}$$

$$= \frac{\sigma_q[\mathrm{E}(r_j) - \mathrm{E}(r_m)]}{x\sigma_j{}^2 + (x - 1)\sigma_m{}^2 + (1 - 2x)\mathrm{Cov}(j, m)}. \qquad (1B.9)$$

The gradient of the curve at M can be found when x equals zero. At this point σ_q must by definition equal σ_m. Substituting into equation (1B.9) gives the desired result:

$$\frac{\mathrm{d}\mathrm{E}(r_q)}{\mathrm{d}\sigma_q} = \frac{\sigma_m[\mathrm{E}(r_j) - \mathrm{E}(r_m)]}{\mathrm{Cov}(j, m) - \sigma_m{}^2}. \qquad (1B.10)$$

This however is equal to the slope of the capital market line, and consideration of Figure 1B.1 gives the following:

$$\frac{\sigma_m[E(r_j) - E(r_m)]}{\text{Cov}(j,\, m) - \sigma_m{}^2} = \frac{E(r_m) - r_f}{\sigma_m} \qquad (1B.11)$$

which simplifies to

$$E(r_j) - E(r_m) = [E(r_m) - r_f]\left[\frac{\text{Cov}(j,\, m)}{\sigma_m{}^2} - 1\right]. \qquad (1B.12)$$

By letting

$$\frac{\text{Cov}(j,\, m)}{\sigma_m{}^2} = \beta_j$$

this simplifies to

$$E(r_j) = [E(r_m) - r_f][\beta_j - 1] + E(r_m) \qquad (1B.13)$$

which, rearranged, gives the basic form of the capital asset pricing model.

Linearity of the capital market line

The derivation given above assumes that the capital market line is linear. This however can be proved as follows.

Given the opportunity to invest in a risk-free asset in addition to a portfolio of risky assets it is possible to create any portfolio lying along r_fMZ as shown in Figure 1B.2. A portfolio P could therefore be formed by altering the proportion of funds, x, invested in M. Thus the expected return on P can be expressed as

$$E(r_p) = xE(r_m) + (1 - x)r_f. \qquad (1B.14)$$

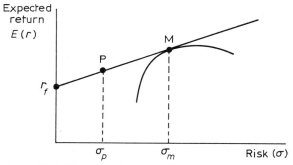

Figure 1B.2 The capital market line.

As this expression involves no second-order powers of x the expected return on the portfolio is therefore linear.

The standard deviation of the portfolio can be expressed as

$$\sigma_p = \sqrt{[x^2\sigma_m^2 + (1 - x)^2\sigma_f^2 + 2x(1 - x)\text{Cov}(r_f, r_m)]}. \quad (1B.15)$$

By definition the risk-free rate of return has a standard deviation (σ_f) of zero so that equation (1B.15) simplifies to

$$\sigma_p = \sqrt{(x^2\sigma_m^2)}.$$

When $\sigma_f = 0$

$$\sigma_p = x\sigma_m. \quad (1B.16)$$

Once again this relationship involves no second-order powers of x proving that the capital market line is linear.

By rearranging equation (1B.14) and substituting for x from equation (1B.16) it can easily be shown that the equation of the capital market line for efficient portfolios is as follows:

$$E(r_p) = r_f + \frac{\sigma_p}{\sigma_m} [E(r_m) - r_f]. \quad (1B.17)$$

Single- and multi-index models

Chapter 1 has shown that it is possible to simplify the inputs to a portfolio analysis by relating the returns on an investment to some index of market movements. This can be done by using either a single or multiple index.

Single index models

The return on two securities A and B can be expressed in terms of an index (I) as follows.

$$r_a = a_0 + a_1I + u. \quad (1B.18)$$

$$r_b = b_0 + b_1I + v. \quad (1B.19)$$

The expected return on A and B will therefore be

$$E(r_a) = a_0 + a_1E(I) \quad (1B.20)$$

and

$$E(r_b) = b_0 + b_1E(I). \quad (1B.21)$$

For each of the returns the deviation from their expected value can be found by subtracting equation (1B.20) from (1B.18), and (1B.21) from (1B.19).

$$r_a - E(r_a) = a_1[I - E(I)] + u. \tag{1B.22}$$

$$r_b - E(r_b) = b_1[I - E(I)] + v. \tag{1B.23}$$

The variance of r_a can be expressed as

$$\text{Var}(r_a) = E[r_a - E(r_a)]^2. \tag{1B.24}$$

Substituting from equation (1B.22) gives

$$\text{Var}(r_a) = E\{a_1{}^2[I - E(I)]^2 + u^2 + 2a_1u[I - E(I)]\}. \tag{1B.25}$$

Applying the expectations operator and noting that the expected value of the error term $E(u)$ equals zero, it will be seen that the above equation simplifies to

$$\text{Var}(r_a) = a_1{}^2 \text{Var}(I) + \text{Var}(u). \tag{1B.26}$$

Similarly,

$$\text{Var}(r_b) = b_1{}^2 \text{Var}(I) + \text{Var}(v). \tag{1B.27}$$

The covariance term can be derived from

$$\text{Cov}(r_a, r_b) = E\{[r_a - E(r_a)][r_b - E(r_b)]\}. \tag{1B.28}$$

By substitution from equations (1B.22) and (1B.23) and again recognizing that $E(u) = 0$ and $E(v) = 0$ it can easily be shown that equation (1B.28) simplifies to:

$$\text{Cov}(r_a, r_b) = a_1b_1\text{Var}(I) \tag{1B.29}$$

The values of a_1 and b_1 represent the volatility of an asset's returns measured relative to an index. These are the beta coefficients. It will be seen therefore that once the β of an asset has been estimated relative to the returns on an index, it is possible to estimate the expected return together with the variance and covariance of returns with a limited amount of data.

Multi-index models

Instead of using one index it is possible to express the return on a security by reference to several indices. Thus the return on a security could be expressed as

$$r_a = a_0 + a_1I_1 + a_2I_2 + a_3I_3 + \ldots a_nI_n + u \tag{1B.30}$$

where $I_1, I_2, \ldots, I_n$ represent the value of a number of indices. The expected value of r_a can therefore be expressed as

$$E(r_a) = a_0 + a_1 E(I_1) + a_2 E(I_2) + a_3 E(I_3) + \ldots a_n E(I_n). \quad (1B.31)$$

Using the same procedure as before it can be shown that the variance and covariance terms can be expressed as

$$\text{Var}(r_a) = a_1{}^2 \text{Var}(I_1) + a_2{}^2 \text{Var}(I_2) +$$
$$\ldots a_n{}^2 \text{Var}(I_n) + \text{Var}(u) \quad (1B.32)$$

and

$$\text{Cov}(r_a, r_b) = a_1 b_1 \text{Var}(I_1) + a_2 b_2 \text{Var}(I_2) + \ldots a_n b_n \text{Var}(I_n). \quad (1B.33)$$

The use of multi-index models has great potential in terms of trying to explain the returns generating process for property. This is an area which should receive greater attention in the future.

Appendix 1C: The expectations operator and other expressions

Appendix 1B has made considerable use of the expectations operator in deriving expressions for expected returns, variances and covariances. As portfolio theory and capital market theory is based on expectations it is useful to present some common operations which make use of the expectations operator.

Although estimating expected values is similar to calculating averages the two processes are conceptually different. Expected values rely upon having some knowledge of the probability of certain outcomes which can change if those probabilities change. An average, however, assumes that each outcome is equally likely. Appendix 1A identified this difference when expressing the different moments of a distribution using both future and historic data.

The following provides, without proof, a series of alternative expressions for common statements relating to two random variables, x and y, which have a joint probability distribution $p(x, y)$, together with constants k, a, b, c and d.

$$E(x + y) = E(x) + E(y) \qquad (1C.1)$$

$$E(kx) = kE(x) \qquad (1C.2)$$

$$E(bx + c) = bE(x) + c \qquad (1C.3)$$

$$Var(x) = E[x - E(x)]^2 \qquad (1C.4)$$

$$Var(x) = E(x^2) - [E(x)]^2 \qquad (1C.5)$$

$$E(x^2) = Var(x) + [E(x)]^2 \qquad (1C.6)$$

If x and y are independent:

$$E(xy) = E(x)E(y) \qquad (1C.7)$$

$$Var(x, y) = [E(x)]^2 \, Var(y) + [E(y)]^2 \, Var(x) + Var(x)Var(y)$$

If x and y are not independent:

$$E(xy) = E(x)E(y) + Cov(x, y) \qquad (1C.8)$$

$$Var(x, y) = [E(x)]^2 \, Var(y) + [E(y)]^2 \, Var(x)$$

$$+ \, Var(x)Var(y) + 2E(x)E(y)Cov(x, y) \qquad (1C.9)$$

This is an approximation of the general case derived by Goodman (1960). If x and y have a joint bivariate Normal distribution the following term should be added to equation (1C.9):

$$\text{Var}(x)\text{Var}(y)(1 + \sigma_{xy}{}^2).$$

Other properties of random variables are as follows:

$$\text{Var}(k) = 0 \tag{1C.10}$$

$$\text{Var}(ax + b) = a^2\,\text{Var}(x) \tag{1C.11}$$

$$\text{Cov}(x, y) = \text{E}(xy) + \text{E}(x)\text{E}(y) \tag{1C.12}$$

$$\text{Cov}(x, k) = 0 \tag{1C.13}$$

$$\text{Cov}[(ax + b), (cy + d)] = ac\,\text{Cov}(x, y) \tag{1C.14}$$

Appendix 1D: Regression analysis

Regression analysis is a statistical tool used to examine the interrelationship between two or more variables. It is frequently used to analyse data which is both cross-sectional and in time-series form.

An example of the former would be a model which specifies the relationship between property values and a number of explanatory variables such as location, area, tenant quality, height of building and so on. The analysis would consider a sample of data taken at one point in time and would try to explain value in terms of its relationship with the independent variables.

Time-series analysis, by contrast, considers data collected for two or more variables over a number of time periods. An example of this would be a model which tries to explain the returns on a property by relating a time series of returns to similar data calculated using a property index.

Because of the importance of regression analysis in the development of asset pricing models this appendix is intended to cover some of the basic properties. A more detailed treatment can be found in a number of textbooks dealing with statistics, such as Johnston (1966), Gujarati (1978), Makridakis, Wheelwright and McGee (1983), Pindyck and Rubinfeld (1981) and Wonnacott and Wonnacott (1972).

The basic model

The basic form of regression model relates one variable to another by a line which minimizes the sum of the squared differences of each observation from the line. This is illustrated in Figure 1D.1.

Given the scatter diagram of y versus x it is possible to draw a straight line between the points so that the error around the line is minimized. Under these conditions it is possible to relate x and y by an equation for a straight line,

$$y = a + bx \qquad (1D.1)$$

where a is the intercept term and b is the slope of the line. If e represents the vertical distance of an observation from the line, each point (j) can be represented by

$$y_j = a + bx_j + e_j \qquad (1D.2)$$

The values of a and b are referred to as the **parameter estimates** of the regression model. Under certain assumptions they can be regarded

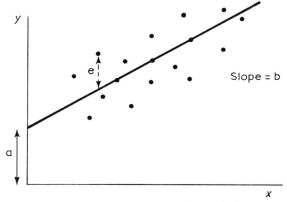

Figure 1D.1 Least squares regression analysis.

as being unbiased, efficient and consistent. These are desirable properties which are essential to the interpretation of a regression analysis and have the following meaning.

Bias

If it were possible to run the regression analysis many times with different sets of data the regression parameter should be equal to its mean value. Thus the mean or expected value of b, for example, should be equal to its true value. The difference in interpretation between biased and unbiased estimators is shown in Figure 1D.2. The estimator will of course have some dispersion round its true value. It is this dispersion which affects its efficiency.

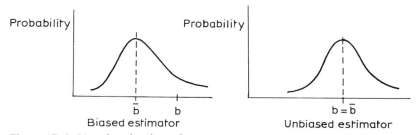

Figure 1D.2 Biased and unbiased estimators.

Efficiency

The slope coefficient b will be an efficient unbiased estimator if its variance is small. One estimator is more efficient than another if it has a smaller variance. Figure 1D.3 illustrates the difference between an efficient and inefficient estimator. Clearly we can be more confident about the expected value of the efficient estimator because it has a smaller dispersion.

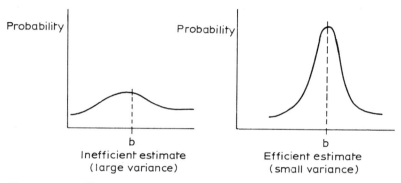

Figure 1D.3 Efficiency.

Consistency

Our parameter estimate will be a consistent estimator if it approaches its true value as the sample size increases. The distribution of the estimator b, for example, will approach the true value as the sample size increases. Figure 1D.4 illustrates the point as sample size increases.

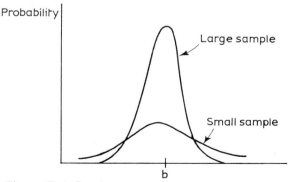

Figure 1D.4 Consistency.

Regression analysis assumptions

To be sure that the regression analysis is providing results which can be interpreted in a meaningful way, the model is derived using the following important assumptions relating to the error term (e).

1. It is random, unbiased and has a mean of zero.
2. It has constant variance for all observations. This property is known as **homoscedasticity**.
3. Each of the error terms is uncorrelated so there is no pattern or serial correlation.
4. The error terms are uncorrelated with the x terms so the errors are independent.

When undertaking a regression analysis it is important to check the residuals to see whether there is any pattern which would violate the above assumptions.

Given these assumptions it is possible to draw inferences about the regression statistics and derive confidence intervals around the regression line.

Regression coefficients

Given that the regression equation (1D.1) is a linear unbiased estimate of y, the parameter estimates for a and b can be calculated from the following expressions:

$$a = \frac{\sum y}{n} - b \frac{\sum x}{n} \tag{1D.3}$$

$$b = \frac{\text{Cov}(x, y)}{\text{Var}(x)}. \tag{1D.4}$$

An alternative way of writing equation (1D.4) is

$$b = \frac{n \sum xy - (\sum x)(\sum y)}{n \sum x^2 - (\sum x)^2} \tag{1D.5}$$

Analysis of variance

The total variance in the dependent variable y can be expressed as the sum of the squared differences from the mean value of y. Part of this variance can be explained by the regression line and part by the residual or unexplained variance. Total variance can therefore be split as follows:

total variance = explained variance + unexplained variance.

The decomposition of variance is shown in Figure 1D.5.

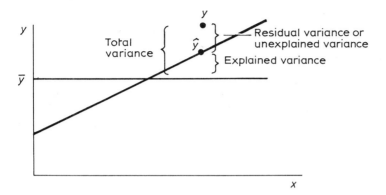

Figure 1D.5 The analysis of variance.

If we represent the mean and fitted values of y by $\bar{y}$ and $\hat{y}$ the total variance can be drafted as follows:

$$\sum (y - \bar{y})^2 = \sum (\hat{y} - \bar{y})^2 + \sum (y - \hat{y})^2 \qquad (1D.6)$$

A further interpretation can be given by dividing by the total variance. This enables the explained and unexplained variance to be expressed as a proportion of the total variance. This is an important concept because it identifies the meaning of the term coefficient of determination (R^2). Algebraically it can be expressed as

$$\frac{\sum (\hat{y} - \bar{y})^2}{\sum (y - \bar{y})^2} = \frac{\text{explained variance}}{\text{total variance}} = R^2. \qquad (1D.7)$$

R^2 is a measure of the explanatory power of the regression model. A figure of 0.75 for example implies that 75% of the variation in y can be explained by the regression. The remaining 25% must be explained by other factors.

It will be evident that the partitioning of the variance in this way is identical to the discussion in Chapter 1 relating the total risk of an investment to market risk and specific risk.

Testing for significance

If the data used for a regression analysis are correctly specified they should be Normally distributed. It is common to undertake a transformation to ensure that this property is maintained, and then under these conditions it is possible to use the t-test for checking the significance of the parameter estimates. The t value can be found by dividing the regression estimate by its standard error. In approximate terms if the resulting t value is close to 2.0 we can say that the figure is statistically significant at the 95% level.

This process however only checks to see whether the parameter estimate is significantly different from zero. A more appropriate model should take into consideration a hypothesized value against which the test should be carried out. The model to use is given in equations (1D.8) and (1D.9).

$$t_a = \frac{a - a_h}{\sigma_a} \tag{1D.8}$$

$$t_b = \frac{b - b_h}{\sigma_h} \tag{1D.9}$$

The values a_h and b_h represent the hypothesized values for the intercept term and slope coefficient against which the test is being carried out. For example it may be necessary to test to whether the slope coefficient in a regression is significantly different from 1.0. Take for example the following regression results which relate the returns on a property (r_p) to a market index (r_m) (standard errors are shown in brackets).

$$r_p = a + br_m$$

Parameter estimates		
a	b	R^2
−0.44	0.85	0.863
(3.36)	(0.05)	

Our prior hypothesis may be that we expect the intercept (a_h) to be zero and the slope coefficient (b_h) to be statistically indistinguishable from 1.00. In order to test this, we use equations (1D.8) and (1D.9). Then as

$$t_a = \frac{-0.44 - 0}{3.36} = -0.13$$

and this figure is less than 2.00, it is safe to say that the intercept term is not significantly different from zero.

The analysis of the slope coefficient is as follows:

$$t_b = \frac{0.85 - 1.00}{0.05} = -3.00.$$

The t value in this case is much greater than 2.00 in absolute terms which indicates that it is significantly different from 1.00. It is also significantly different from zero. Even though 0.85 may be considered to be reasonably close to 1.00 it cannot be regarded as being statistically close.

Multiple regression

The above discussion has considered the relationship between two variables. It is possible to extend the analysis to encompass a much wider range of independent variables. The interpretation of the statistics given above is the same irrespective of the number of independent variables under consideration. There are however some added complications and the reader who is interested in pursuing this topic further should refer to Johnston (1966), Gujarati (1978), Makridakis, Wheelwright and McGee (1983), Pindyck and Rubinfield (1981) and Wonnacott and Wonnacott (1972).

Appendix 1E: Continuous rates of return

Rates of return can be drafted either in discrete time or continuous time. The difference in calculation between the two is shown in equations (1E.1) and (1E.2) where V_t and V_{t-1} represent values at the end and beginning of a period and a represents the income received.

Discrete time:

$$r_t = \frac{V_t - V_{t-1} + a}{V_{t-1}}. \tag{1E.1}$$

Continuous time:

$$r_t = \ln\left(\frac{V_t + a}{V_{t-1}}\right). \tag{1E.2}$$

Equation (1E.2) can also be drafted as

$$r_t = \ln(V_t + a) - \ln(V_{t-1}). \tag{1E.3}$$

Although portfolio theory and capital market theory have been developed within a single-period framework there is nothing which defines the length of that period. Calculating rates of return within a continuous time framework overcomes this problem, so this is a strong reason for using continuous rates of return.

Another reason for using continuous rates of return is based on the recognition that the lower bound to rates of return is −100% because it is impossible to lose more than 100% of an investment. However it is possible to earn positive returns which can be well in excess of 100%. For this reason it is not uncommon to find that the returns from assets such as stocks and property are positively skewed and do not conform to a Normal distribution. Under this assumption it is desirable to use continuous returns because taking the natural log of value relatives has the effect of pulling in the higher rates of return but has less effect on the lower returns. This transformation tends to make the returns distribution closer to Normal.

Although portfolio theory is drafted in terms of single-period expectations there is no loss of generality caused by using continuous returns.

Another advantage of working in continuous time is that returns over longer periods can be found easily merely by adding intermediate figures. The statistics produced using continuous returns tend to produce lower means and variance, and the distributions tend to have less skewness in comparison with similar figures using discrete returns.

Generally speaking because the distributions of continuous returns tend to be closer to Normal distributions than discrete returns, estimated risk statistics such as β will tend to be more efficient than those calculated using discrete returns.

Unless otherwise stated continuous returns are used throughout the remainder of this book.

References

Baum, A. (1989) *A critical examination of the measurement of property investment risk*, Discussion Paper No. 22, Department of Land Economy, University of Cambridge.

Brennan, M. (1971) Capital market equilibrium with divergent borrowing and lending rates, *Journal of Financial and Quantitative Analysis*, 6, December.

Brown, G. R. (1985) An empirical analysis of risk and return in the UK commercial property market, unpublished PhD dissertation, University of Reading.

David, H. A., Hartley, H. O. and Pearson, E. S. (1954) The distribution of the ratio, in a single normal sample, of range to standard deviation, *Biometrika*, 61.

Fama, E. (1965) The behaviour of stock prices, *Journal of Business*, January, 34–99.

Fama, E. (1970) Multiperiod consumption–investment decisions, *American Economic Review*, March.

Findlay, M., Hamilton, C. W., Messner, S. D., and Yormark, J. S. (1979) Optimal real-estate portfolios, *AREUEA Journal*, 7(3) 298–317.

Friedman, H. C. (1970) Real-estate investment and portfolio theory, *Journal of Financial and Quantitative Analysis*, March, 861–74.

Goodman, L. A. (1960) On the exact variance of products, *Journal of the American Statistical Association*, 708–13.

Gujarati, D. (1978) *Basic Econometrics*, McGraw–Hill, New York.

Johnston, J. (1966) *Econometric Methods*, Englewood Cliffs, N.J., Prentice Hall.

Lintner, J. (1965) Security prices, risk and maximal gains from diversification, *Journal of Finance*, December, 587–615.

Locke, S. M. (1987) Performance assessment indexes and capital asset pricing models, *Journal of Valuation*, 5, 230–48.

Makridakis, S., Wheelwright, S. and McGee, V. (1983) *Forecasting: methods and applications*, John Wiley & Sons, New York.

Mandelbrot, B. (1963) The variation of certain speculative prices, *Journal of Business*, October, 394–419.

Markowitz, H. (1959) *Efficient Diversification of Investments*, John Wiley & Sons, Inc., New York.

Mayers, D. (1972) Nonmarketable assets and capital market equilibrium under uncertainty, reprinted in *Studies in the Theory of Capital Markets* (ed. Jensen, M. C.), Praeger, New York.

Miles, M. and Rice, M. (1978) Towards a more complete investigation of the correlations of real estate investment yield to the rate evidenced in the money and capital markets: the individual investor's perspective, *Real Estate Appraiser and Analyst*, November–December, 8–19.

Mossin, J. (1966) Equilibrium in a capital asset market, *Econometrica*, October, 768–83.

Pindyck, R. S. and Rubinfeld, D. L. (1981) *Econometric Models and Economic Forecasts*, McGraw–Hill, New York.

Roll, R. (1977) A critique of the asset pricing theory's tests, *Journal of Financial Economics*, (4), 129–76.

Rosenberg, B. and Marathe, V. (1973) *The prediction of investment risk: systematic and residual risk*, reprint 21, Berkeley Working Paper Series.

Samuelson, P. (1965) Proof that properly anticipated prices fluctuate randomly, *Industrial Management Review* 6, Spring, 41–9.

Sharpe, W. (1963) A simplified model for Portfolio Analysis, *Management Science*, January, 277–93.

Sharpe, W. F. (1964) Capital asset prices: a theory of market equilibrium under conditions of risk, *Journal of Finance*, September, 425–42.

Ward, C. W. R. (1979) Methods of incorporating risk in the analysis of commercial property investments, unpublished PhD dissertation, Reading University.

Wonnacott, T. H. and Wonnacott, R. J. (1972) *Introductory Statistics for Business and Economics*, John Wiley & Sons, New York.

2
Market efficiency and its effect on pricing

One of the most important ideas in modern finance is that prices reflect all knowable information. The value of an asset is therefore a reflection on both the quantity and quality of available information.

In a well-ordered society most markets tend to be reasonably efficient. In other words the prices at which assets sell are on average a fair reflection of their true value. If this is true then it will be difficult to discover those assets which are consistently mispriced. An efficiently operating market is also important for the interpretation of such aspects as asset allocation and performance measurement.

The concept of market efficiency was first proposed in relation to stock and bond prices. It does, however, have a general relevance and is particularly important as far as property is concerned since it is frequently contended that the property market is inefficient.

This chapter looks at the background to market efficiency by looking at the type of information available and assessing its importance in establishing value. The basic concepts of market efficiency will be discussed and a series of appendices will examine the matter in more detail.

2.1 The importance of information in assessing value

If valuations are an accurate reflection of information then they will indicate the best way in which resources should be allocated. Thus, in looking at the question of how valuable is information, we are also looking at another problem which relates to the efficiency of the property market. Our investigation should therefore say something in answer to the following questions.

1. What information is important in assessing value?
2. What does such imformation say about market efficiency?

3. Is it possible to earn abnormal returns by trying to obtain better information about individual properties or locations?

In those situations where a single value can be misleading it has been suggested that a range of values might be more meaningful. An example of this would be an obsolete multi-storey industrial building let on a long lease to a tenant with moderately good convenant.

Producing a range of values might also imply that the methodology employed differs according to the type of valuation being carried out. However, if valuations are an accurate reflection of information then the methodology should be essentially the same. What will differ is the type of information to be incorporated and the relevance placed on it by the valuer.

The most common type of valuation will consist of a cash flow extended into the future, discounted at a rate of return which compensates for the riskiness of the property. The cash flow will be assessed by the valuer after carrying out a detailed survey of the property and its location and will reflect his expectations concerning the future potential of the property. The rate of return used to discount the cash flow will reflect the fact that there is a trade-off between risk and return so high risk investment will require higher expected returns than low risk investments.

Because investors generally combine assets into portfolios, they are trying to diversify away much of the risk of holding those assets separately. Investors therefore cannot expect to be compensated for the risk they can eliminate, only that risk which remains after diversification. This aspect was discussed in Chapter 1 and it is this element of risk which determines the rate of return used to discount the cash flows.

The notion of considering value in a portfolio sense is a fundamental truth which applies to all risky assets and only that information which is relevant to the valuation has any importance.

Valuations can cover a number of different requirements, some of which are given in the following list:

1. open market value;
2. current use value;
3. redevelopment value;
4. insurance value;
5. mortgage value;
6. stock exchange value;
7. going concern value.

A number of these are specialist valuations reflecting a specific subset of information. However, each can be drafted in very general terms which would take the following form:

$$E(V) = f(a, b, c, d, e, f, \ldots n) \qquad (2.1)$$

where a, b, c, d, ..., n represent different factors which affect the valuation. Depending on the type of valuation being undertaken the weight applied to each of the factors will vary. Note also that the valuation is drafted in terms of expectations because we cannot be certain about the outcome of each of the factors.

Valuations will vary not only between each other but also from period to period depending on the type of information which is relevant and how the valuer assesses that information. Current use value for example will be a reflection of the existing use of a property on the assumption that planning permission would not be granted for any material development. Similarly redevelopment value will reflect more of the future potential of the property assuming planning permission would be granted. In both cases a cash flow could be estimated, based on the judgement of the valuer, which must then be discounted at a rate of return which provides adequate compensation for the risks undertaken.

Of the values referred to above, it is probably open market value which is most important. This is intended to represent

the best price at which an interest in property might reasonably be expected to be sold by Private Treaty at the date of the valuation assuming:

1. a willing seller;
2. a reasonable period within which to negotiate the sale, taking into account the nature of the property and the state of the market;
3. values will remain static throughout the period;
4. the property will be freely exposed to the market;
5. no account is to be taken of an additional bid by a special purchaser.

RICS guidance note No. 22 (2nd edn.)

These are the assumptions recommended by the RICS under which open market values should be assessed generally. It is important to note that within this definition open market valuations are drafted in terms of expectations and the subset of information is very clearly specified. By sampling a large number of valuers it would be possible to produce a probability distribution of open market values for an individual property. The shape of the curve would be peaked round the expected value but would also have tails on either side reflecting the influence of special purchasers or forced sales, as illustrated in Figure 2.1.

In making up this distribution the value given for a property will vary from valuer to valuer depending on his expectations concerning the subset of information at his disposal. If the valuer is uncertain about the future he cannot be sure about the present value of the income from the property. He can only say that under one set of circumstances it will have one value and under another set, another value. Each of the possible values could be ascribed a probability and would contribute to the distribution curve. However the expected value of the distribution should be close to the true economic value of the property.

Figure 2.1 shows a distribution of open market values, but it would be just as possible to draw up a distribution of insurance values or redevelopment values. Each represents a different information set and will have its own expected value. The rôle of the valuer is to ensure that the information set is clearly defined and to interpret only that information which is relevant to the valuation. In many cases the distinction between the different types of value may not be clear cut.

However, this is not the end of the story as far as open market values are concerned since we are also interested to know whether a distribution of values is likely to be the same as a distribution of prices for the same property. In other words, is the same information subset

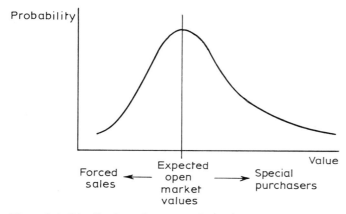

Figure 2.1 Distribution of open market values.

being used by all players in the market when assessing open market values?

Given a distribution of values the price at which a property trades in the market should be chosen randomly from the distribution of values. Valuations and prices do not have to coincide but we want to be sure that on average the same information subset is being used so that no significant bias exists between the values and prices.

If this were not the case, it could have serious consequences for the property industry. Professional advice would be meaningless and performance measurement would be a fruitless exercise.

The market therefore should be making the same assessment concerning expectations as the valuer. This is important because confusion can arise in believing that valuations are not a good proxy for prices. For example Sykes (1983) argues that valuations are always in error due to the difficulty of forecasting rental values and yields. However, as valuations are drafted in terms of expectations, they will conform to some probability distribution depending on different views concerning growth potential. If valuers are making the same assessment of future expectations as the market then the sales price should be drawn randomly from that distribution. Moving through time, valuers as well as the market will revise their expectations in the light of changing conditions. This should cause no problems as far as capital allocation is concerned unless there is consistent bias between valuations and prices. Empirical tests of this hypothesis (Appendix 2A) indicate that there is a close relationship between valuations and prices.

From the point of view of the valuer, difficulties would arise if there was significant bias between valuations and prices and if that bias was maintained over long periods. Although it is common to find reports suggesting the valuation process is flawed and values bear no relationship to prices, it is important to realize that the whole basis of professional property advice rests on the assumption that the valuations are a good proxy for prices. This is not to say that there should be a one-to-one correspondence between valuations and prices, only that on average one is a good proxy for the other. If this were not the case then it would be impossible to provide meaningful advice to institutional investors on the allocation of funds within their portfolios and performance measurement would be difficult to justify without liquidating a portfolio.

Although this is an important point it must be understood in relation to the subset of information under consideration. The hypothesis that valuations are a good proxy for prices is valid only if the information subset is the same for both prices and valuations. If for example open market values are being compared with special purchase prices then the relationship falls down. The information subset has changed and because it differs from the open market approach it could signal an opportunity for profitable arbitrage.

Correctly assessing information is therefore the central issue in determining value. The information relevant to determining open market values for example could contain an element of both current use and potential use. The agreed open market value could represent a weighted average of these two figures. A newly completed development should have its current use value equal to its redevelopment value. In this case there is no possibility that a new development will be carried out so the open market value will represent 100% of current use value. Over time, current use value will decline and redevelopment value will increase. Other external influences may bring this about more quickly if for example political changes favour redevelopment. The probability factor that could be assigned to the redevelopment option will therefore increase so the open market value may well be made up of, say, 40% current use value and 60% redevelopment value. As open market value represents the best price there will come a point when, assuming planning permission has been granted, redevelopment value assumes the major proportion of the open market value. Thus by altering the likelihood of certain events taking place the valuer can track the sensitivity of changes in the open market value of a property and can advise his client accordingly.

It would be incorrect though to suggest that valuers are constantly making this assessment, as the majority of properties will not require this type of analysis. Some, however, will. Take for instance the case of a redevelopment site which consists largely of small shops or residential property. A developer buys the properties on a piecemeal basis over a number of years. The first purchase will reflect very little in the way of redevelopment value and be largely current use value. At the beginning of the site assembly, the chances of redevelopment taking place in the near future may well be slight and the developer could be relying very much on hope. As more property is acquired the planning scene may become clearer, and so the later purchases will reflect a greater proportion of redevelopment value. In these situations it has not been unusual for a developer to acquire the properties by forming several different companies in order to avoid the impression that a redevelopment is likely to take place and hence prevent an individual owner from holding him to ransom. By doing this the developer is artificially restricting information, so the valuation of the individual properties will only reflect that information which is available.

2.2 Efficiency of the market

What does this discussion say about the efficiency of the property market? What in fact is an efficient market?

A market is efficient if prices reflect all known information. If valuations are a good proxy for prices then valuations should reflect all known information. Thus for the market to function efficiently all available information must be impounded into valuations.

It has frequently been argued that because property is lumpy, cannot easily be split up, is difficult to sell and incurs high transaction costs, it is not efficient. Although these points are important they will only affect the operational efficiency of the market. As far as open market valuations are concerned and particularly in relation to portfolio performance we are more interested in allocational efficiency. In other words, if valuations are a fair reflection of what is happening in the market-place then they can be used as the correct method for allocating investment funds. The high transaction costs associated with trading in property, however, will prevent the market from being operationally efficient, but this aspect is not unique to the property market. It is possible to have gross imperfections in the property market and yet it can still be efficient.

Why is this important? The reason is that in an efficient market it is difficult to earn a return in excess of that which would compensate for the risk of the asset. In terms of the security market line described in Chapter 1 this means locating an asset which lies above the line. Although from time to time it has been reported that the market is inefficient this is unlikely to be consistently true. There is very little empirical evidence to suggest it is grossly inefficient particularly if adjustments are made for changes in the information subset. On the whole valuers are probably doing a good job of impounding information into values. It is important however to be clear about the level of market efficiency to which we are referring.

A market is said to be efficient if it responds to new information. By definition, if the information is new then valuations from period to period should be independent of each other. The valuation of a property will change only in response to new information, and this should be the case irrespective of the period over which the valuations are measured. This is important because short-term changes in property values are just as relevant as long-term changes. If we consider the allocation of funds between different types of investment to be important then the optimal allocation of funds will be determined by short-term changes in the market. Investors however do not have an infinitely long time-horizon but will switch funds depending on short-term performance. Moving in and out of property is difficult due to marketing problems and high transaction costs, but will only cause investors to divert funds to other more profitable investments, not necessarily to completely liquidate their property holdings.

This is the weak form of market efficiency and at this level the property market responds well. It is also possible to test empirically (Appendix 2B). Although as we become more stringent about the type of information available, the possibility that the market remains efficient is probably reduced. For example an investor with inside information on the redevelopment potential of a site may well earn abnormal returns because he has access to information not generally available. This would also cover the developer referred to earlier, who bought a site using several different companies. At this level the market is probably inefficient although it is difficult to test empirically. Similarly the effect of special purchasers may introduce inefficiencies also.

These factors do not mean that at a general level the equilibrium of the market will be upset. Why then should we be so concerned about the efficiency of the market and what would be the implications of the market being grossly inefficient?

The fact that efficient markets do exist enables us to say something about the way assets should be priced. If the market is a fair game then investors should be compensated for that part of total risk which they cannot eliminate through diversification. An efficient market also implies that valuers are doing a good job of impounding information into valuations.

If the property market were grossly inefficient it would imply that at those times when property was performing exceptionally well, all other markets would be abandoned in favour of property because it would be easy to earn abnormal returns. Conversely when property was performing badly everybody would liquidate their holdings. Clearly this does not happen in practice; there is always some level of activity and property changes hands at prices which on average probably reflect an equilibrium situation at the time of trading. The fact that there may be times when investment in property is low is merely a reflection of the desire to change the percentage of funds in property without liquidating the portfolio. Indeed there are sound economic reasons for believing that investment funds should hold up to about 30% of their total portfolio in property.

2.3 Capitalizing on information

If markets were truly efficient it would be impossible to earn abnormal returns. Abnormal in this sense means a return higher than that needed to compensate for the riskiness of the asset. Without the possibility of being able to earn such abnormal returns there is then no incentive to acquire information because properties selected at random would generate returns which compensated for their risk. Capitalizing on information, therefore, requires the use of valuation models which are capable of processing information in a useful manner.

It is at this point that the rôle of valuation models must be questioned. Why for example are they needed? In an efficient market the process of buying and selling properties should generate sufficient information which, together with the valuer's experience and knowledge of the properties concerned, should enable their values to be assessed. This was the proposition described in Chapter 1, to which two responses suggest themselves.

Firstly, valuation models are useful because they formalize the process by which value is assessed and identify the critical factors. They draw upon information which is available in the market-place and define the economic relationship between the critical variables.

Secondly, and this is probably the most important function, they should be used to establish equilibrium market values which can then be used to determine whether a property is under- or over-priced. Clearly, if we can identify a value for a property which is a reflection of prevailing market conditions and that property is being offered for sale below its equilibrium value then, if bought, it would generate a rate of return higher than required to compensate for its level of risk and therefore would be of substantial benefit to the investor. The valuation model therefore is trying to define equilibrium values.

The best estimates of equilibrium value will depend on the quality of information available. Abnormal returns can be earned only by acquiring better information than other investors. By utilizing costly information it is possible to out-perform those investors who do not have access to similar information. This out-performance will be more pronounced at the gross level, but after taking costs into consideration, out-performance, though the degree be reduced, should still be possible.

If by better analysis it is possible to locate those properties which are under-priced then they should give positive abnormal returns. After taking costs into consideration the advantage however may be eroded although the principles still remain valid.

This approach has implications as far as performance measurement is concerned. If for example a portfolio does exceptionally well in one period, it may well be as a result of better information concerning an individual property or group of properties. Over longer periods the ability to consistently capitalize on information may not be as marked so it becomes difficult to show out-performance when returns are measured over longer and longer periods. Awareness of this fact does point to the need to improve the quality of information used to select properties in order to identify those strategies which could improve performance.

2.4 Valuation models

It should be clear from the above that for valuation models to have a positive role in the selection process they should assist in identifying whether a property is under- or over-priced. The definition of a valid model is therefore a matter of economics, not mathematics. Whereas mathematically correct models can be derived once the economic principles have been established, it does not follow that the reverse is true. This distinction is important if the market is to make efficient use of valuation models.

In order to advance our understanding of valuation models it is worthwhile establishing a general approach to valuation and then contrasting it with some commonly used models.

2.5 A general approach to valuation

The current value of any asset can be determined by taking its value next year and discounting it back to its present value at a rate of return which reflects the riskiness of that asset. The difficulty with this approach is that next year's value is unknown. However, by applying the same logic to next year's value it will be evident that this can be expressed in terms of the following year's value and so on. The process can be continued indefinitely so eventually, by substitution, the present value of the asset can be expressed in terms of a final value which occurs in the distant future.

Consider this now in property terms. The current expected value, $E(V_0)$, of a property with an expected income of $E(a_1)$ in the first year can be expressed in terms of next year's expected value $E(V_1)$ as follows.

$$E(V_0) = \frac{E(a_1) + E(V_1)}{1 + E(r_1)}. \tag{2.2}$$

The expected value of the property at the end of the first year, $E(V_1)$, can be expressed in terms of the following year's expected value, $E(V_2)$, together with the expected income to be received in the second year, $E(a_2)$.

$$E(V_1) = \frac{E(a_2) + E(V_2)}{1 + E(r_2)}. \tag{2.3}$$

Note that the expected rate of return for the second year is different from that for the first year. In general the return used for each period will be determined by the riskiness of the asset and the term structure of interest rates which prevail at that time. By substitution, the present value of the property $E(V_0)$ can be expressed in terms of its value two years hence as follows:

$$E(V_0) = \frac{E(a_1)}{[1 + E(r_1)]} + \frac{E(a_2) + E(V_2)}{[1 + E(r_1)][1 + E(r_2)]} \tag{2.4}$$

If this process were to be continued indefinitely it would be possible to produce a valuation model drafted entirely in terms of the income received in each period, discounted at a rate appropriate to each period. Although extremely cumbersome, this approach is fundamental to all valuation models because it embodies three important factors which ensure its economic correctness.

1. Each of the cash flows is expressed in nominal terms. They are not in current day prices terms but are drafted in terms of the price structure ruling at the time they occur.
2. Each of the discount rates used is expressed in nominal terms and therefore embodies investors' expectations concerning inflation. Nominal returns can be assumed to be approximately equal to the sum of the real rate of return and the expected rate of inflation.
3. The required rate of return also embodies a premium for risk and therefore explicitly recognizes that higher risk assets require higher expected returns.

It is usual to consider valuations in nominal terms because interest rates observed in the market are expressed in this way. The option is available to define valuations in real terms and both approaches will give exactly the same answer. Whichever is adopted, the clear message is that nominal cash flows should be discounted at nominal rates and real cash flows should be discounted at real rates.

2.6 Simplifying the model

Having established the economic principles it is possible to introduce simplifications which will make the model more usable. This can be achieved by making assumptions concerning both the income stream and the required rate of return.

Taking the income stream first, it will be evident that instead of expressing this in terms of discrete annual amounts it could be drafted in terms of an initial income which is then assumed to grow at a constant annual rate. This growth figure would in effect be the average of all the annual growth rates in income in perpetuity.

The required rate of return used to discount the cash flow can be considerably simplified by expressing it as a single figure. Here again the rate chosen is effectively the average of all the future annual rates of return used to discount each of the cash flows. The starting point for determining this figure is to look at the yield on long-term gilts. These figures represent the average of the market expectations concerning short-term interest rates. Thus if the market expects short-term interest rates in the future to rise then long-term rates will generally exceed current short-term rates. Conversely if a drop is anticipated then long-term rates will be below short-term rates.

The return on gilts represents the riskless situation. However as there is risk associated with investment in property it is necessary to add a premium, the extent of which will vary from property to property. It must be stressed that no two properties are likely to be of equal risk, so the use of a global premium of, say, 2% is unlikely to be universally correct.

Given these simplifications, a property let with annual reviews would have a current expected value expressed as:

$$E(V_0) = \frac{E(a)}{E(r) - E(g)} \qquad (2.5)$$

$E(a)$ = expected initial rent;
$E(r)$ = long-term expected required rate of return;
$E(g)$ = long-term expected growth rate in rent.

The rôle of the valuer is to assess independently the required rate of return, suitably adjusted for risk, and the expected growth rate in income, having regard to the type of property, its condition and location together with the economic prospects of the area. Different valuers will have different expectations concerning these two figures so that the expected value of the property is likely to have some variation associated with it. This variation should not matter as long as it is random. In other words if there is an equal chance of a property being either under- or over-valued in any period then over time these errors should cancel out.

It has been stressed earlier that what is important is whether the valuation serves as a good proxy for the price it would achieve in the open market and whether there is any significant bias between valuations and prices. For instance, are there times when valuers estimates are consistently above or below market prices? If valuers are doing a good job and efficiently processing information, there should be no significant difference between valuations and prices. Errors in valuation should be random and over time they should cancel out. The evidence to date suggests that this is the case.

Although valuers are aware of required rates of return and growth rates, for simplicity they prefer to make use of yields. In the example given above the income stream a_1, a_2, a_3, . . ., a_n could be capitalized at a single yield figure which would be the difference between the required rate of return and the growth rate.

However this basic model is interpreted, it is still economically correct as cash flows and rates of return are both expressed in nominal terms. As long as the yield figure embodies the correct assumptions concerning the required rate of return and the growth rate, this model can be used to establish equilibrium values. Once these have been established the model forms the basis for identifying under- or over-priced property from information available in the market-place.

Introducing periodic rent reviews does not alter this basic interpretation; it merely produces a more complex relationship.

2.7 Alternative valuation models

Having established a basic approach to the development of a valuation model it is now possible to examine alternatives to see if they are economically valid. The following models are considered:

1. the equivalent yield model;
2. the equated yield model;
3. the rational valuation model.

2.8 The equivalent yield model

This is probably the most commonly used valuation model. It expresses the capital value of a property in terms of a fixed income stream received in perpetuity with the reversion expressed as the difference between the current full rental value and income stream. Algebraically this is expressed as

$$V_0 = \frac{a_0}{y} + \frac{R_0 - a_0}{y(1 + y)^n} \tag{2.6}$$

where

a_0 = current income;
R_0 = current rental value;
n = number of years to reversion;
y = equivalent yield.

Although not generally acknowledged, equation (2.6) must relate to an expected value. The model is expressed in two parts. The first part is merely the current income capitalized in perpetuity at the equivalent yield. At this point it is important to recognize that the income is fixed in nominal terms although it is declining in real terms. To be consistent, the equivalent yield must therefore be expressed in nominal terms. The second part of the equation however introduces an anomaly. The reversionary element, which is the difference between the rental value and the income, is drafted using present-day prices but occurs at some time in the future. It is capitalized in perpetuity at the equivalent yield and then discounted back to its present value over the period to the reversion (n years). While this may sound logical, the anomaly occurs because the future reversion is drafted in terms of a present-day price structure and not at the price structure ruling at the time of the reversion, i.e. it is drafted in real terms.

The equivalent yield model therefore incorporates cash flows which are both nominal and real although both elements use the same discount rate, i.e. the equivalent yield. Although the equivalent yield is truly the internal rate of return, the conflict between real and nominal cash flows makes it a difficult figure to interpret in economic terms. This also makes it difficult to compare it with yields from other investments which do not suffer from the same problem. This is a severe criticism of the model which restricts its use for analytical work without adjustment, but its popularity probably relies on the fact that it provides a convenient way of relating income, rental value and the number of years to reversion in a manner which valuers can readily grasp, and uses information which is generally available in the market-place. As the equivalent yield for a property is often determined subjectively by reference to known equivalent yields or to prime yields of similar property, there is probably an equal chance of it being overestimated as underestimated. If these errors are random then they should cancel out over time. Even though the model may not be defensible in economic terms it may still produce valuations which closely approximate those observed in an equilibrium market.

Although the model can be criticized on economic grounds it has considerable merit on practical grounds and for this reason it cannot be rejected as a viable method for determining value.

2.9 The equated yield model

The equated yield model overcomes many of these objections. The income stream generated by the property is drafted in nominal terms so that the model includes the expected growth rate, and in addition the periodic rent review pattern is included. The resulting cash flows are discounted at the required rate of return reflecting the riskiness of the property. This is the equated yield, algebraically expressed as

$$V_0 = \frac{a}{r} \left[\frac{(1+r)^p - 1}{(1+r)^p - (1+g)^p} \right] \qquad (2.7)$$

where

p = period between rent reviews;
g = annual growth rate in income.

Like equation (2.6) this model defines expected value. It can be adjusted to allow for the fact that the number of years to reversion is different from the interval between rent reviews, as follows:

$$V_0 = \frac{a_0[1 - (1+r)^{-n}]}{r} + \frac{R_0(1+g)^n}{(1+r)^n} \left[\frac{(1+r)^p - 1}{(1+r)^p - (1+g)^p} \right] \qquad (2.8)$$

where

R_0 = current rental value;
n = number of years to the rent review.

The first part of the expression is merely the present value of an annuity for n years. The income (a_0) is fixed in nominal terms and is discounted at the nominal required rate of return (r).

The second part expresses the current rental value in nominal terms by inflating R_0 at $g\%$ per annum for n years, up until the first rent review. The remainder of the expression is merely an adjustment to take account of the periodic rent reviews. With some simple manipulation the equated yield model can also cope with more than one assumption concerning growth.

The equated yield model therefore partly satisfies the requirement of being economically correct. To use it properly the valuer must make an assessment of the required rate of return and the expected growth rate.

These two factors are independent of each other. The required rate of return is determined in the market-place by reference to other assets of equivalent risk and the growth rate is determined by macro- and micro-economic factors affecting the property. It is in essence the difference between these two figures which determines the property yield. Contrast this with the interpretation given by Sykes and McIntosh (1985) who state that it is

'the differential exhibited by the opportunity cost of money and the property capitalization rate which determines the implied rental growth rate not (as is commonly and erroneously considered to be the case) the cost of money/rental growth differential which determines the property investment yield rate'.

The first part of this statement must be incorrect if it is accepted that the expected return and growth rate are independent variables. However, the equated yield model can be used to analyse transactions in order to determine expected growth rates, but it does require the valuer to make a valid estimate of the expected rate of return.

For practical valuation purposes the equated yield model is cumbersome, and its principal value is in its use as an analytical tool, although with the correct inputs it should produce exactly the same answers as the equivalent yield model.

2.10 The rational valuation model

The rational valuation model developed by Sykes (1981) is a hybrid version of the equated yield model. It is based on the earlier work of Greaves (1972) and is an attempt to overcome some of the problems inherent in the equivalent yield model. Although not specifically recognized by Sykes, the model should be drafted in terms of expectations and takes the following form:

$$V_0 = \left[\frac{a_0}{r} - \frac{a_0}{r(1 + r)^n} \right] + \frac{R_0(1 + g)^n}{y_0(1 + r)^n} \qquad (2.9)$$

where

a_0 = current income;
R_0 = current rental value;
r = opportunity cost of finance;
y_0 = rack-rented equivalent yield;
g = implied growth rate;
n = number of years to next rent review.

If it is assumed that the property is rack-rented so that a_0 equals R_0, and n equals p, then the value of the property, V_0, can be represented by a_0/y_0. Substituting this into equation (2.9) it is possible to solve for the growth rate as follows:

$$g = \left\{ \left[\frac{r - y_0}{r} \right] [(1 + r)^p - 1] + 1 \right\}^{1/p} - 1. \qquad (2.10)$$

It will be seen from equation (2.9) that the rational valuation model is merely a variation of a discounted cash flow approach which recognizes that cash flows should be expressed in nominal terms. It therefore adjusts the current income by using the expected growth rate.

It will be seen also that the model expresses the valuation in terms of both the rack-rented yield and the opportunity cost of finance, the argument being that it uses information familiar to the valuer. No guidance is given on selecting an appropriate figure for the opportunity cost of finance despite this being a fundamental part of the model.

It should be recognized also that since the rack-rented yield is a function of the required rate of return and the expected growth rate, the model will be economically valid only if these figures are used consistently throughout. This may not be the case as some valuers may choose a rate of return which is completely different to that implied by the rack-rented yield. It also follows that the growth rate implied by the yield may not be the same as that incorporated in the model.

The procedure adopted for over-coming this problem is to calculate a growth rate given information concerning the yield. Here again difficulty arises as transformation of the model expresses the growth rate as a function of the rack-rented yield. There will be only one solution therefore which will occur when the required rate of return implied in the rack-rented yield is the same as that specified in the model. Assuming that the two rates of return do coincide, it will be seen that the growth rate is determined within the system of equations and not by reference to macro- or micro-economic factors. It is possibly using this approach to arrive at growth figures which merely justify the mathematical ralationship but completely ignore the under- lying economics.

Under very restrictive conditions, however, the rational valuation model will produce economically correct results. Those conditions are that the required rate of return and the expected growth rate specified in the model are exactly the same as those implied in the rack-rented yield. In order to specify these figures correctly the valuer would need to undertake the same type of analysis required for the equated yield model. Given this situation there appears to be little advantage in utilizing the rational model as opposed to the equated yield model, which does not suffer from the same problems. In addition if the valuer wanted to make more than one assumption within the model concerning expected growth rates this could not be dealt with easily by the rational model.

The choice of the required rate of return is of course critical to all valuation models and it is not unusual for valuers to utilize the return on long-dated gilts for this figure. If used in the rational model this will introduce errors into the resulting valuations, the magnitude of which will depend on the difference between the gilt rate and the required return implied in the yield.

There is no reason to believe that the rational model produces valuations which are any better in an economic sense than, say, the equivalent yield model. As with all the models described here it is far from being a true description of the underlying economic processes.

2.11 Reconciliation

Much of the debate which has surrounded the development of valuation models in recent years has concentrated on mathematical consistency and refinement. Very rarely is the economic validity of the models considered, although really this is the principal issue, and the concept of expected value is usually totally ignored. The equivalent yield is commonly used in the market-place and is the means by which most valuations are established, being widely practised and capable of adapting to a wide variety of situations. Even though it can be criticized on many levels, including economic grounds, it cannot be assumed that it will produce invalid valuations. To do this requires a totally different approach to establishing equilibrium values, based on a better understanding of the way capital markets operate.

The development of complex discounted cash flow models as a means of establishing equilibrium values is unlikely to produce worthwhile results as the practical value of the model diminishes as the number of unknown variables increases. The most promising area for research is more likely to be in the application of cross-sectional multi-factor models which relate value to a series of explanatory variables. This approach is similar to that adopted in both the USA and UK for the analysis of stocks.

In the absence of an approach to valuation which has some economic rationale, it is impossible to identify whether individual properties are under- or over-priced. It follows that it is also impossible to exploit any inefficiencies which may exist within the property market. Any abnormal returns which occur are therefore likely to be due entirely to chance rather than skill.

2.12 Conclusions

This chapter has shown that the property market is probably efficient at the weak form level. It has shown also that the value of a property depends on the quality of information in the relevant information subset. As the access to information becomes more restricted it is more than likely that the market will become progressively more inefficient so that there is a greater probability of earning abnormal returns. What is not certain is whether abnormal returns can be earned consistently from period to period and whether those using current valuation models are capable of indentifying under-priced properties.

In exploring the validity of valuation models it was pointed out that it is the economic factors which are important. Mathematical accuracy is merely a by-product of economic correctness. Even though a poor model is being used there is no guarantee that it will produce poor valuations. The most common method of valuation is by comparison with similar properties. Although this will give a guide to the best value that can be achieved in the market-place the question which remains unanswered is whether the property is under- or over-priced in an economic sense. Conventional valuation models are unable to answer this as they have no economic reference of market equilibrium.

The elements in a valuation model which still need to be addressed are the risk class of the underlying property and the expected growth rate. As these are more technical aspects they are considered within the following appendices:

2A: Valuations versus prices
2B: An analysis of weak form market efficiency in the commercial property market
2C: Term structure and its potential impact on valuation
2D: An analysis of the changing risk profile of the commercial property market
2E: The assessment of systematic risk using a scenario approach
2F: The assessment of systematic risk using a certainty equivalent approach
2G: Assessing the risk premium for property
2H: The decomposition of property yields

Appendix 2A: Valuations versus prices

The hypothesis that valuations act as a good proxy for prices can be tested by analysing a sample of properties which have both a transaction price and a contemporaneous independent valuation. Although such data are difficult to obtain, a random sample of 29 properties was collected for the period 1975–80 covering a broad spectrum of types and quality. The data consisted of transactions prices together with the most recent prior independent valuation, as obtaining contemporaneous valuations is almost impossible to achieve.

The principal condition imposed was that the transaction prices should be based on the open market difinition given by the RICS. This is important because the effect of special purchasers, forced sales or specialized valuations needs to be excluded from the analysis. Similarly, each of the valuations had to be made on an open market basis. They were carried out independently before the date of sale by different firms of surveyors. This avoids any problems which might arise due to firm bias.

The methodology involves regressing the valuation for each of the properties onto its price. This can be expressed as

$$V = a_0 + a_1 P + e \qquad (2A.1)$$

where V and P relate to the valuation and price and a_0 and a_1 are the regression coefficients. The final term (e) represents the error in the model not explained by the regression.

If the hypothesis is correct there should be a one-to-one correspondance between valuations and prices. In particular we are testing to see whether a_1 is close to 1.0 and statistically significant. To overcome problems of heteroscedasticity the regression is run in terms of values and prices per square foot, thus ensuring that the data are in comparable units. As a further refinement the data are normalized by taking natural logs. The results are shown in Table 2A.1, and portrayed graphically in Figure 2A.1.

Table 2A.1 Valuations versus prices (1975–80)

Independent variables		$\bar{R}^2$
a_0	a_1	
−0.20	1.02	0.99
(−0.05)	(0.021)	

Standard errors are shown in brackets.

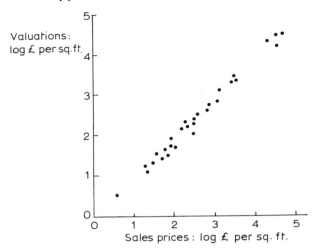

Figure 2A.1 Valuations versus prices (1975–80).

The one-to-one relationship appears to be confirmed as the a_1 coefficient is statistically indistinguishable from 1.0. In addition the high $\bar{R}^2$ value indicates that prices explain about 99% of their equivalent valuation. Although the intercept term a_0 is significantly different from zero this can be attributed to the fact that the valuations and prices were not exactly synchronous. In fact over the analysis period the market was rising so the negative intercept is consistent with the view that prices had moved up relative to their earlier valuations.

The high correlation between prices and valuations should not be interpreted as meaning they should always be equal. All this analysis is saying is that valuers are using the same information as the market and that on average the difference can be attributed to random errors.

A more extensive analysis has been carried out by Investment Property Databank and Drivers Jonas (Drivers Jonas, 1988) using a sample of 1442 properties within the IPD database. Each of the properties was sold between January 1982 and March 1988 and had at least two open market valuations in the two consecutive years prior to the sale. All the valuations occurred between January 1980 and December 1987.

Various tests were undertaken but the principal one concerned an examination of prices versus valuations. The regression model used differed from the analysis given in equation (2A.1) because valuations were used as the independent variable, thus:

$$P = a + bV + e \tag{2A.2}$$

The data was adjusted for heteroscedasticity by converting to units per square foot. The resulting transformation was sufficiently Normal so no further adjustment was required.

Although no information was given as to whether the prices represented open market transactions it is assumed that with such a large sample size the effect of special situations would be diversified away. No tests for significance were supplied but the results of the basic model were as shown in Table 2A.2.

Table 2A.2 Prices versus valuations (1982–8)

Independent variables		
a	b	$\bar{R}^2$
3.56	1.061	0.934

Source: IPD/Drivers Jonas.

These results show a slope coefficient (*b*) which is close to 1.0 and confirms the findings of the previous analysis. The positive intercept term (*a*) is due again to the fact that there was a lag between valuation and transaction dates. Because the model has used valuations as the independent variables the positive intercept is consistent with the fact that the market was rising over the period of the analysis.

Further analyses were undertaken which included the lag between the valuation and transaction date. These showed that the intercept term was unstable and was probably statistically indistinguishable from zero and that the lag term was significant. The basic hypothesis that there is a one-to-one relationship between valuations and prices remained unchanged.

Both of these analyses are reassuring from the point of view of the valuation profession since they add credence to the proposition that valuers are correctly interpreting information. If this were not the case then the validity of professional advice would be thrown into disarray.

As this is such an important area it would be reassuring for similar tests to be carried out over other periods to ensure that the results are consistent.

Valuations versus valuations

If valuations are a good proxy for prices it is also reasonable to assume that valuations prepared by one firm are a good proxy for valuations prepared by another firm. If both firms have access to the same set of information then although they may interpret that information differently at the portfolio level they should be statistically indistinguishable from each other.

This hypothesis can be tested by taking a group of properties which have valuations prepared by two different firms on a regular basis. This can occur when one firm is employed to provide check valuations in order to reveal any bias that may be present.

Regressing the valuations onto each other would produce a model of the following form, where A and B represent the firms involved.

$$A = a_0 + a_1 B + e \qquad (2A.3)$$

If inter-firm valuations are a good proxy for each other then a_1 should be statistically indistinguishable from 1.0 and a_0 should be statistically distinguishable from zero.

The sample of properties all belong to one fund and are typical of institutional holdings. Twenty-six properties have been analysed over a four-year period, 1981–4. As with the earlier analysis all data have been converted to square foot values and normalized by taking logs. The results are summarized in Table 2A.3, and the comparison of valuations for each firm is shown graphically in Figure 2A.2.

In all cases the a_0 coefficients are close to zero and statistically insignificant. This is a more stringent test than valuations versus prices. The earlier analysis allowed the intercept term to differ from zero because of differences in timing. In this case however it is essential that the intercept term be indistinguishable from zero otherwise it suggests that one firm may consistently value either above or below the other firm.

The a_1 coefficients are also statistically indistinguishable from 1.0 implying that, throughout the valuation range, both firms are valuing in the same way. The one-to-one relationship between the valuations prepared by each firm should not be miscontrued as implying that the valuations for individual properties are identical. It is still possible for there to be reasonable differences. At the portfolio level the differences

Table 2A.3 Regression results of inter-firm valuations

	a_0	Standard error	a_1	Standard error	$\bar{R}^2$
1981	0.108	0.138	0.985	0.035	0.98
1982	0.071	0.122	0.993	0.030	0.98
1983	−0.002	0.100	1.003	0.029	0.98
1984	0.000	0.123	1.006	0.025	0.99

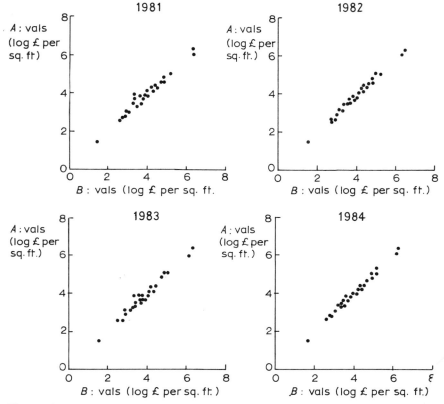

Figure 2A.2 Regression results of inter-firm valuations (1981–4).

should be diversified away. The amount of scatter shown in F 2A.2 illustrates the differences which can occur when valuatio prepared by different firms.

The $\bar{R}^2$ values are all very high indicating that the va prepared by firm A could explain about 98% of the variatic valuations provided by firm B.

Given that this analysis has been based on a sample properties and if, in addition, it can be assumed that the representative of the whole market then valuations prepare ent firms should be good substitutes for each other. Unde the principle that both firms have access to the sam databases of comparable information. Bias would occur tion subset being used by each firm differed.

These results however suggest that there is no e between the valuations prepared by different firms.

that by interpreting relevant information it should not be possible for firms to compete with each other purely on the quality of their valuations.

Appendix 2B: An analysis of weak form market efficiency in the commercial property market

Because property is infrequently traded valuations assume greater importance in the market-place. This has a direct bearing on the efficient allocation of funds. Appendix 2A showed that valuations could act as good proxy for traded prices. This appendix examines how good valuations are, in responding to new information. By implication it is also an examination of how good valuers are at impounding new information.

Market efficiency

A market is efficient if prices fully and instantaneously reflect all available, relevant information. Then the price at which an asset will trade will be an accurate signal for capital allocation.

Although emphasis in the property market must be switched from prices to valuations it is nevertheless essential to know whether valuations are efficient. If there are significant differences between prices and valuations this could signal the conditions under which an investor could earn excess returns.

The conditions necessary for an efficient market can be contrasted with those of a perfect market, in which case the following condition must exist:

1. Markets must be frictionless, i.e. there should be no transaction costs or taxes and all assets must be perfectly divisible and marketable.
2. Information should be costless and received simultaneously by all individuals.
3. All investors should be rational expected-utility maximizers.

If a perfect capital market exists then that market will be both allocationally and operationally efficient. In other words funds will be distributed optimally, without cost.

The notion of a perfect capital market is of course very restrictive and generally not essential to ensure that a market is efficient. For example a market can still be efficient even if it involves transaction costs and assets are not capable of infinite divisibility. In addition a market may exhibit imperfect competition yet still be efficient. Similarly the existence of costless information is not necessarily a precondition for market efficiency.

These points are of course important as far as property is concerned because its lumpiness prevents investors from acquiring a small proportion of the equity other than through some financial intermediary such as a property bond or unit trust. In addition, transaction costs are relatively high, preventing frequent trading.

These factors will mean that the property market is imperfect but this does not imply that it is inefficient.

Fama (1970) has formalized the notion of market efficiency depending on the level of information available, and has identified three forms as follows.

1. **Weak form efficiency**: no investor can earn excess returns from trading rules based on a past series of prices.
2. **Semi-strong form efficiency**: no investor can earn excess returns from trading rules based on publicly available information.
3. **Strong form efficiency**: no investor can earn excess returns from any information whether publicly available or not.

Although each of these forms of efficiency is important to the investor in property it is the weak form which is undoubtedly the easiest to test. It is also likely to be the most relevant for many institutions as their standing investments could dominate, in terms of value, all new purchases or developments. If the market is inefficient at this level then it would imply that institutional investors should trade more actively in property.

At the semi-strong level, the type of information which is most publicly made available through the professional press is that relating to reversionary sales, i.e. property for sale under a current lease agreement with an imminent reversion to a full market rental. This type of property is very popular and some commentators have suggested that the reason for this is because they are always undervalued (Sykes 1983a). It is not clear, however, whether the term undervalued implies some trade-off between risk and return although the implication is that purchase of such properties would lead to excess returns. If the market is efficient at the semi-strong level then this type of property should be priced so that it would give a return which adequately compensated for its risk. The fact that information concerning the property is made publicly available should ensure that it is priced fairly.

One reason this type of property is popular may be because of clientèle effects. A property with an imminent reversion will generate a higher income stream. For gross funds this increase in income will prove to be more attractive than unrealized gains to non-paying tax funds.

At the strong form level of market efficiency there is probably more opportunity to earn excess returns. This could well be the case where a developer acquires property at its current use value and then by carrying out a development is able to convert the property to a higher valued use. Under such conditions he could well earn excess returns, but this should be measured net of costs. To give an example, during the early 1960s and 1970s a number of developers capitalizing on certain aspects of planning law or as a result of monopolistic information concerning the development potential of sites were able to earn substantial excess returns. Many became millionaires. History, however, is silent on the number who went bankrupt!

Unfortunately no data are available to test a hypothesis relating to strong form efficiency. There is one study (Greer, 1974) which has been carried out to investigate the allocational efficiency of the residential real-estate market in the Denver County area of Colorado. The research was based on data from 135 transactions between 1968 and 1973 and investigated whether a group of traders with insider knowledge, i.e. agents with advance information on forthcoming properties, were able to earn excess returns. Using the efficient markets model this study rejected the hypothesis that the real-estate market was allocationally inefficient.

No other tests are available on strong form market efficiency which cover the commercial property market although it is probably at this level where most of the excess returns are likely to be earned.

Weak form market efficiency

The idea that an efficient market reflects all information is so general that it is not testable. In order to formalize the informational content of prices Fama (1970) has classified efficient markets into fair game, martingale (or submartingale), and random walk models, the latter ones being special cases of fair game models.

The basic idea behind a fair game model is that the return on an asset is a function of its risk. This can be expressed as

$$e_{j,t+1} = r_{j,t+1} - \mathrm{E}(r_{j,t+1}|\phi_t) \qquad (2\mathrm{B}.1)$$

where

$e_{j,t+1}$ = difference between actual and predicted returns;
$r_{j,t+1}$ = return on asset j from period t to $t + 1$;
ϕ_t = information subset available at time t.

The expected value of the difference between actual and predicted returns is zero, thus

$$E(e_{j,t+1}) = E[r_{j,t+1} - E(r_{j,t+1}|\phi_t)] = 0. \qquad (2B.2)$$

For a fair game to exist on average across a large sample the expected return on an asset must equal its actual return. This does not imply that returns will be positive, only that expectations will not be biased.

A fair game which is a martingale requires that tomorrow's price be greater than today's price. In returns form this implies that expected returns are positive, i.e.

$$E(r_{j,t+1}|\phi_t) > 0. \qquad (2B.3)$$

A martingale would exist if tomorrow's price was expected to equal todays's price. This would imply an expected return of zero, i.e.

$$E(r_{j,t+1}|\phi_t) = 0. \qquad (2B.4)$$

The random walk model implies that there is no difference between a distribution of returns conditional on a subset of information and an unconditional distribution. In returns form this can be expressed as

$$f(r_{j,t+1}|\phi_t) = f(r_{j,t+1}). \qquad (2B.5)$$

The random walk model requires much stronger conditions than fair game and martingale models because they require the return parameters to be the same with or without the information subset. If the returns follow a random walk then the mean of the underlying distribution does not change over time and a fair game results.

The empirical implication of a random walk is that all drawings be taken independently from the same distribution. Thus a random walk requires the serial correlation between returns to be zero for all lags. A fair game is not as stringent as this, and significant serial correlation is not inconsistent with a fair game.

If we consider the weak form of market efficiency it will be seen from equation (2B.2) that $e_{j,t+1}$ represents the deviation of the return in period $t + 1$ from its expected value. This is the residual return and for a fair game it must have zero serial correlation of returns for all time lags. Note also that the subset of information for weak form efficiency, i.e. ϕ_t is equal to the past series of returns namely, $r_{j,t}$, $r_{j,t-1}$, $r_{j,t-2}$, ... $r_{j,t-n}$. As the expected return for period $t + 1$ can depend on the return observed in period t the serial correlation of returns need not be zero.

Thus serial correlation within one-period returns is not inconsistent with a fair game model but is inconsistent with a random walk.

The random walk hypothesis described above has been tested (Brown, 1985) by examining the serial correlation coefficients for a large sample of properties. Valuations and cash flows were collected on a monthly basis from January 1979 to December 1982 covering a sample of 135 properties comprising 46 retail, 39 office and 50 industrial properties. Continuously compounded returns were computed thus enabling returns to be obtained for periods longer than one month merely by adding returns.

The serial correlation coefficients for the sample properties are given in Tables 2B.5–7 for monthly, quarterly and half-yearly returns over increasing lags. Table 2B.1 provides a summary of the average values for each sector.

In all cases the absolute value of the coefficients is low with only a small number being more than twice their standard error. In addition the χ^2-test of the null hypothesis that the serial correlation coefficients were all significantly different from zero at the 5% level was rejected for all lags and holding periods.

The consistently low coefficients would seem therefore to indicate that the property market is efficient at the weak form level. It is not a random walk but complies with the requirements of a fair game. As the martingale is a special case of the fair game model, and discounted present values follow a martingale, this also provides evidence in support of the belief that valuations are present values.

At the portfolio level the coefficients are again small. These are summarized in Table 2B.2 for both equally and value-weighted portfolios.

Because of the longer holding periods generally associated with investment in property it might be expected that annual returns exhibit greater serial dependence. This hypothesis was tested utilizing continuously compounded returns from the Jones Lang Wooton index over the period from January 1967 to January 1983.

Table 2B.1 Average serial correlation coefficients for each sector

Sector	*Monthly returns*						*Quarterly returns*			*Half-yearly returns*
	Lag						*Lag*			*Lag*
	1	2	3	4	5	6	1	2	3	1
Office	−0.027	−0.107	0.087	−0.023	0.048	−0.011	−0.077	−0.053	0.003	−0.233
Retail	0.027	−0.037	0.024	0.002	−0.021	0.003	−0.012	0.015	−0.021	−0.020
Industrial	−0.039	−0.003	0.041	0.004	0.009	0.016	0.017	0.005	−0.072	−0.104

Table 2B.2 Serial correlation coefficients for equally- and value-weighted portfolios
(January 1979–December 1982)
Equally-weighted portfolio

Sector	Monthly returns						Quarterly returns			Half-yearly returns
			Lag					Lag		Lag
	1	2	3	4	5	6	1	2	3	1
Office	0.234	−0.162	0.188	0.032	−0.271	−0.062	−0.010	0.047	0.196	−0.161
Retail	0.038	0.192	0.094	−0.153	0.069	−0.010	0.115	0.212	0.215	0.367
Industrial	0.375	0.364	0.244	0.057	0.098	0.148	0.266	0.090	−0.088	−0.123
PF(EW)	0.346	0.096	0.220	−0.056	−0.080	0.021	0.131	0.068	0.175	−0.026

Value-weighted portfolio

Sector	Monthly returns						Quarterly returns			Half-yearly returns
			Lag					Lag		Lag
	1	2	3	4	5	6	1	2	3	1
Office	0.221	−0.094	0.009	−0.018	−0.154	0.043	−0.119	0.041	0.228	−0.051
Retail	0.274	0.223	0.175	−0.010	0.174	0.016	0.303	0.279	0.296	0.405
Industrial	0.184	0.213	0.187	−0.025	0.025	0.146	0.085	0.117	−0.067	−0.242
PF(VW)	0.375	0.108	0.165	−0.017	0.033	0.094	0.104	0.119	0.248	0.053

The results (Table 2B.3) are consistent with those presented in Tables 2B.5–7 which show the serial correlation coefficients for each property and sector within the sample analysed. The null hypothesis that each of the coefficients was greater than zero was rejected at the 5% level.

Examination of the signs shown in Tables 2B.5–7 reveal the patterns for first-order serial correlation, shown in Table 2B.4.

With the exception of quarterly returns for the industrial sector there is a preponderance of negative signs for both the office and industrial sectors. By contrast the retail sector is more evenly distributed with regard to sign. The pattern exhibited is consistent with the performance of each sector of the property market over the period examined

Table 2B.3 Serial correlation coefficients for annual continuously compounded returns (January 1967–January 1983)

Years					
1	2	3	4	5	6
0.007	−0.079	−0.334	−0.184	−0.136	0.058

Table 2B.4 Pattern of signs for first-order serial correlation

Sector		Monthly returns	Quarterly returns	Half-yearly returns
Office	−	24	25	33
	+	15	14	6
Retail	−	22	25	24
	+	24	21	22
Industrial	−	33	20	33
	+	17	30	17

(January 1979 to December 1982), but as the coefficients are always small they are not necessarily indicative of any consistent pattern.

For any period the serial correlation coefficients will be determined partly by market-wide factors and partly by other factors specific to each sector. Although further research may find some evidence of stronger serial dependence the direction of that dependence is unlikely to be consistent.

To summarize, therefore, the evidence produced by the serial correlation model would seem to indicate that there is little dependence between successive changes in property valuation. What evidence there is, is insufficient to enable an investor to construct profitable trading strategies based on a time-series examination of property valuations, assuming that valuations are a good proxy for traded prices.

This evidence is also important in terms of assessing the rôle of valuers in the valuation process. The lack of serial correlation at the individual property level indicates that valuers are doing a good job of adjusting valuations in response to new information. This is important because it also implies that the property market conforms to the requirements of a fair game so investors will be compensated for higher returns only by taking on additional risk.

At the weak form level the property market appears to be reasonably efficient. Although the analysis carried out in this appendix has been based on a relatively short time span the figures produced a remarkable consistency between sectors. With the growth in databases it would be worth carrying out similar analyses using more extensive samples over different time periods. A precondition of such an analysis is that returns are accurately measured by taking into consideration expenditure incurred on each property as well as income received.

Further research is also required to test whether the above results hold true at the semi-strong and strong form levels.

Table 2B.5 Serial correlation coefficients: **office sector** (January 1979–December 1982)

Property	Monthly returns						Quarterly returns			Half-yearly returns
	1	2	3	4	5	6	1	2	3	1
01	−0.123	−0.432*	0.235	0.146	0.039	−0.137	−0.120	−0.152	0.074	−0.484
02	0.060	−0.154	0.078	−0.071	−0.046	−0.052	0.155	−0.186	−0.167	−0.370
03	−0.065	−0.391*	0.014	0.109	−0.010	−0.146	−0.373	−0.051	−0.055	−0.518
04	0.240	−0.127	0.201	0.192	−0.266	−0.234	0.230	−0.347	−0.431	−0.391
05	0.072	−0.202	0.035	−0.025	−0.196	−0.063	−0.346	0.074	0.050	−0.550
06	0.007	−0.016	0.070	−0.110	0.019	0.102	−0.067	0.093	−0.090	−0.067
07	−0.017	−0.117	0.012	0.051	−0.064	0.045	−0.206	−0.019	−0.159	−0.372
08	−0.214	0.066	−0.040	−0.145	0.004	−0.112	−0.272	−0.218	0.061	−0.803
09	−0.054	−0.051	−0.107	0.093	−0.032	0.251	0.033	−0.009	0.137	0.124
10	−0.107	−0.214	0.212	0.030	−0.071	0.039	0.062	−0.089	0.067	−0.008
11	−0.073	−0.105	0.077	−0.060	−0.119	−0.040	−0.101	−0.229	0.104	−0.329
12	0.076	−0.167	0.164	0.019	−0.134	−0.042	0.209	0.158	0.124	0.182
13	−0.123	−0.017	0.140	−0.217	0.145	0.024	0.097	−0.050	0.128	−0.105
14	0.345*	−0.089	−0.010	−0.002	0.055	−0.038	−0.015	0.014	0.290	0.000
15	0.201	0.141	0.061	−0.009	−0.116	−0.016	0.034	−0.036	0.031	0.028
16	0.032	0.045	0.012	−0.170	0.162	−0.049	−0.109	−0.001	−0.124	−0.158
17	−0.122	−0.168	0.332*	−0.183	−0.056	0.029	0.026	−0.022	−0.191	−0.285
18	−0.167	−0.021	0.175	−0.075	0.012	−0.115	−0.029	−0.349	0.335	−0.187
19	0.310*	−0.230	−0.263*	−0.126	−0.096	−0.053	−0.366	−0.109	−0.273	−0.589
20	−0.120	−0.326*	0.277*	−0.046	−0.316*	0.108	−0.318	0.074	0.253	−0.040
21	−0.338*	−0.220	0.307*	−0.106	−0.222	0.143	−0.452	−0.295	0.582*	−0.424
22	0.330*	−0.163	−0.129	−0.056	−0.178	0.029	−0.232	−0.016	−0.013	−0.235
23	−0.041	0.103	−0.004	0.068	−0.031	−0.053	−0.020	−0.043	−0.118	−0.131
24	−0.160	−0.258	0.062	0.125	−0.165	0.098	0.050	0.302	0.219	−0.205
25	0.143	−0.046	0.245	0.046	−0.077	−0.057	0.283	−0.109	−0.021	−0.154
26	−0.125	0.257	0.014	0.099	−0.097	−0.069	0.201	0.153	0.082	0.263
27	−0.273	0.008	0.124	−0.231	0.045	0.047	0.018	−0.023	−0.449	−0.158
28	−0.040	−0.134	−0.093	−0.071	0.105	−0.018	−0.376	0.002	0.154	0.019
29	−0.245	−0.336*	0.301*	−0.011	−0.296*	0.136	−0.486	0.222	0.155	−0.225
30	−0.359*	0.156	−0.223	−0.078	0.154	−0.132	−0.233	−0.001	−0.118	−0.162
31	0.059	−0.020	0.365*	0.305*	0.030	−0.032	0.539*	0.028	−0.191	−0.006
32	−0.249	−0.190	0.153	0.045	0.089	−0.022	−0.240	0.065	0.129	−0.215
33	−0.010	−0.034	0.278	−0.025	0.015	−0.146	0.220	−0.175	−0.021	−0.143
34	−0.140	0.061	0.060	−0.185	−0.049	−0.022	−0.225	−0.194	0.008	−0.650
35	0.203	−0.105	−0.002	−0.012	−0.070	−0.008	−0.023	−0.030	−0.189	−0.390
36	0.142	−0.235	0.047	−0.150	−0.223	−0.080	−0.336	−0.287	0.293	−0.463
37	0.009	0.001	0.055	0.041	−0.114	0.088	−0.021	0.055	−0.084	−0.363
38	−0.046	−0.140	0.069	−0.107	0.006	0.214	−0.187	0.021	−0.485	−0.282
39	−0.087	−0.293	0.092	−0.006	0.275	−0.034	−0.021	−0.283	0.025	−0.247
Average	−0.027	−0.107	0.087	−0.023	0.048	−0.011	−0.077	−0.053	0.003	−0.233

* Observation is >2 standard errors from zero.

Table 2B.6 Serial correlation coefficients: **retail sector** (January 1979–December 1982)

Property	Monthly returns						Quarterly returns			Half-yearly returns
	1	2	3	4	5	6	1	2	3	1
01	−0.066	0.032	0.110	−0.071	−0.018	0.065	−0.004	0.274	−0.190	−0.006
02	−0.005	−0.019	0.058	−0.000	0.054	−0.037	0.008	0.005	−0.035	−0.083
03	−0.139	0.132	−0.041	−0.173	−0.020	−0.050	−0.108	−0.149	0.008	0.002
04	−0.007	−0.213	−0.068	−0.065	0.098	−0.098	−0.368	0.144	0.035	−0.171
05	−0.056	−0.149	−0.025	−0.021	−0.042	−0.028	−0.173	−0.145	−0.200	−0.337
06	0.416*	−0.101	−0.071	−0.071	−0.060	−0.070	0.027	−0.023	−0.102	0.413
07	0.198	0.044	0.110	−0.035	−0.001	−0.156	0.082	−0.149	−0.493	−0.488
08	0.030	−0.031	−0.011	−0.038	−0.048	−0.008	−0.022	−0.075	0.505	0.267
09	0.237	−0.004	−0.077	−0.214	−0.019	−0.091	0.109	−0.027	0.171	0.431
10	−0.055	0.075	0.002	−0.013	0.302*	−0.120	0.067	0.154	−0.123	0.068
11	0.381*	−0.041	0.076	0.086	0.065	0.292	0.129	0.339	0.016	0.402
12	0.113	−0.077	−0.126	−0.014	−0.178	−0.023	−0.208	−0.063	0.012	−0.423
13	−0.061	−0.074	0.137	−0.072	−0.059	−0.099	−0.006	−0.181	0.111	−0.285
14	−0.199	−0.091	0.100	−0.069	−0.089	0.249	0.036	0.203	0.069	0.393
15	0.163	−0.043	0.082	0.188	0.018	−0.008	0.377	0.206	−0.086	−0.140
16	0.068	−0.174	0.020	0.187	0.040	−0.110	−0.110	−0.043	0.314	−0.147
17	0.105	0.248	−0.042	0.071	0.014	0.238	0.175	0.356	−0.119	0.303
18	−0.165	−0.212	0.077	0.135	−0.092	−0.028	−0.006	−0.218	−0.448	−0.324
19	−0.050	−0.036	−0.017	0.017	−0.075	0.155	−0.042	0.067	0.012	0.108
20	0.008	0.037	0.286	0.002	0.018	0.032	0.306	0.080	0.223	0.108
21	0.057	−0.215	0.019	0.198	0.104	−0.085	0.239	0.084	0.053	0.182
22	0.043	−0.047	−0.010	−0.134	−0.127	−0.027	−0.135	−0.110	−0.169	−0.439
23	0.048	−0.076	−0.091	0.179	−0.017	−0.042	−0.004	−0.103	−0.037	−0.304
24	0.124	0.200	0.050	0.223	0.027	−0.010	0.318	−0.055	−0.234	0.098
25	0.088	0.014	0.081	0.014	0.017	0.067	0.259	−0.230	−0.121	−0.188
26	−0.311*	−0.071	0.178	−0.165	0.004	0.131	−0.062	−0.009	−0.315	−0.548
27	−0.031	−0.050	0.003	−0.020	−0.411*	0.008	−0.484	−0.017	0.209	−0.077
28	0.105	0.139	0.109	0.020	0.108	−0.079	0.222	0.380	0.286	0.505
29	0.163	−0.022	0.221	−0.064	−0.033	−0.040	0.122	−0.171	0.135	−0.060
30	0.113	−0.077	−0.126	−0.014	−0.178	−0.023	−0.208	−0.063	0.012	−0.423
31	0.313*	0.095	0.000	0.044	−0.014	0.014	0.121	−0.040	−0.280	−0.261
32	0.211	−0.130	0.004	0.002	−0.082	−0.046	−0.060	0.249	0.382	0.268
33	−0.043	0.081	−0.027	0.029	0.084	−0.083	0.336	−0.002	0.260	0.134
34	−0.072	−0.108	−0.053	0.050	0.048	0.007	−0.194	−0.013	0.297	0.058
35	−0.025	0.015	0.124	−0.170	0.080	−0.140	0.003	−0.138	−0.274	−0.374
36	−0.027	−0.058	0.158	−0.005	0.024	0.032	0.122	−0.080	−0.211	0.089
37	0.110	−0.153	0.118	0.182	−0.097	−0.024	−0.042	−0.168	0.262	0.406
38	−0.030	−0.075	0.053	0.285	−0.020	0.145	0.219	0.201	0.065	0.285
39	−0.091	0.217	−0.066	−0.098	0.024	−0.036	0.121	−0.103	−0.291	−0.183
40	−0.094	−0.019	−0.091	−0.150	0.012	−0.074	−0.264	−0.121	−0.087	−0.419
41	−0.346*	0.167	−0.064	0.060	−0.011	0.048	−0.299	0.413	−0.153	0.282
42	0.016	−0.127	0.007	−0.031	−0.029	−0.006	−0.158	−0.077	0.028	−0.162
43	0.013	−0.133	−0.006	−0.075	−0.068	−0.166	−0.217	−0.289	0.318	0.282
44	−0.112	−0.242	0.093	−0.209	0.165	0.053	−0.220	0.078	−0.497	0.049
45	0.106	0.056	−0.146	−0.014	−0.021	0.148	−0.221	0.113	−0.209	−0.198
46	−0.022	−0.402*	−0.034	0.103	−0.039	0.275	−0.334	0.197	−0.096	−0.171
Average	0.027	−0.037	0.024	0.000	−0.021	0.003	−0.012	0.015	−0.021	−0.020

* Observation is >2 standard errors from zero.

Table 2B.7 Serial correlation coefficients: **industrial sector** (January 1979–December 1982)

Property										

	Monthly returns						Quarterly returns			Half-yearly returns
Property	1	2	3	4	5	6	1	2	3	1
01	−0.225	0.049	−0.158	0.062	−0.109	−0.006	−0.080	−0.128	0.086	−0.347
02	−0.112	−0.049	0.084	−0.087	0.068	0.190	−0.140	0.500	−0.135	0.387
03	−0.012	−0.157	−0.011	0.067	−0.039	−0.039	−0.173	−0.123	−0.129	−0.710
04	0.196	0.151	0.121	−0.016	0.022	−0.034	0.014	−0.063	−0.362	−0.515
05	−0.063	−0.219	0.077	−0.051	−0.020	−0.144	−0.300	−0.136	0.392	−0.263
06	−0.078	0.147	0.153	−0.185	−0.062	0.173	0.197	0.022	−0.209	−0.211
07	−0.254	0.175	−0.118	0.287	−0.059	0.191	0.165	0.169	0.305	0.408
08	0.004	0.012	0.067	−0.045	0.015	−0.420*	0.144	−0.307	−0.123	−0.412
09	0.003	0.099	0.046	−0.016	−0.021	−0.027	0.141	0.036	−0.291	−0.253
10	−0.031	−0.039	0.032	0.100	−0.024	0.003	0.090	0.352	−0.021	0.165
11	0.089	−0.010	−0.029	−0.087	0.006	−0.047	0.008	−0.110	−0.081	0.580
12	0.111	−0.007	−0.165	−0.223	−0.102	−0.152	−0.149	−0.092	−0.019	−0.376
13	−0.046	0.204	−0.041	0.220	0.242	−0.122	0.254	0.038	−0.108	0.304
14	−0.114	0.045	−0.032	0.009	−0.019	0.049	−0.218	−0.226	0.115	−0.514
15	0.217	−0.019	0.127	−0.021	0.066	0.100	−0.022	0.039	−0.137	−0.200
16	−0.017	−0.182	−0.108	−0.024	0.158	−0.044	−0.218	−0.029	−0.408	−0.656
17	0.018	−0.202	−0.183	−0.016	0.068	−0.021	−0.437	0.241	−0.104	−0.164
18	0.051	−0.196	−0.049	0.119	0.197	−0.165	0.082	−0.036	−0.182	−0.415
19	0.025	−0.025	−0.072	−0.001	0.178	−0.057	−0.138	0.110	−0.413	−0.579
20	−0.022	−0.125	0.135	0.274	0.063	0.061	0.317	0.233	−0.128	0.244
21	0.034	0.006	0.116	0.016	0.077	−0.201	0.172	−0.214	0.218	−0.182
22	0.017	−0.052	0.315*	−0.114	0.118	−0.006	0.180	−0.169	−0.228	−0.223
23	0.062	0.152	−0.018	−0.099	−0.204	0.219	−0.134	0.022	0.360	0.070
24	−0.051	0.005	0.289	0.019	0.125	−0.176	0.286	−0.354	−0.088	−0.382
25	−0.024	0.023	0.007	0.073	0.019	0.057	0.090	0.066	−0.393	−0.278
26	0.326*	0.264	0.217	0.162	0.065	0.152	0.413	0.006	−0.213	0.051
27	0.107	0.059	0.079	−0.080	0.074	−0.048	0.004	0.043	−0.087	−0.157
28	−0.070	−0.291	0.051	−0.046	0.138	0.003	−0.427	0.131	−0.159	−0.497
29	−0.111	−0.054	0.257	−0.084	−0.099	0.216	0.109	−0.062	−0.170	−0.162
30	−0.219	−0.065	0.160	−0.015	−0.104	0.075	0.092	0.138	0.248	0.128
31	−0.121	0.019	−0.044	0.207	−0.047	−0.042	0.122	−0.208	0.237	0.256
32	−0.026	0.460*	0.024	−0.004	−0.072	−0.096	0.024	−0.143	−0.132	−0.062
33	−0.058	−0.191	0.220	−0.042	−0.129	0.035	−0.132	0.001	−0.018	0.310
34	0.103	−0.244	0.138	0.046	−0.140	−0.068	0.240	−0.214	−0.284	−0.359
35	−0.199	−0.029	0.038	0.062	−0.114	0.107	−0.112	0.095	0.029	0.191
36	−0.013	−0.048	0.014	0.095	0.101	−0.030	0.167	0.127	−0.187	−0.037
37	−0.178	−0.049	0.028	0.291	−0.356*	0.146	0.064	0.181	−0.110	0.172
38	−0.126	0.036	0.255	0.031	0.069	0.004	0.395	−0.015	−0.025	−0.047
39	−0.081	−0.219	−0.031	−0.013	0.086	−0.086	−0.141	−0.176	−0.110	−0.282
40	−0.122	0.023	0.108	−0.033	0.003	0.065	−0.029	0.125	−0.265	−0.110
41	0.214	−0.190	−0.312*	−0.331*	0.157	0.208	−0.406	−0.021	0.274	−0.062
42	−0.105	0.150	0.002	0.228	−0.306*	0.080	0.202	0.228	−0.031	−0.054
43	−0.043	0.220	−0.024	−0.042	−0.015	0.032	0.230	−0.084	−0.227	−0.101
44	−0.146	0.054	0.099	−0.193	0.013	0.183	0.001	−0.066	0.252	0.166
45	−0.097	0.026	−0.084	−0.082	0.147	−0.068	−0.165	0.073	−0.143	−0.330
46	−0.293	0.107	0.107	−0.184	0.030	0.032	0.054	−0.070	0.046	−0.028
47	−0.237	0.148	−0.019	−0.165	0.068	−0.067	−0.134	−0.029	−0.038	−0.062
48	−0.135	−0.151	0.057	0.143	−0.145	−0.042	0.028	−0.034	0.072	0.083
49	0.146	0.096	0.105	−0.026	0.192	0.363	0.122	0.388	−0.121	0.308
50	−0.196	−0.057	0.005	0.014	0.062	−0.036	−0.018	0.003	−0.359	0.028
Average	−0.039	−0.003	0.041	0.004	0.009	0.016	0.017	0.005	−0.072	−0.104

* Observation is >2 standard errors from zero.

The only other published test of market efficiency in the property market is that undertaken by George Gau (1984) in British Columbia. The tests were based on specially constructed indices of apartment and commercial buildings in Vancouver. Like findings presented in this appendix the serial correlation tests showed a general absence of significant dependence between monthly returns. Gau concluded that this evidence provided support for the view that the price behaviour in property markets conformed to a fair game model.

Appendix 2C Term structure and its potential impact on valuation

The term structure of interest rates describes the relationship between interest rates and the term to maturity. Figure 2C.1 shows the relationship between the redemption yields on government stock and the term to maturity as at 5th June 1990.

The slope of this curve is almost horizontal. It does not however remain constant. From time to time it can be either upward or downward sloping.

It will be seen from this illustration, however, that there is a relationship between interest rates and term to maturity. Three theories have been put forward to explain why this happens.

1. The **expectations hypothesis** states that long-term bond yields are the average of short-term yields. If short-term interest rates are expected to rise the yield curve will be upward sloping. If they are expected to fall the curve will be downward sloping.
2. The **liquidity preference hypothesis** states that investors pay a premium on short-term interest rates in order to avoid the interest rate risk associated with long-term maturities.
3. The **market segmentation hypothesis** states that the yield curve is made up of independent maturity segments and that the yield on each segment is separately determined by supply and demand.

For the sake of illustration only the expectations hypothesis will be considered here.

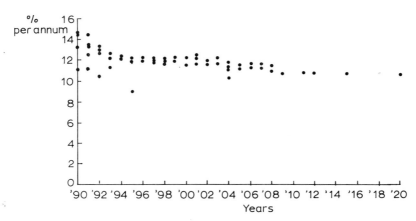

Figure 2C.1 The term structure of interest rates as at 5th June 1990.

The pure expectations hypothesis rests on the belief that the return on long-dated bonds are equal to the geometric mean of the short-term rates over the holding period. This can be expressed as follows by letting $_0s_n$ represent the observed spot rate published in the financial press for a loan that starts immediately (i.e. at time $t=0$) and is repaid n years in the future. This is related to a series of forward rates $_tf_{t+n}$ which represents a loan which starts at period t and matures n years later at time $(t+n)$. This is an implied rate as it cannot be observed directly. Using this convention the current spot rate can be expressed as follows.

$$(1 + {}_0s_1) = (1 + {}_0f_1). \tag{2C.1}$$

$$(1 + {}_0s_2)^2 = (1 + {}_0f_1)(1 + {}_1f_2). \tag{2C.2}$$

$$(1 + {}_0s_3)^3 = (1 + {}_0f_1)(1 + {}_1f_2)(1 + {}_2f_3). \tag{2C.3}$$

In general terms this relationship can be expressed as

$$(1 + {}_0s_n)^n = (1 + {}_0f_1)(1 + {}_1f_2) \ldots (1 + {}_{n-1}f_n). \tag{2C.4}$$

How this relationship works in practice can be demonstrated by a simple example. Assume that an investor is considering an investment opportunity which has a two-year horizon. He has £1000 to spend and can consider two possible strategies:

1. purchase a two-year gilt with a yield of 6% p.a.; or
2. purchase a one-year gilt yielding 7% p.a. and reinvest the proceeds in another one-year gilt at the end of the first year.

The first alternative will give a final value of

$$£1000 \times 1.06 \times 1.06 = £1123.60.$$

If however he chooses the second alternative then the value of the investment will depend on the yield on the one-year bond during the second year, thus the value is

$$£1000 \times 1.07 \times (1 + {}_1f_2) = £1070 \times (1 + {}_1f_2).$$

The expectations hypothesis says that this alternative must be equal to investment in a two-year bond, thus

$$£1070 \times (1 + {}_1f_2) = £1123.60$$

so

$$_1f_2 = 5.00\%.$$

The 5.00% represents the one-year forward rate investors expect in the second year given current expectations.

This principle can be extended to find the implied one-period forward rate at any period in the future given information about current spot rates and maturities.

The direct implication of this analysis for property is that changes in the shape of the yield curve may not be fully accounted for if long-term bond yields are always used as the reference point for establishing values. To illustrate this point consider an investment which generates an income stream of £100 per year over the next five years. Let us assume that the yield curve is rising so that current short-term interest rates are lower than long-term interest rates. The cash flow in each period should be discounted at the interest rate appropriate to that period, as shown in Table 2C.1. The present value of the cash flow in year 5 should be discounted at 8.00% for one year back to year 4. The result should be added to the cash flow in year 4 and then discounted at the one-year forward rate back to year 3 at the forward rate for year 4 and so on. This procedure will give a present value of £418.79.

The alternative procedure is to use the five-year gilt yield to discount all the cash flows at the same rate. This is the geometric mean of each of the one year rates and will produce a present value of £412.33. The reason for the difference in present values is that with a rising yield curve long-term rates will be higher than short-term rates and will more heavily discount the early cash flows.

If the yield curve was falling, long-term rates would be lower than current short-term rates. Reversing the one-year rates in the above illustration so that year 1 has 8.00% and year 5 has 5.00%, the present value of the cash flow becomes £406.03. The geometric mean return remains unchanged at 6.79% and so the present value using this rate remains the same, i.e. £412.33.

When a property is valued the assumption is that the equivalent yield chosen automatically adjusts for changes in the shape of the bond yield

Table 2C.1 Rising yield curve

End year	1 year forward rates	5 year gilt rate	Cash flow
1	5%	6.79%	£100
2	6%		£100
3	7%		£100
4	8%		£100
5	8%		£100

curve. Athough this may be true it clearly places a burden on the valuer to correctly incorporate the change. Failure to understand the implications of the term structure can result in an incorrect analysis of property values. This aspect is as yet unresolved.

Appendix 2D: An analysis of the changing risk profile of the commercial property market

The riskiness of the property market is not constant over time. Experience of differences in expectations shows this to be the case particularly when there are boom markets and considerable activity in both traded property and new development.

This appendix carries out a simple analysis using publicly available data to plot the changes in risk which have occurred in

1. the market for real property and
2. the property share market.

Although these are interrelated they form two distinct markets in terms of how they respond to risk.

The real property market

At this level the interest is in how the market risk of property has changed over time. The basic data for undertaking this analysis are estimated from the standard deviation of returns calculated from a property index.

The data chosen for this analysis are published by Jones Lang Wooton, who compute an index of total returns going back to 1966. Apart from the long time series, the index has very little serial correlation in its periodic returns implying that it is free from smoothing even though it is based on a relatively small sample size.

Changes in market risk are estimated by calculating the standard deviation of returns for five-year overlapping periods. The time-horizon chosen can be severely criticized as being too short to be statistically valid since each calculated figure will have a high standard error. Although this is true it nevertheless gives a good indication of how the market risk of the property sector has been changing over time. The purpose of the analysis is therefore illustrative rather than quantitative. A graph of the annual rates of return calculated from the Jones Lang Wooton data is shown in Figure 2D.1 and the overlapping five-year standard deviations are plotted in Figure 2D.2.

This clearly shows that property carried a high level of market risk during the early 1970s, and from Figure 2D.1, how the market fell during this period. This was when the collapse of the secondary banking market caused may property companies to go into liquidation and there was a general collapse of the property market. Following this

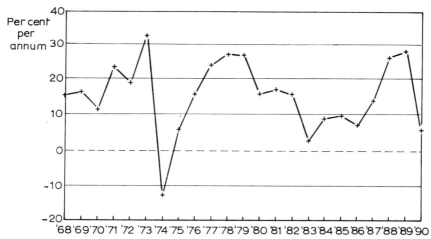

Figure 2D.1 Annual returns: Jones Lang Wooton (1968–90).

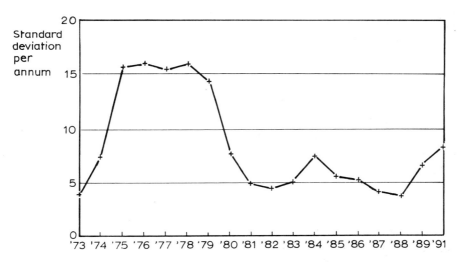

Figure 2D.2 Changes in property market risk (1968–90).

it will be seen that the riskiness of the market significantly reduced as confidence was restored. The low market risk in the mid to late 1980s was characterized by a boom in the market. The market risk appears again to be increasing at a time when there is a major downturn in activity.

Apart from plotting the changes in market risk it may well be possible that this approach could be helpful in predicting the future direction of change in market risk.

The property share market

The property share market is not a direct indicator of changes in the property market. The reason for this is that those property companies which are traded on the stock market may well represent a combination of both development and investment; they may also be involved in other areas of business and are likely to be highly geared.

It is useful nevertheless to plot changes in market risk of the property share market as this should reveal something about the way the market is reponding to external factors. In this case the measure of market risk being plotted is the beta coefficient calculated by reference to the FT All Share index. In order to appreciate what is happening it is necessary to understand how the beta coefficient of property companies is likely to change.

The β of the underlying property assets is the weighted average of the β of the traded equity shares and the amount of debt finance in the company structure. If we let D and E equal the amount of debt and equity in the company the beta coefficient of the underlying property assets can be represented by the following expression:

$$\beta_{\text{property}} = \beta_{\text{equity}} \frac{E}{D + E} + \beta_{\text{debt}} \frac{D}{D + E} \qquad (2D.1)$$

What is traded in the market is of course the equity shares and it is the beta coefficient of the equity, β_{equity}, which is the point of interest.

If we assume that the beta coefficient of the debt, β_{debt}, is zero it will be seen that β_{equity} can be found by transforming equation (2D.1) as follows.

$$\beta_{\text{equity}} = \beta_{\text{property}} / \left(\frac{E}{D + E}\right). \qquad (2D.2)$$

The beta coefficient of the equity shares will therefore depend on any changes which may take place in the beta coefficient of the underlying property together with the proportion of funds committed to property.

The beta coefficient of the underlying property will depend on the covariance of returns between property and the FT All Share index. It is unlikely that this will change substantially over time as it would imply a fundamental change in the nature of property. For the purposes of this example assume that β_{property} is in the order of 0.20 measured relative to the returns on the FT index.

The other factor affecting the beta coefficient of equity shares is the level of gearing employed by property companies. This will of course vary from company to company and it is not possible to determine what the average is likely to be for the whole market. It is possible however to estimate what would happen to β_{equity} as changes in the level of gearing occur.

This is shown in Table 2D.1, which clearly illustrates that as the level of debt financing decreases, the proportion of equity increases so that the beta coefficient of the equity approaches the beta coefficient of the underlying property. With high levels of debt finance the beta coefficient of the equity increases substantially.

Table 2D.1 Changes in the beta coefficient of property shares in relation to changes in the equity/debt + equity ratio.

$\dfrac{Equity}{Debt + equity}$	$\beta_{property}$	β_{equity}
0.10	0.20	2.00
0.15	0.20	1.33
0.20	0.20	1.00
0.40	0.20	0.50
0.60	0.20	0.33
0.80	0.20	0.25
1.00	0.20	0.20

As was shown in Chapter 1, beta with coefficients in excess of 1.00 will be more volatile than average and will therefore respond badly during times when there is a decline in the market. In an upturn in activity they will of course perform better than average.

It has been a characteristic of property companies that they have been highly geared and this has led to the fact that they are generally regarded as being very risky. This position was made very clear during the property market collapse of the early 1970s after which it was common to see property companies changing their financial structure so that they were less dependent on high levels of debt. If this was a strategy being followed by most property companies then their beta coefficients should decline over time. Figure 2D.3 plots this data since 1979, when the beta coefficient was approximately 1.375, and shows that there has been a consistent decrease in market risk until 1987 when it had reached a level of 0.67. Since 1987 there has been a substantial increase in market risk so that it is now close to 1.0.

An alternative way of looking at the changes in the underlying property risk is to plot the periodic rates of return for the market together with the changes in standard deviation. This is shown in Figure 2D.4 using the Jones Lang Wooton index together with the standard deviations computed on an annual basis.

Figure 2D.3 Changes in beta for property companies (1979–88).

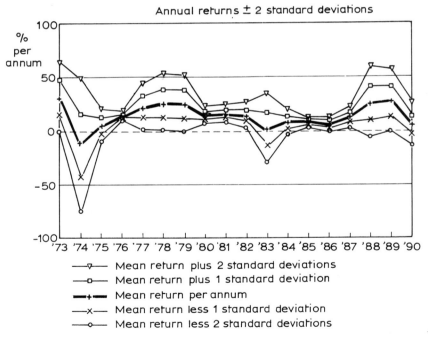

Figure 2D.4 Changes in market risk on an annual basis using the Jones Lang Wooton index.

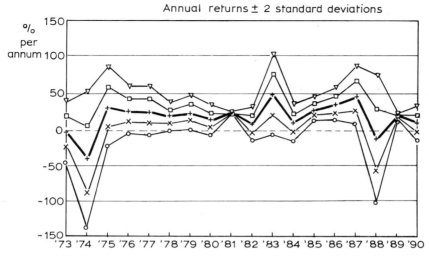

Figure 2D.5 Changes in market risk on an annual basis using the FTA index.

Two standard deviations have been plotted relative to the mean return so that the 99% confidence band has been covered. This clearly shows the cycles that exist in the market. Although they can be recognized after the event it is difficult to forecast when they are going to occur and how long they are likely to last. Figure 2D.5 shows the same approach applied to total returns computed for the FTA index.

Appendix 2E: The assessment of systematic risk using a scenario approach

Portfolio theory is drafted in terms of expectations. Although historic data is useful as a means of testing hypotheses and establishing historic risk measures, its use in an expectations format is limited without considerable adjustment. When considering risk in a property framework the lack of historic data, particularly for a new building, means that a method for assessing risk which does not rely upon past data becomes more important. This appendix shows how this can be done using a scenario approach to assess systematic risk. Once this has been established it can be used to estimate the required return which would compensate for the risk class of the asset. Given this information the identification of whether a property is under- or over-priced can then be made.

The method suggested here can be applied to any asset and is particularly useful for deciding on an appropriate discount rate for development projects. Contrary to the commonly held view, the rate at which a project is financed is not necessarily the correct rate to appraise the project. The target rate is determined by reference to projects of similar risk and is established in the capital markets. This is an interpretation of the security market line discussed in Chapter 1. A good project is one which will generate a positive net present value when discounted at the target rate. Once identified the raising of finance becomes a much simpler matter. Ignoring tax aspects the decision to invest can be treated separately from the financing decision. It is not possible to fundamentally improve the performance of a development project merely by changing the way it is financed. This is why it is important to establish an accurate measure of the target rate of return.

The scenario approach

The scenario approach requires an estimate of the expected outcome for both the market and a property over a defined time-horizon under different economic conditions. Assume that the investor has a five-year time-horizon and would consider disposing of a property if the performance within that period was not satisfactory. This approach is easier to implement over short periods as it is difficult to make reliable estimates of future outcomes when the time-horizon is very long.

To simplify the analysis three basic economic conditions are specified, namely above average growth, average growth and below average growth. Knowing the current purchase price of a property the valuer must forecast the value in five years' time given each of these scenarios.

For example assume that a property could be bought for £1 000 000 and generates an income of £50 000 per annum. The next rent review is in five years' time so intermediate changes in income can be ignored. Using the best forecasting methods at his disposal the valuer constructs a table as shown in Table 2E.1.

Table 2E.1 Property values under different scenarios

Current value	Income	Economic conditions	Expected value in 5 years	Return
£1 000 000	£50 000	Above average growth	£3 546 23	+30.00%
£1 000 000	£50 000	Average growth	£2 418 923	+22.00%
£1 000 000	£50 000	Below average growth	£2 073 131	+18.00%

A probability is assigned to each outcome and a similar estimate is made for the returns on the property market over the next five years. Table 2E.2 shows the results.

Table 2E.2 Scenario analysis for the market

Economic conditions	Prob	Property market return (r_m)	Property return (r_p)
Above average growth	0.25	+20%	+30%
Average growth	0.50	+15%	+22%
Below average growth	0.25	+10%	+18%

Given this information it is possible to estimate expected returns and variances together with the covariance.

Expected returns: Property market

$$E(r_m) = (0.25 \times 20.00\%) + (0.50 \times 15.00\%) + (0.25 \times 10.00\%)$$
$$= 15.00\%$$

Expected returns: Property

$$E(r_p) = (0.25 \times 30.00\%) + (0.50 \times 22.00\%) + (0.25 \times 18.00\%)$$
$$= 23.00\%$$

Variance of returns for the property market

$$Var(r_m) = E[r_m - E(r_m)]^2 \qquad (2E.1)$$
$$Var(r_m) = 0.25(20.00 - 15.00)^2$$
$$+ 0.50(15.00 - 15.00)^2$$
$$+ 0.25(10.00 - 15.00)^2$$
$$= 12.50\%$$

Covariance of returns

$$Cov(r_p, r_m) = E\{[r_p - E(r_p)] \, [r_m - E(r_m)]\} \qquad (2E.2)$$
$$= 0.25[(30.00 - 23.00) \, (20.00 - 15.00)]$$
$$+ 0.50[(22.00 - 23.00) \, (15.00 - 15.00)]$$
$$+ 0.25[(18.00 - 23.00) \, (10.00 - 15.00)]$$
$$= 15.00\%$$

This provides enough information to estimate the market risk.

Market risk

$$\beta_p = \frac{Cov(r_p, r_m)}{Var(r_m)} = \frac{15.00}{12.50} = 1.20. \qquad (2E.3)$$

The property is therefore assessed as being 20% more risky than the market. The required return on the property over the next five years can be estimated from the security market line as follows assuming that the five-year risk-free rate of return is 14%.

Required return $= r_f + \beta_p \ [E(r_m) - r_f]$

$$= 14.00\% + 1.20(15.00\% - 14.00\%)$$

$$= 15.20\%.$$

Given the economic conditions specified, the expected return for the property has been calculated as 23.00%. The abnormal return for the property (23.00% − 15.20%) is 7.80% and this being positive indicates that the property would add value to the firm considering buying by generating a positive net present value. The effect of transactions costs should be taken into consideration to determine whether the abnormal return would still remain positive in the event of a sale. Note however that even if the abnormal return drops to zero buying the property would still earn a gross return of 15.20%.

Appendix 2F: The assessment of systematic risk using a certainty equivalent approach

Determining the systematic risk of property investments using regression analysis would generally require a time series of returns together with a similar time series for the market. It is frequently the case, however, that this information is not available for individual properties. Where such information is available the time series is usually too short to enable reliable regression estimates to be obtained.

A similar exercise using portfolio data instead of individual properties can introduce further problems due to the fact that the variance of returns on portfolios which are increasing in terms of numbers will not be constant. Thus one of the conditions of ordinary least squares regressions analysis is violated (see Appendix 1D). Although such heteroscedasticity can be overcome, additional problems are likely to be introduced due to the fact that indices of property returns are smoothed generally because they involve a degree of averaging. The net effect of this is that beta coefficients obtained by regression analysis will be biased relative to their true values.

One further problem concerns the fact that regression estimates must by definition be historic, whereas what is needed is an estimate of expected β if it is to have any use in terms of valuation theory, performance measurement or capital allocation. This appendix derives an estimate of expected β based on certainty equivalents. The background to this analysis is derived in the following section.

The relationship between yield and growth

It is well-known that in a single-period context there is a negative relationship between expected growth and yield. In other words, high and low yielding properties are expected to exhibit low and high levels of growth respectively.

Under the terms of a property lease, the income received is fixed between rent reviews in money terms and for most practical purposes can be regarded as risk-free. The fact that rent ranks above many other claims in the event of liquidation merely emphasizes this fact. It follows that if a property exhibits zero growth then its yield should be close to the risk-free rate of return. Whether this is the case can only be decided by empirical analysis.

Equation (2F.1) shows, in a single-period context, the relationship between rate of return, income yield and growth for property which has annual rent reviews.

$$r_t = y_t + g_t \qquad (2F.1)$$

The total return, r_t, is simply the sum of the income yield, y_t and the annual capital growth, g_t. Introducing periodic rent reviews blurs the interpretation of income yield so that a straight comparison with the capital growth becomes extremely difficult. Allowing for this fact the contention is that there is some yield figure which overcomes these difficulties and either confirms or rejects the hypothesis that the return on a property with zero growth will approach the riskless rate of return.

This hypothesis can be tested empirically by regressing income yields against capital growth to see whether the intercept term is statistically indistinguishable from the riskless rate of return. For the reasons given above however this test is unlikely to produce conclusive results. The variation in periodic rent reviews means that the income yield is a function of the lease structure which prevails at the beginning of the period. As these will differ for each property, data collected on income yields and capital growth will not be strictly comparable.

This can be demonstrated by taking a sample of 173 properties with capital growth and income yield figures measured over a one-year period from 1983 to 1984. A regression of yield (y) versus capital growth (g) will be of the following form.

$$y = a_0 + a_1 g + e. \qquad (2F.2)$$

The regression should test to see whether a_0 is statistically indistinguishable from the riskless rate of return. The results are shown in Table 2F.1.

Although both coefficients are statistically significant, the explanatory power of the model is low (0.12) and the intercept term a_0 differs considerably from the riskless return, which over the same period was estimated to be 9.68%. The model does however confirm that there is a negative relationship between growth and yield which is significant.

Table 2F.1 Regression analysis of income yield versus capital growth (1983–4)

a_0	a_1	$\bar{R}^2$	n
6.79 (0.217)	−0.11 (0.024)	0.12	173

Standard errors are given in brackets.

One approach which attempts to deal with the different lease terms is to use the equivalent yield. It will be evident that if expected growth is zero the equivalent yield will equal the income yield. Regressing equivalent yields against capital growth produces the results given in Table 2F.2.

Table 2F.2 Regression analysis of equivalent yield versus capital growth (1983–4)

a_0	a_1	$\bar{R}^2$	n
7.99	−0.176	0.39	173
(0.174)	(0.018)		

Standard errors are given in brackets.

This shows a marked increase in explanatory power (0.39) and also an increase in the significance of the regression coefficients. The intercept term however still differs from the riskless return. The reason for this is that each property is valued part-way through a review period and reflects different reversionary potential. These factors taken in combination cause the equivalent yield to vary in relation to a property which is rack-rented. The equivalent yield is also difficult to interpret in an economic sense because it incorporates elements of both real and nominal returns whereas the riskless return is measured in nominal terms (see Chapter 2, section 2.8).

Moving from a model which has annual reviews to one which has periodic reviews therefore causes problems in defining equivalent measures of income yield. Trying to find a suitable yield which confirms the original hypothesis that properties with zero growth should have a return equal to the riskless return is difficult to test empirically. Therefore an alternative approach is needed.

The certainty equivalent yield

One approach to solving this problem is to tackle it from a different direction by constructing a model assuming zero growth and inferring what the intercept of the regression equation based on equivalent yields should be when discounted at the risk-free rate of return. If the figures are the same it should confirm the hypothesis stated earlier.

For a reversionary property valued part-way through a rent review its capital value (V_0) is given by

$$V_0 = \frac{a_0[1 - (1+r)^{-n}]}{r} + \left(\frac{R_0(1+g)^n}{r(1+r)^n}\right)\left(\frac{(1+r)^p - 1}{(1+r)^p - (1+g)^p}\right) \quad (2F.3)$$

where

p = rent review period;

n = number of years to next rent review;

a_0 = current income;

R_0 = current rental value;

g = expected growth rate.

Under conditions of zero growth the current income will be the same as the current rental value so V_0 should equal a_0/y, where y is the equivalent yield. (It will be recalled from equation (2.6) that

$$V_0 = \frac{a_0}{y} + \frac{R_0 - a_0}{y(1 + y)^n}$$

which simplifies to $V_0 = a_0/y$ when $R_0 = a_0$). By replacing V_0 with a_0/y and assuming an expected growth rate, g, of zero, equation (2F.3) can be rearranged in terms of the following equivalent yield when discounted at the risk-free rate of return as follows.

$$y = \frac{r_f(1+r_f)^n}{(1+r_f)^n - 1 + R_0/a_0} \quad (2F.4)$$

The term R_0/a_0 on the right-hand side of the equation is introduced because the sample of properties is valued part-way through a term so an adjustment due to the difference between the observed rental value and income needs to be made. It will be evident from equation (2F.4) that if R_0 equals a_0 then the equivalent yield will be equal to the riskless rate of return. This was the hypothesis put forward earlier.

To adjust for the differences in rental value and income and to estimate y from equation (2F.4) some additional information is required concerning the average number of years to the next rent review together with the ratio of rental value to current income (i.e. R_0/a_0). This was derived for the period 1983–4 using the sample of 173 properties and is summarized in Table 2F.3.

Table 2F.3 Analysis of property sample

Average number of years to next review	Rental value / Current income
$n = 2.43$ Standard error = 0.11	$R/a = 1.23$ Standard error = 0.024

The average number of years to the next rent review for the sample analysed was 2.43 years and the current rental value was 23% greater than the current income. Both these figures are significant at the 99% level.

By substituting the one-year risk-free rate of return into equation (2F.4) assuming a flat yield curve and using the data from Table 2F.3, it is possible to estimate the average expected equivalent yield for property with zero growth.

Recognizing also that the reversionary potential (R_0/a_0) varies inversely with the number of years to the next rent review, it is possible to estimate 95% confidence limits for the yield as shown in Table 2F.4. It will be seen that the regression estimate of 7.99%, given in Table 2F.2, lies within the 95% confidence limits and is very close to the mean value of 8.18%.

Table 2F.4 Estimated equivalent yields and their confidence limits based on zero growth.

	Mean	±95% confidence limits	
n	2.43	2.65 (+)	2.21 (−)
R/a	1.23	1.18 (−)	1.28 (+)
Yield	8.18%	8.48%	7.88%

It should be noted also that if the income from the property is truly riskless under conditions of zero growth, then current income and current rental value arising at some time in the future should be perfect substitutes for each other. Any difference should be accounted for by the riskless rate of return. This proposition can be formalized as

$$a_0 = \frac{R_0}{(1 + r_f)^n}.$$
(2F.5)

Rearranging in terms of the reversionary potential gives

$$R_0/a_0 = (1 + r_f)^n.$$
(2F.6)

Substituting into equation (2F.4) gives

$$y = \frac{r_f(1 + r_f)^n}{2(1 + r_f)^n - 1}.$$
(2F.7)

Given that the risk-free rate of return over the period was 9.68%, it is possible to describe confidence limits for the yield based on the 95% range of values calculated for n, and these are shown in Table 2F.5.

Table 2F.5 Equivalent yields based on equation (2F.7)

Mean value	*Yield values for 95% confidence limits for n*	
y	+95%	−95%
8.06%	7.95%	8.17%

Once again the empirical estimate from the earlier regression model of 7.99% lies within the 95% confidence band (see Table 2F.2).

This evidence suggests that under conditions of zero growth the yield on a property will approach the risk-free rate of return. It is important to note that in expectations form, and in the absence of any other information, investors should take the view that if a property has zero growth its yield will approach the risk-free rate of return. It is suggested that ex-ante this is the case for all properties. There may however be differences ex-post.

Because of differences in the interpretation of conventional property yields, the only measure which justifies this condition in expectations form is the **certainty equivalent yield**. This is computed by subtracting the certainty equivalent growth rate from the risk-free rate of return. The advantage of this procedure is that all properties can be expressed in a form which is directly comparable. Given this scenario it is suggested that certainty equivalent yields can be used as a means of estimating the market risk of property.

A certainty equivalent expectations model of market risk

Consider now a portfolio of property with annual reviews representing the market. This can be proxied by an index. Assume also that the portfolio is large enough for it to contain no residual risk. In certainty equivalent form, the expected return on this portfolio will equal the riskless rate of return and can be expressed in terms of yield and growth as follows:

$$E(r_m) = E(\hat{y}_m) + E(\hat{g}_m) \qquad (2F.8)$$

where

$E(r_m)$ = expected certainty equivalent market return equal to the riskless rate of return;
$E(\hat{y}_m)$ = expected certainty equivalent yield;
$E(\hat{g}_m)$ = expected certainty equivalent growth.

In equilibrium this portfolio will lie on a downward sloping line relating certainty equivalent (CEQ) growth to the CEQ yield. This is shown as point M in Figure 2F.1.

Consider now portfolio P which is also highly diversified. This too will lie on the downward sloping line and in certainty equivalent form will also have a return equal to the riskless rate of return. This is expressed as

$$E(r_f) = E(\hat{y}_p) + E(\hat{g}_p) \tag{2F.9}$$

where

$E(\hat{y}_p)$ = expected certainty equivalent yield for P;
$E(\hat{g}_p)$ = expected certainty equivalent growth for P.

Given that the income stream is constant, the expected CEQ growth on portfolio P can be expressed as a linear function of the market, M, as follows:

$$E(r_f) = E(\hat{y}_p) + k_p E(\hat{g}_m) \tag{2F.10}$$

$$k_p = E(\hat{g}_p)/E(\hat{g}_m). \tag{2F.11}$$

In equilibrium k_p is a measure of the change in the CEQ growth of portfolio P relative to the market. It is a random variable which depends on the probability distribution of the respective certainty equivalent growth rates.

The negative relationship illustrated in Figure 2F.1 can be used in a

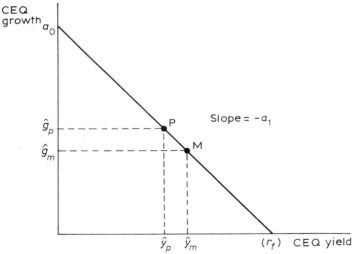

Figure 2F.1 Relationship between certainty equivalent growth and certainty equivalent yield.

single-period context to derive expressions for the certainty equivalent growth of both portfolio P and the market. These are:

$$E(\hat{g}_p) = a_0 - a_1 E(\hat{y}_p) \tag{2F.12}$$

$$E(\hat{g}_m) = a_0 - a_1 E(\hat{y}_m). \tag{2F.13}$$

The intercept and slope coefficients for both these equations are identical because in equilibrium both portfolios will lie on the same line when drafted in CEQ form. In fact all properties will lie at some point along this line when expressed in certainty equivalent form. The precise location of a property on the line will depend on the degree of certainty which can be attached to its value. This aspect is covered in the next section.

From equation (2F.11) it will be seen that the value of k_p can be drafted as:

$$k_p = \frac{a_0 - a_1 E(\hat{y}_p)}{a_0 - a_1 E(\hat{y}_m)}. \tag{2F.14}$$

This can be further simplified by deriving an expression for a_1 based on the relationship shown in Figure 2F.1.

$$a_1 = \frac{a_0}{r_f}. \tag{2F.15}$$

By substitution into equation (2F.14) the value k_p can be written as

$$k_p = \frac{r_f - E(\hat{y}_p)}{r_f - E(\hat{y}_m)}. \tag{2F.16}$$

This is a measure of the change in the expected certainty equivalent growth of a portfolio relative to the market. In equilibrium it is also a measure of the portfolio certainty equivalent β based on certainty equivalent yields. This can be simply demonstrated as follows.

From the capital asset pricing model we know that in equilibrium the β of any asset can be expressed as

$$\beta_p = \frac{E(r_p) - r_f}{E(r_m) - r_f}. \tag{2F.17}$$

In certainty equivalent form we know also that $E(r_p)$ and $E(r_m)$ must equal the expected riskless return. By substituting from equations (2F.8) and (2F.10) into (2F.17) we can derive the certainty equivalent beta, $\hat{\beta}_p$, as follows.

$$\hat{\beta}_p = \frac{E(\hat{y}_p) + k_p E(\hat{g}_m) - r_f}{E(\hat{y}_m) + E(\hat{g}_m) - r_f}. \tag{2F.18}$$

Substituting for k_p from equation (2F.16) and rearranging gives

$$\hat{\beta}_p = \frac{[E(\hat{y}_p) - r_f][r_f - E(\hat{y}_m)] + [r_f - E(\hat{y}_p)]E(\hat{g}_m)}{[r_f - E(\hat{y}_m)][E(\hat{y}_m) + E(\hat{g}_m) - r_f]} \qquad (2F.19)$$

which simplifies to

$$\hat{\beta}_p = \frac{r_f - E(\hat{y}_p)}{r_f - E(\hat{y}_m)}. \qquad (2F.20)$$

or

$$\hat{\beta}_p = \frac{E(\hat{y}_p) - r_f}{E(\hat{y}_m) - r_f}. \qquad (2F.21)$$

By using certainty equivalent yields it is possible to derive comparable expressions of certainty equivalent market risk for both the market and each property.

By recognizing that the income stream from a property can be regarded as fixed it is possible to show that systematic risk estimated in terms of capital growth is identical to similar figures calculated in terms of total returns. (Taking a random sample of 20 properties and estimating historic betas in terms of both total returns and growth rates it was shown that the resulting estimates were statistically indistinguishable from each other. The regression equation of β_r versus β_g was $0.045 + 0.96\beta_g$. The intercept was statistically indistinguishable from zero and the slope coefficient was statistically indistinguishable from 1.0. In addition the $\bar{R}^2$ value was 0.95.)

Equation (2F.21) can therefore be used as a proxy for systematic risk. It is drafted in expectations form and represents an estimate of expected market risk assessed at the beginning of the period. The assumption is that in expectations form a property with zero growth will have a return equal to the riskless rate of return. Equation (2F.21) can be interpreted in this manner. It derives a certainty equivalent expected β based on the assumption that, ex-ante, properties with zero growth will have a return equal to the riskless rate of return. The yields used in equation (2F.21) are certainty equivalent yields. They are merely the difference between the riskless rate of return and the riskless growth rate. The expression can therefore be simplified by recognizing this fact, thus:

$$\hat{\beta}_p = \frac{r_f - [r_f - E(\hat{g}_p)]}{r_f - [r_f - E(\hat{g}_m)]}. \qquad (2F.22)$$

$$\hat{\beta}_p = \frac{E(\hat{g}_p)}{E(g_m)}. \qquad (2F.23)$$

Strictly speaking this should be written as:

$$\hat{\beta}_p | \varphi_{t-1} = \frac{E(\hat{g}_p)}{E(\hat{g}_m)} | \varphi_{t-1} \qquad (2F.24)$$

subject to $\hat{\beta}_p > 0$ for upward only reviews.

Equation (2F.24) shows that given the subset of information available at time $t-1$, the certainty equivalent beta of a portfolio can be derived from an estimate of the certainty equivalent growth rate for both the portfolio and the market. This result is appealing because it enables an estimate of market risk for a portfolio to be made on a period by period basis. Taking into consideration differing rent review patterns does not alter the basic relationship. The model is therefore capable of adapting to different lease structures and also recognizes the effect of changes in the term structure of interest rates.

Adjusting point estimates for valuation error

Equation (2F.24) is based on portfolios and assumes that in equilibrium any errors in valuation can be diversified away. If the same procedure is applied to individual properties the estimation of certainty equivalent beta will be biased and will depend on the subset of information available in estimating the value of the property.

If the subset of information is complete and agreed by all parties this will be reflected in the valuation of the property. This will represent an equilibrium market position. If the subset of information is not complete the value of a property is unlikely to be in equilibrium with the market and so an opportunity may exist for profitable arbitrage. In terms of the CEQ model, individual properties will plot at different points along the line in Figure 2F.1 depending on the information subset.

Unless there is consistent bias in valuations, it will be evident that large portfolios will be able to diversify away any valuation error. The market portfolio will therefore plot at a point which represents an equilibrium position.

Empirical evidence (Brown, 1985a;1985b), suggests that consistent bias in valuations may not be a problem at the portfolio level as long as it is well diversified across all sectors. However in order to use the model for analysing individual properties, estimates of β based on current valuations will have to be adusted to take account of valuation error.

Research by Blume (1975) has shown that there is a tendency for beta coefficients to regress towards 1.0. In other words, assets with high growth will, over time, tend to achieve levels of growth which are more in line with the average for the market. Similarly assets with low initial growth will also tend to approach the average over time. If there is a tendency for beta coefficients to move towards the grand average it would appear sensible to take this fact into account. This is particularly important in estimating the beta coefficients for individual properties.

One approach is to average the estimated β with the market. Beta coefficients which are higher or lower than average would be adjusted towards 1.0. This method assumes that all properties have similar levels of error in their valuations which in practice is unlikely to be the case. A more desirable approach would be to make an adjustment based on the degree of uncertainty concerning the valuation. Thus the greater the error, the greater the adjustment towards the mean.

In order to develop a model which has practical application it is desirable to use data which are readily available in the market-place. To this end a weighting system based on the variance of the yield estimates used to calculate the property values is suggested. This can be incorporated in the following adjustment:

$$\hat{\hat{\beta}}_j = \hat{\beta}_m \frac{\sigma_j^2}{\sigma_j^2 + \sigma_m^2} + \hat{\beta}_j \frac{\sigma_m^2}{\sigma_m^2 + \sigma_j^2} \qquad (2F.25)$$

where

$\hat{\hat{\beta}}_j$ = certainty equivalent beta of property j adjusted for valuation error;
$\hat{\beta}_j$ = unadjusted certainty equivalent beta for property j;
$\hat{\beta}_m$ = certainty equivalent beta of the market;
σ_j^2 = variance of yield estimate for property j;
σ_m^2 = variance of yield estimate for the market.

This is a Bayesian adjustment from which it will be evident that if there is no uncertainty concerning the variance of the property yield, σ_j^2 will equal zero so the adjusted beta will be exactly the same as the point estimate. This is more likely to happen when the subset of comparable information used to value a property is comprehensive.

Testing the model

One of the problems with the model derived above is that it is drafted in terms of expectations and is impossible to test. This of course is the very basis on which portfolio theory has been derived. Because investors' expectations are not known at the beginning of a period it is impossible to make a comparison with realized returns. As a result it is not possible to take a time series of returns, compute beta coefficients in the traditional way, compare them with betas estimated using equation (2F.21) and draw any meaningful conclusions.

This type of model is more likely to be used in the area of performance measurement and in predicting possible future change in sectors. If it is really picking up expectations any differences between observed returns may well provide useful information about the future.

To illustrate this point the model was used to predict sector returns for the period from 1978 to 1985 using the Richard Ellis property market indicators. Actual returns were then regressed against expected returns. The reason for this was twofold. Firstly it was important to examine the intercept term to see whether it picked up any abnormal returns and whether they were in line with expectations. Secondly the slope coefficent was checked to see whether it was statistically indistinguishable from 1.0. This would indicate that the underlying long-term returns generating process was in line with expectations. The results of this analysis are shown in Table 2F.6, and can be interpreted as follows.

Office sector

The a_0 term is statistically indistinguishable from zero and the slope coefficient a_1 is statistically indistinguishable from 1.0. The explanatory power of the model at 0.94 is very high. This would imply that over the period analysed the office sector showed no abnormal performance relative to expectation and as a sector was fairly priced.

Table 2F.6 Regression of actual returns versus expected returns using the Richard Ellis property market indicators (1978–85)

	$r_s = a_0 + a_1 E(r_s)$		
Sector (S)	a_0	a_1	$\bar{R}^2$
Office	−0.42 (1.61)	0.91 (1.56)	0.94
Retail	7.79 (3.44)	0.95 (0.20)	0.78
Industrial	−8.66 (2.47)	1.34 (0.15)	0.93
Total	−0.25 (0.06)	1.02 (0.004)	0.99

Standard errors are given in brackets.

Retail sector

Over the period 1978–85 the retail sector performed well and this is reflected in the regression results. The intercept term a_0 shows a statistically significant figure of 7.99%. There were factors affecting the performance of the retail sector which contributed to a higher rate of return than expected. The a_1 coefficient is statistically indistinguishable from 1.0 implying that the long-term growth potential for the sector is in line with expectations. The positive abnormal performance is therefore more likely to be the result of chance events affecting that sector. It may well have been caused by the buoyancy in retail spending contributing to a temporary mispricing. This chance event could of course be eroded in time. The long-term position revealed in the slope coefficient is that retail properties will on average be priced in line with expectations. The model also has a high explanatory power.

Industrial sector

This sector performed badly over the analysis period as can be seen from the statistically significant a_0 coefficient (−8.66%). Economic events during this period adversely affected the performance of the industrial sector and contributed to the temporary mispricing.

What is more interesting, however, is the slope coefficient which at 1.34 is 2.27 standard errors from 1.0. This would imply that in the long term the industrial sector has a higher growth potential than expected. This could occur if there had been a continual down valuation of the sector. In practice it means that on average the value of industrial property at the beginning of a period was much lower than it should have been, even allowing for the adverse economic conditions. Given that the intercept term is probably a chance event the high slope coefficient would seem to imply that there is considerable growth potential within the industrial sector yet to be tapped. The regression also has a high explanatory power.

This particular result is interesting because the period after 1985 showed a significant improvement in the industrial sector and by 1988 it was the highest performing sector. Whether this is a random result can only be determined by more extensive tests over longer periods. If this finding can be applied consistently then it would imply that the model has considerable potential in predicting the future direction of movement.

Overall this analysis shows that the model produces results which are generally in line with investors' expectations concerning the performance of each sector. This is encouraging because it indicates that the model may have value in determining appropriate risk-adjusted discount rates for individual properties. While this is the first stage in identifying under-priced properties, much remains to be done.

Appendix 2G: Assessing the risk premium for property

It is a widely held belief that the premium earned from investing in property is in the order of 2% per annum over the risk-free rate of return. This figure is often adopted without question as the basis for establishing target rates of return and is applied consistently across each sector of the market irrespective of differences in risk class.

This appendix examines three alternative approaches to calculating the risk premium using empirical evidence wherever possible. The main purpose of this exercise is to see whether the observed risk premium is close to 2% and under what conditions this is likely to be justified.

Method A: Direct observation

This is the most direct method of obtaining estimates of the risk premium and involves subtracting the risk-free rate of return from the returns earned on a property index.

The property returns used are calculated from published property indices and represent annual returns over different time spans. The risk-free rate of return is calculated from Treasury Bill rates and represents the guaranteed return that could be earned on an annual basis. This figure is then subtracted from the property return for each period to arrive at the risk premium. Table 2G.1 shows the results together with the standard deviation and standard error of the mean, which is important because the time series used in each case are merely samples drawn from a much larger population and so it is necessary to be able to describe confidence intervals for the average premium. More specifically it enables a *t*-statistic to be established which will verify whether the observed risk premium figures can be regarded as being statistically different from 2%. It will be seen from Table 2G.1 that the risk premium for each index varies considerably and no clear pattern appears to emerge. As the sample size for each index varies it is inevitable that there will be random noise associated with the premium figures reflecting the performance of the constituent properties. This is picked up in the standard error of the mean and the resulting *t*-value gives an indication of whether the premium figures are statistically different from 2%.

In all cases the low *t*-values indicate that we cannot reject the hypothesis that the true risk premium is 2%. The figure will clearly vary from period to period but in the absence of any other information the use of 2% is not unreasonable. It should also be noted that, with the exception of the Richard Ellis and Jones Lang Wooton indices,

Table 2G.1 Average risk premium figures estimated from property indices

		Years	Average % risk premium per annum	Standard deviation % per annum	Standard error % per annum	(2.00%) t-value
JLW	1967–84	17	5.42	11.32	2.75	1.24
WGS	1979–88	9	3.21	8.05	2.68	0.45
IPD	1980–89	9	2.29	8.07	2.69	0.11
RE	1978–89	11	5.17	8.26	2.49	1.27
PI	1981–89	9	1.97	8.78	2.93	−0.01
HP	1973–88	16	8.90	18.22	4.56	1.51
MGL	1977–88	11	4.24	7.35	2.21	1.01

JLW:	Jones Lang Wooton
WGS:	Weatherall Green & Smith
IPD:	Investment Property Databank
RE:	Richard Ellis
PI:	The Property Index
HP:	Hillier Parker
MGL:	Morgan Grenfall Laurie

none of the premium figures is statistically different from zero. It is generally believed however that investment in property is expected to provide compensation for risk so there should be a requirement for a positive premium.

Method B: Cash flow analysis

The above method concentrated on publicly available information concerning property indices. Although this gives some evidence of the likely premium to be earned a better indication would be given by an analysis of the cash flows generated by a large portfolio of property.

Simply calculating the internal rate of return on a portfolio and subtracting from it the redemption yield of a government stock with the same maturity is inappropriate because the difference in cash flow between the two assets will vary. The way around this problem is to redraft the cash flows for the property portfolio by taking out the influence of risk, and then to calculate the internal rate of return. The resulting figure will be the risk premium. The methodology involved can be developed as follows.

In a single-period context, the risk premium is merely the difference between the actual return and the riskless rate of return, so

$$\text{premium} = r_p - r_f. \qquad (2G.1)$$

This can be drafted in terms of value relatives:

$$\text{premium} = \left(\frac{V_1 - V_0}{V_0}\right) - \left(\frac{I_1 - I_0}{I_0}\right) \qquad (2G.2)$$

where

$V_0 =$ value of property at the beginning of the period;
$V_1 =$ value of property at the end of the period;
$I_0 =$ riskless index in period 0;
$I_1 =$ riskless index in period 1.

Taking logs gives

$$\ln(\text{premium}) = \ln\left(\frac{V_1}{V_0}\right) - \ln\left(\frac{I_1}{I_0}\right) \qquad (2G.3)$$

$$= \ln\left(\frac{V_1}{I_1}\frac{I_0}{V_0}\right) \qquad (2G.4)$$

and the second part of this expression (I_0/V_0) can be eliminated if the initial value of the riskless index is assumed to be the same as V_0.

The principle involved is to divide each of the cash flows by the riskless index for each period so that the cash flows are expressed in risk premium form. This is exactly the same procedure as would be adopted in obtaining cash flows adjusted for inflation. It was also the principle followed by Emary (1985) who analysed a sample of 350 properties with cash flows stretching over a period of 29 years, 1956–85. The resulting money-weighted premium for each sector over different sub-periods is given in Table 2G.2.

There are two important points to note from this analysis. Firstly the average risk premium measured over the whole period, for the total portfolio, is close to 2%, and secondly, the spread of premium figures in each sub-period decreases as the period over which the premium is measured increases.

Table 2G.2 Money-weighted risk premium figures

| | Risk premium in per cent per annum for different sub-periods | | | |
	1956–85	1980–5	1984–5	n
Portfolio	1.80	−2.20	−4.80	350
Office	0.70	−1.80	−6.70	94
Retail	3.70	0.10	3.60	144
Industrial	0.80	−4.90	−9.40	112

The negative risk premium figures over the shorter periods indicates that it is not always possible to achieve positive returns so the common view concerning the 2% risk premium only has validity in terms of long-term expectations. In other words the longer a property is held the more likely it is that our expectations concerning the risk premium will be realized.

Method C: Using portfolio theory

It was established in Chapter 1 that total risk can be partitioned into two components, namely market risk and residual risk, and can be expressed algebraically as

$$\sigma_p^2 = \beta^2 \sigma_m^2 + \sigma_e^2. \tag{2G.5}$$

If a portfolio is efficiently diversified it will contain no residual risk so σ_e^2 will approach zero as the portfolio includes more assets. It was also shown that there is a linear relationship between efficiently diversified portfolios, that is they will all lie along a straight line.

With this information it is possible to estimate the expected premium on property given the average premium earned on equities. The procedure follows from equation (2G.5) assuming that the residual is zero.

$$\sigma_p^2 = \beta_p^2 \sigma_m^2 \tag{2G.6}$$

so

$$\beta_p = \frac{\sigma_p}{\sigma_m}. \tag{2G.7}$$

Thus a proxy beta for the property sector relative to the equity market can be established from knowledge of the standard deviation of returns from both a property and equity index. The relationship in terms of calculating the risk premium can be established from Figure 2G.1.

It will be readily seen that the risk premium for the property sector can be established from

$$r_p - r_f = \frac{\beta_p}{\beta_m} (r_m - r_f). \tag{2G.8}$$

We know β_m must by definition equal 1.00 so equation (2G.8) simplifies to

$$r_p - r_f = \beta_p (r_m - r_f). \tag{2G.9}$$

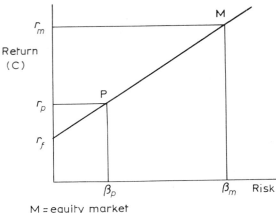

M = equity market
P = property market

Figure 2G.1 Establishing the risk premium for property.

To estimate the property risk premium two pieces of information are required:

1. a proxy beta for property measured relative to the return on equities;
2. a measure of the expected premium on equities.

Proxy beta

The proxy beta for property can be obtained using equation (2G.7) by dividing the standard deviation of returns for property by a similar figure for equities, which is easily obtained from equity returns and on average has a value of approximately 30% per annum. The standard deviation of returns for property however is more difficult to ascertain because smoothing effects tend to cause the standard deviation of returns on an index to be understated. Figure 2D.2 in Appendix 2 showed that it could vary from about 5% to 15% with the higher figures being recorded during the property collapse of the early 1970s. In terms of long-term averages a figure somewhere between 5% and 10% per annum would seem appropriate. Taking 7.5% gives an estimate for β using equation (2G.7) as follows:

$$\beta_p = \frac{\sigma_p}{\sigma_m} = \frac{7.5}{30} = 0.25.$$

The expected equity risk premium

The model shown in equation (2G.9) is drafted in terms of long-term expectations so $(r_m - r_f)$ represents what investors expect to achieve on average by holding a portfolio of equities over long periods. By subtracting the return on Treasury Bills from the return on equities it can be shown that the average premium earned on equities over long periods is in the order of 9.5% per annum.

Given these two pieces of information it is possible to establish a proxy value for the expected risk premium for property as follows.

$$r_p - r_f = 0.25(9.5) = 2.38\%.$$

Despite the broad assumption underlying this analysis it is encouraging to see that the resulting premium is close to 2%.

Conclusion

The three approaches given above have each shown that there is some validity in the proposition that investors on average expect to earn a premium of about 2% per annum from holding property. The conditions under which this applies are as follows.

1. The 2% premium only applies to a portfolio consisting of all properties. The premium for individual sectors will vary according to their risk profile.
2. The 2% premium only applies to property if held long-term. Observed premium figures over short periods are likely to approach the grand average.
3. In the absence of any specific forecasting knowledge the best estimate of the premium for the next period is likely to be in the order of 2%.

As more extensive databases of property are now available it should be a relatively simple matter to carry out more detailed tests to establish with greater accuracy the realized risk premium from holding property.

Appendix 2H: The decomposition of property yields

The expected risk premium earned on each sector of the property market is not directly observable. It should differ for each sector of the market reflecting the fact that there are differences in market risk, and although the risk premium is not defined it is implied in the yield figures used.

This appendix uses the certainty equivalent model derived in Appendix 2F to decompose equivalent yields in order to estimate the expected risk premium. The approach adopted is based on some broad assumptions concerning lease structure and the average market premium.

From the capital asset pricing model, the expected equilibrium return of any sector of the property market can be expressed as

$$E(r_s) = r_f + \beta_s[E(r_m - r_f]. \tag{2H.1}$$

In risk premium form this gives

$$E(r_s) - r_f = \beta_s[E(r_m) - r_f]. \tag{2H.2}$$

The right-hand side of this expression represents the sector premium and is calculated as the product of the market risk of the sector and the average market premium, which long-term is generally assumed to be 2%. It is not essential to maintain a constant assumption concerning the average market premium but it is nevertheless convenient for this discussion.

Using average market yields it is possible to estimate expected risk levels for each sector as follows.

Assume that on average the property market comprises 50% office property, 25% retail property and 25% industrial property. Again this is not essential but is useful for this discussion. The market risk of each sector can be estimated using

$$\hat{\beta}_s = \frac{(\hat{g}_s)}{(\hat{g}_m)}, \tag{2H.3}$$

but in order calculate these sector betas, certainty equivalent growth rates need to be estimated from readily available market data. The starting point for this exercise is the equivalent yield model which expresses value in the following form.

$$V = \frac{a}{y} + \frac{R - a}{y(1 + y)^n} \tag{2H.4}$$

where

$$a = \text{current income;}$$

R = current rental value;
n = number of year to the next review;
y = equivalent yield.

Dividing through by V gives

$$1 = \frac{\hat{y}}{y} + \frac{\hat{R} - \hat{y}}{y(1 + y)^n} \qquad (2H.5)$$

where

$\hat{y}$ = income yield;
$\hat{R}$ = rental value yield.

Recognizing that the reversionary potential (RP) of a property is the percentage by which the current income falls short of the current rental value, it can be expressed as follows.

$$RP = 1 - \frac{a}{R} \qquad (2H.6)$$

so

$$R = \frac{a}{1 - RP}. \qquad (2H.7)$$

Dividing through by V provides an expression for the rental value yield ($\hat{R}$).

$$\hat{R} = \frac{\hat{y}}{1 - RP} \qquad (2H.8)$$

Substituting into equation (2H.5) and rearranging enables an expression to be derived for the income yield as follows.

$$1 = \frac{\hat{y}}{y} + \frac{\hat{y}}{(1 - RP)y(1 + y)^n} - \frac{\hat{y}}{y(1 + y)^n} \qquad (2H.9)$$

$$\hat{y} = \frac{(1 - RP)y(1 + y)^n}{(1 - RP)(1 + y)^n + RP} \qquad (2H.10)$$

The income yield for each sector can therefore be derived from equivalent yield data together with an estimate of reversionary potential. It will be evident that if the reversionary potential (RP) equals zero the income yield will equal the equivalent yield. This will occur when the income is equal to the rental value.

This information can now be used in the equated yield model in order to derive an estimate of certainty equivalent growth. For a property valued part-way through a rent review period, its value can be expressed as

$$V = a\left[\frac{1 - (1 + r)^{-n}}{r}\right] + \frac{R(1 + g)^n}{r(1 + r)^n}\left[\frac{(1 + r)^p - 1}{(1 + r)^p - (1 + g)^p}\right]. \quad (2H.11)$$

Dividing through by V and substituting for the income yield from equation (2H.10) gives the following expression drafted in terms of the equivalent yield and the reversionary potential.

$$1 = \frac{(1 - RP)y(1 + y)^n}{(1-RP)(1 + y)^n + RP}\left\{\left[\frac{1 - (1 + r)^{-n}}{r}\right]\right.$$
$$\left. + \frac{(1 + g)^n}{r(1 - RP)(1 + r)^n}\left[\frac{(1 + r)^p - 1}{(1 + r)^n - (1 + g)^p}\right]\right\} \quad (2H.12)$$

By substituting the risk-free return for r and assuming that the number of years to the next rent review period, n, is approximately half the rent review period, p, it is possible to solve for the certainty equivalent growth rate for any value of the reversionary potential. By weighting the results for each sector of the market it is possible to

Table 2H.1 Expected risk premia in % per annum (1968–89)

	Office	Retail	Industry	Market
1968	3.08	1.84	0.00	2.00
1969	2.78	2.44	0.00	2.00
1970	2.92	2.14	0.00	2.00
1971	3.04	1.94	0.00	2.01
1972	3.24	1.56	0.00	2.01
1973	2.42	2.34	0.86	2.01
1974	2.76	2.48	0.00	2.00
1975	2.36	2.36	0.90	2.00
1976	2.24	2.24	1.28	2.00
1977	2.66	2.66	0.00	2.00
1978	2.20	2.36	1.24	2.00
1979	2.08	2.18	1.66	2.00
1980	2.04	2.14	1.76	2.00
1981	2.06	2.16	1.72	2.00
1982	2.06	2.16	1.72	2.00
1983	2.10	2.30	1.48	2.00
1984	2.08	2.40	1.42	2.00
1985	2.04	2.56	1.36	2.00
1986	2.30	3.42	0.00	2.01
1987	2.36	3.28	0.00	2.00
1988	2.28	2.98	0.46	2.00
1989	2.12	2.42	1.34	2.00
Average	2.42	2.38	0.78	2.00

establish the certainty equivalent growth for the total market. It is then a simple matter to establish the certainty equivalent market risk.

Once the market risk has been established it can then be used to estimate risk premium figures for each of the sectors.

Table 2H.1 shows the Morgan Grenfall Laurie average yield data from 1968 to 1989 decomposed into expected risk premium figures for each sector of the market. The average market risk is assumed to be 2.00%. The clear message which emerges from this is that the industrial sector carries the lowest expected risk premium. In other words investors holding industrial property long-term would expect to earn a rate of return below the average for the market. If abnormal returns are earned in this sector it is probably because industrial property becomes marginal thus creating an excess demand which drives up prices.

Table 2H.2 shows the average property yields used in the analysis together with the derived expected returns and the returns on Consols which has been used as the reference riskless rate of return.

Table 2H.2 Property yields and expected returns

	Yields (% per annum)			Expected return (% per annum)			(% per annum)
	Office	Retail	Industry	Office	Retail	Industry	Consols
1968	5.87	6.37	8.00	10.17	8.93	7.09	7.09
1969	5.87	6.12	8.55	10.68	10.34	7.90	7.90
1970	5.75	6.06	8.00	9.82	9.04	6.90	6.90
1971	5.25	5.37	8.50	8.62	7.52	5.58	5.58
1972	5.00	5.37	8.00	8.94	7.26	5.70	5.70
1973	6.20	6.37	9.50	13.58	13.50	12.02	11.16
1974	7.00	7.50	11.50	14.23	13.95	11.47	11.47
1975	6.50	6.50	9.00	12.78	12.78	11.32	10.42
1976	6.00	6.00	8.50	13.83	13.83	12.87	11.59
1977	6.50	6.50	8.50	9.39	9.39	6.73	6.73
1978	6.00	5.75	7.50	11.51	11.67	10.55	9.31
1979	5.50	5.00	7.25	15.61	15.71	15.19	13.53
1980	5.50	5.00	7.00	17.00	17.10	16.72	14.96
1981	5.50	5.00	7.00	15.86	15.96	15.52	13.80
1982	5.50	5.00	7.00	15.86	15.96	15.52	13.80
1983	5.75	5.25	7.25	12.60	12.80	11.98	10.50
1984	5.75	5.00	7.25	12.38	12.70	11.72	10.30
1985	6.25	5.00	7.75	12.64	13.16	11.96	10.60
1986	6.50	5.25	9.00	11.20	13.32	8.90	8.90
1987	6.50	5.50	9.00	11.26	12.18	8.90	8.90
1988	6.50	5.60	8.75	11.58	12.28	9.76	9.30
1989	6.10	5.65	8.25	11.22	11.52	10.44	9.10

The information from Tables 2H.1 and 2H.2 is shown graphically in figures 2H.1 and 2H.2.

The information contained in this appendix concerning risk premium figures should be interpreted as the market's perception of the long-term premium for each sector assuming that on average investors expected to earn 2% over the risk-free rate of return for holding the market. There is no guarantee that the expected premium for each sector will remain constant over time. This is clearly shown in Figure 2H.2 and is merely a reflection of the fact that investors' expectations concerning future prospects for each sector are changing over time. The figures should not be confused with realized premium figures for each sector which can vary considerably from period to period. The premium figures estimated here form the basis for establishing target rates of return appropriate to each sector.

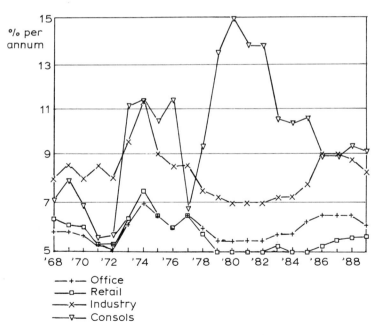

Figure 2H.1 Property yields and return on consols.

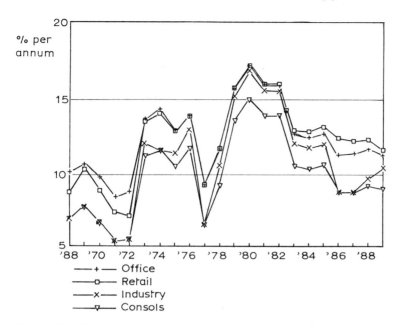

Figure 2H.2 Expected sector returns.

References

Blume, M. (1975), Betas and their regression tendencies, *Journal of Finance*, June, **XXX** (3).

Brown, G. R. (1985), An empirical analysis of risk and return in the UK commercial property market, unpublished PhD dissertation, Reading University.

Brown, G. R. (1985a), Property investment and performance measurement: a reply, *Journal of Valuation*, **4**, 33–44.

Brown G. R. (1985b), The information content of property valuations, *Journal of Valuation*, **3**, (4).

Drivers Jonas, (1988), Technical appendix to *The variance in valuations* Investment Property Databank.

Emary, R. H. (1985) Property risk premia, unpublished M.Phil dissertation, Reading University.

Fama, E. (1970), Efficient capital markets: a review of theory and empirical evidence, *Journal of Finance*, May, 383–417.

Gau, G. (1984), Weak form tests of the efficiency of real estate investment markets, *The Financial Review*, Nov, **19**, (4).

Greaves, M. J. (1972), The investment method of property valuation and analysis: an examination of some of its problems, unpublished PhD thesis, University of Reading.

Greer, G. (1974), Risk, return and efficiency in the market for real property, unpublished PhD dissertation, University of Colorado.

Investment Property Databank, Drivers Jonas (1988), The variance in valuations.

Sykes, S. G. (1981), Property valuation: a rational model, *The Investment Analyst*, (61), 20–6.

Sykes, S. G. (1983), The uncertainties in property valuation and performance, *The Investment Analyst*, (67).

Sykes, S. G. (1983a), Valuation models: action or reaction, *Estates Gazette*, **267**, September, 1108–12.

Sykes, S. G. and McIntosh A. P. J. (1985), *A guide to institutional property investment*, MacMillan, London.

3
Hedging against inflation

Historically, property has been regarded as a good hedge against inflation and has probably formed a major part of institutional investment portfolios purely on this basis.

This chapter considers this and investigates the tests that need to be carried out in order to establish whether property adequately hedges against inflation and performs better or worse than other assets. There have been a number of studies in the USA which have dealt with this problem in terms of a range of assets but very few comparable studies covering property. In the UK there are fewer still studies with virtually no coverage of property. This is partly due to the lack of good time-series data on which to carry out an analysis and partly due to the fact that property is frequently regarded as a specialist area. Nevertheless with the prospect of an inflationary economy it becomes more important to examine this aspect because it has a direct bearing on the way portfolios should be constructed.

3.1 Development of inflation

The evidence of the last thirty years suggests that there is no single cause for inflation. There are however some initiating influences on the demand and supply side which can be seen to contribute. If, for example, the demand for goods and services exceeds that available then their prices will be bid up. In this case the direction of cause is from demand to inflation. In other words there is too much money chasing too few goods. A good example of this occurred in 1922 when the German Central Bank printed billions of bills of paper marks which then went into circulation chasing too few goods. Prices rose causing demand-pull inflation with a vengeance.

This is essentially the monetarist view of inflation which anticipates a continuous inflationary spiral if the quantity of money is increased as prices rise. Not unnaturally the monetarist cure is to restrict the money supply as prices rise maintaining its increase at a rate appropriate for the real rate of growth of the economy.

Inflation can however also be started on the supply side causing what is known as cost-push inflation. An example of this was the five-fold increase in oil prices in 1973–4 which triggered off world-wide inflation. Cost-push inflation usually follows from demand-pull. Once prices start to rise trade unions seek compensating wage rises related not only to current increases but also to the expectation of future price rises. Thus prices are bid up.

In simple terms this is what causes inflation although it is difficult to identify the two effects separately so we cannot generally distinguish between cost-push and demand-pull inflation.

As far as capital assets are concerned, and this of course includes property, inflation will have the effect of increasing the monetary value of future earnings or rents which will in turn be reflected in capital values. Clearly some assets will respond better to inflation than others. From the investor's point of view there is a need to protect the purchasing power of his savings and so he will tend to seek out those assets which he believes will act as a hedge against inflation. Institutional investors are also alive to this problem as they have a long-term liability in terms of providing pensions.

To determine which assets are a hedge against inflation it is necessary to understand a little about the theory of inflation hedging.

3.2 Hedging against inflation: the theory

An understanding of the problems of inflation hedging can be gained by comparing a series of index numbers for different assets in relation to an index of price movements. Table 3.1 compares the retail price index with the returns on the Jones Lang Wooton index, the FTA All Share index and the Long-dated Gilts index.

By re-basing the index at different dates it is possible to see how each asset has performed relative to inflation. For example over the whole period 1967–88, each asset out-performed the retail price index. However, over shorter periods different results emerge. The period 1967–76 saw only property out-performing inflation and over the period 1973–80 none of the assets hedged against inflation. The most recent period, from 1984–88 showed each asset outperforming inflation.

Table 3.1 Inflation and index comparison

June	JLW index				FTA index				Long-dated gilts				Retail price index			
1967	26	100			36	100			61	100			34	100		
1968	30	115			54	150			58	95			36	106		
1969	35	135			51	142			54	89			37	109		
1970	39	150			48	133			58	95			40	118		
1971	48	185			66	183			66	108			43	126		
1972	57	219			83	231			71	116			46	135		
1973	76	292	100		81	225	100		70	115	100		51	150	100	
1974	66	254	87		47	131	58		55	90	79		59	174	116	
1975	70	269	92		62	172	77		67	110	96		74	218	145	
1976	81	312	107		79	219	98		81	133	116		85	250	167	
1977	100		132		100		123		100		143		100		196	
1978	127		167		119		147		117		167		107		209	
1979	160		211		149		184		133		190		120		235	
1980	185		243		171		211		142		203		145		284	
1981	217				213				154				161			
1982	251				232				188				176			
1983	257				346				259				182			
1984	280			100	383			100	270			100	192			100
1985	307			110	499			130	310			115	205			107
1986	328			117	683			178	380			141	210			109
1987	374			134	1014			265	420			156	219			114
1988	470			168	882			230	445			165	229			119
Hedge:	+	+	−	+	+	−	−	+	+	−	−	+				

Although this type of analysis is quite common it is insufficient as a basis for concluding that the assets have fully hedged against inflation. Examining index numbers does not convey the whole message because it provides insufficient information about the underlying processes. To determine whether an asset is a hedge against inflation requires a more rigorous approach and a definition for a hedge against inflation.

3.3 Defining a hedge against inflation

The expected nominal return on any asset can be expressed as the sum of the expected real rate of return and the expected rate of inflation. This however is only an approximation and really only applies when the figures involved are small. The full expression involves the product of two figures as follows.

$$[1 + E(r_n)] = [1 + E(r_r)][1 + E(i)] \qquad (3.1)$$

where

$$E(r_n) = \text{expected nominal return;}$$
$$E(r_r) = \text{expected real return;}$$
$$E(i) = \text{expected inflation rate.}$$

The expected nominal return can therefore be found from

$$E(r_n) = E(r_r) + E(i) + E(r_r)E(i). \qquad (3.2)$$

The final term is the product of the expected real return and the expected rate of inflation, which for small values can be considered negligible. For example, assume that the expected real return and expected inflation rate are 4% and 5% respectively. Substituting these figures gives the following:

$$E(r_n) = 0.04 + 0.05 + (0.04 \times 0.05)$$

$$= 0.092$$

$$= 0.09 \text{ approximately (i.e. 9\%).}$$

As the product of 0.04 and 0.05 is very small it can be ignored. In the above calculation it affects only the third decimal place.

In terms of pricing, the market will use all available information and fix the price of the asset at the beginning of the period so that the expected nominal return will be the sum of the appropriate expected real return and the best possible assessment of expected inflation.

This relationship was first put forward in 1930 by Irving Fisher (1930). He argued that the expected real return on an asset is determined by factors such as the productivity of capital, the investor's time preference and his taste for risk. He also argued that expected real returns and expected inflation are unrelated.

This general approach to the definition of nominal returns is applicable irrespective of the time period over which it is measured. Thus as a first attempt at getting closer to deciding whether property is a hedge against inflation we can compare the internal rate of return of a number of portfolios back to their date of purchase with rates of inflation calculated from the retail price index over the same period. The internal rates of return calculated for each portfolio take account of the initial value and current value together with the size and timing of each of the acquisitions and cash flows for each property. The rate of return calculated in this way is money-weighted because it takes account of cash flows in and out of the portfolio. The comparable rate of return for the retail price index is found by taking index values at the same dates as the initial and current portfolio values and measuring the annual increase over the period. This is actually a time-weighted rate of return but because there are no intermediate cash flows it will be exactly the same as the money-weighted rate of return. The two returns are therefore comparable.

Using this approach internal rates of return were estimated for 27 portfolios and compared with the retail price index; Figure 3.1 plots the results. The hypothesis is that if the nominal returns on each portfolio incorporate the effects of inflation then the internal rate of return calculated for a group of portfolios should show a positive relationship with returns on the retail price index. As expected this is what happens and almost without exception all the returns are above the retail price index line indicating that over long periods, property is likely to show positive real rates of return.

An alternative way of looking at this is to strip out the effects of inflation from the cash flows of each of the properties in order to arrive at a cash flow in real terms. The relationship between a real cash flow and a nominal cash flow can be accounted for by the rate of inflation. As cash flows are fixed in nominal terms they embody the effects of inflation. The relationship between the two is given by

$$a_n = a_r(1 + i) \tag{3.3}$$

where

$$a_n = \text{nominal cash flow;}$$
$$a_r = \text{real cash flow;}$$
$$i = \text{rate of inflation.}$$

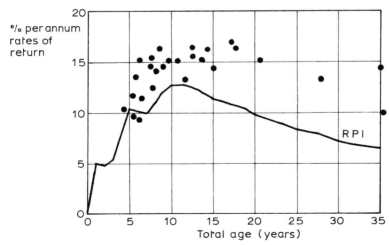

Figure 3.1 Property portfolio returns and inflation (from 1983).

The real cash flow can be found by transposing.

$$a_r = \frac{a_n}{(1 + i)}.$$ (3.4)

But we know that $(1 + i)$ can be calculated from an index so that the real cash flow can be estimated as

$$a_r = \frac{a_n}{I_n/I_0}$$ (3.5)

$$a_r I_0 = a_n/I_n$$ (3.6)

As I_0 is a constant (usually 100) the real cash flow can be estimated by dividing each nominal cash flow figure by the retail price index number for the corresponding period.

The internal rate of return of the resulting cash flow gives an internal rate of return in real terms. Figure 3.2 shows a plot of these figures against the total age of each portfolio.

Regressing the real returns against total age, it is possible to see whether age has any impact on explaining real returns. The regression line is close to horizontal, indicating that there is no significant relationship. Thus the age of a portfolio appears to have no impact on determining real returns. From this analysis it is also possible to show that on average, over a total period of 35 years, investors have received a real rate of return in the region of 2.77% per annum. (If short-term riskless interest rates are used as a proxy for expected inflation then this calculation is similar to stripping out the effect of risk on the cash flows so that the average return figure is an approximation of the risk premium on property. The figures given here are comparable with those estimated in Appendix 2G to Chapter 2.)

We can also say there is a 95% probability that the real return has

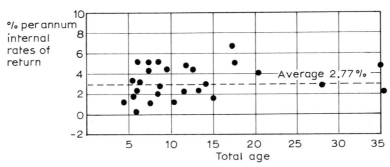

Figure 3.2 Real rates of return and portfolio age (from 1983).

been in the region of 1.77% to 3.77%. If the past is any guide to the future we can say that investors in property on average can expect to earn real rates of return of this order.

Although this analysis gives some indication of the quality of property as a hedge against inflation it is still not a conclusive test. In fact we have yet to provide a suitable definition and test for a hedge against inflation.

To tackle this problem we have to look in more depth at the original definition of the nominal return on an asset. To recap, the expected nominal return can be expressed as the sum of the expected real rate of return and the expected rate of inflation. The important point to notice from this definition is that everything is drafted in terms of expectations, even inflation. Observed changes in the retail price index, however, not only include expected inflation but also an additional shock, either negative or positive, which will alter the final outcome. Thus if investors have to forecast what inflation is going to be next year the consensus would represent an expected value based on the best estimate of economic conditions. In twelve months' time economic conditions may turn out to be completely different causing the retail price index to differ from expectations. Thus inflation can be split into two components.

inflation = expected inflation + unexpected inflation.

This separation into components gives a better way of defining a hedge against inflation. We can now hypothesize that if there is a one-to-one relationship between the returns on an asset and expected inflation then that asset is a hedge against expected inflation. Similarly if there a one-to-one relationship between the returns on an asset and unexpected inflation then that asset is a hedge against unexpected inflation. If the asset shows a one-to-one relationship with both expected and unexpected inflation then it can be regarded as a complete hedge against inflation. This approach is economically sound and can be tested over a number of time periods.

The classic work in this area is a paper by Fama and Schwert (1977) who established the methodology and examined the hedging characteristics of a wide range of assets, including residential real estate, in the United States over a period from 1953 to 1971. Fama formalized the definition of nominal returns propounded by Irving Fisher in the following manner.

$$E(r_{jt}|\varphi_{t-1}) = E(i_{jt}|\varphi_{t-1}) + E(\Delta_t|\varphi_{t-1}) \qquad (3.7)$$

where

φ_{t-1} = information set available at time $t - 1$;
j = asset j;
t = time subscript;
E = expectations operator;
r_{jt} = nominal return on asset j;
i_{jt} = real return on asset j;
Δ_t = rate of inflation.

In setting the nominal rate of return for the period from $t - 1$ to t the market uses the information set available at the beginning of the period, φ_{t-1}, to determine the expected rate of inflation and expected real rate of return, including an adjustment for risk. This assumes that the market is an efficient processor of information.

Fisher also hypothesized that the real and monetary sectors of the economy were independent of each other. Thus the expected real rate of return given in equation (3.7) will be determined by factors such as the productivity of capital, time preference, the taste for risk, and will be independent of the expected rate of inflation.

Assuming it is possible to measure the expected rate of inflation the regression counterpart of equation (3.7) can be used to test the joint hypothesis that:

1. the market is efficient;
2. the expected real return and the rate of inflation are independent.

The form of regression model used to test this hypothesis is

$$r_{jt} = \alpha_j + \beta_j E(\Delta_t | \varphi_{t-1}) + e_{jt} \tag{3.8}$$

which relates nominal returns to expected inflation. This regression should produce the following results.

1. α_j should be equal to the real rate of return.
2. β_j should be statistically indistinguishable from 1.0 if the asset is a hedge against expected inflation. This is also consistent with the belief that real returns and inflation are unrelated. In other words inflation will affect the value of the nominal returns but will have no effect on the expected real rate of return.
3. e_{jt}, i.e. the error term or residuals, should be serially uncorrelated. In other words there should be no pattern in the residual returns indicating that the market is efficient.

This is a simple model relating nominal returns to expected inflation. However, we are interested in knowing also how nominal returns are related to unexpected inflation. This can be defined algebraically as

$$\Delta_t - E(\Delta_t|\varphi_{t-1}) \tag{3.9}$$

where Δ_t is the observed rate of inflation in period t. The full regression model is therefore

$$r_{jt} = \alpha_j + \beta_j E(\Delta_t|\varphi_{t-1}) + \gamma_j[\Delta_t - E(\Delta_t|\varphi_{t-1})] + n_{jt} \tag{3.10}$$

and this regression model should produce the following results:

1. α_j should be equal to the real rate of return;
2. β_j should be statistically indistinguishable from 1.0 implying that the asset is a hedge against expected inflation;
3. γ_j should be statistically indistinguishable from 1.0 if the asset is a hedge against unexpected inflation;
4. if $\beta_j = \gamma_j = 1.0$ then the asset is a complete hedge against inflation.

The Fisher model implies that for all assets the coefficient β_j should be equal to 1.0 for expected inflation. We have no prior hypothesis however about the relationship with unexpected inflation although it is likely to differ for different assets. As far as property is concerned, if the generally held belief that it is a hedge against inflation is correct, the coefficient relative to unexpected inflation should be positive.

Note also that since expected and unexpected inflation are by definition uncorrelated, a test of the ability of an asset to hedge against expected inflation using equation (3.10) will be identical to similar tests using equation (3.8).

3.4 Assessing expected inflation

The analysis described above relies upon an estimate of expected inflation, $E(\Delta_t|\varphi_{t-1})$, being available although it is not directly observable. The way Fama overcame this problem was to use the returns on Treasury Bills as a proxy for expected inflation. The justification for this approach is that because they are short-term investments the price of Treasury Bills will incorporate expected inflation and will not have time to adjust to any unexpected changes. The return on a Treasury Bill (b_t) which matures at time t will be known in advance at period $(t-1)$. Fama (1975) argued that if the bill market is efficient and real returns are constant, the nominal return on the bill should be equal to the expected real return plus the expected rate of inflation. This can be formally expressed as

$$b_t = E(i) + E(\Delta_t|\varphi_{t-1}) \qquad (3.11)$$

where

b_t = return on 90-day Treasury Bills;
$E(i)$ = expected real rate of return.

The equation can be rearranged to give the expected rate of inflation,

$$E(\Delta_t|\varphi_{t-1}) = -E(i) + b_t \qquad (3.12)$$

which can then be tested using the following regression model:

$$\Delta_t = \alpha + \beta b_t + e_t. \qquad (3.13)$$

This is merely a regression of observed inflation rates versus Treasury Bill rates. The hypothesis being tested is that β is statistically indistinguishable from 1.0. If this is the case then Treasury Bill rates can be used as a proxy for expected inflation. The coefficient for α should also represent the real rate of return. The results which Fama obtained over the period 1953–71 are shown in Table 3.2.

Each of these regressions show slope coefficients which are statistically indistinguishable from 1.0 and the serial correlation coefficients are all close to zero. This implies that the bill market is efficient and that Treasury Bill interest rates are good proxies for expected inflation. On this basis the unexpected component of inflation can be calculated by subtracting Treasury Bill rates from observed rates of inflation. So,

$$r_{jt} = \alpha_j + \beta_j b_t + \gamma_j[\Delta_t - b_t] + n_{jt}. \qquad (3.14)$$

Before presenting the results of Fama and Schwert's analysis it is as well to point out that this method of estimating expected inflation has

Table 3.2 Treasury Bill rates as proxies for expected inflation (1953–71)

b_t	Sample size	α	β	$\bar{R}^2$	Serial correlation for following lags 1	2	3
Monthly	223	−0.0007 (0.0003)	0.98 (0.10)	0.29	0.10	0.12	−0.02
Quarterly	74	−0.0023 (0.0011)	0.93 (0.11)	0.48	0.00	0.04	0.10
Half-yearly	24	−0.0097 (0.0024)	1.06 (0.10)	0.82	0.00	−0.04	0.16

Return on six-month Treasury Bills were only available from 1959.
Standard errors are shown in brackets.

been criticized on the grounds that it assumes constant real rates of return. Although this was true over the period Fama and Schwert analysed, it has transpired that in other periods, real rates of return were not constant. This aspect has been addressed by Fama and Gibbons (1982) and has been considered in relation to inflation hedging for USA commercial property by Hartzell, Hekman and Miles (1986). In this latter paper, regression tests of Treasury Bills and inflation produced the results shown in Table 3.3 when analysed over the period 1973–83.

From this it will be seen that over the period 1973–83 Treasury Bills acted as a poor proxy for expected inflation. The same was also true for the subperiods examined. The Durbin–Watson statistic tests for the presence of no serial correlation in the residual error terms obtained from the regression. It lies in the range of 0 to 4 with 2 representing zero serial correlation. The low figures given in Table 3.3 indicate there is some evidence of positive serial correlation, implying that real rates of return were not constant.

The alternative approach for estimating expected inflation is to use a moving-average process. This is the technique proposed by Fama and Gibbons and subsequently used by Hartzell, Hekman and Miles. The process involves estimating the ex-post real rate of return as

$$r_t = R_{t-1} - \Delta_t. \tag{3.15}$$

Using an integrated moving-average process forecasts of the expected real rate of return are generated. The expected rate of inflation is then found by taking the difference between the nominal rate of return and the forecast value for the real rate of return, thus

$$E(\Delta_t) = R_t - r_t. \tag{3.16}$$

Estimates of the unexpected rate of inflation can then be found by

Table 3.3 Treasury Bill returns as proxies for expected inflation: 1973–83

	α	β	$\bar{R}^2$	*Durbin–Watson*
1973–83	0.013	0.338	0.08	0.89
	(0.004)	(0.183)		
1976–83	0.010	0.393	0.11	0.98
	(0.005)	(0.203)		
1978–83	0.007	0.500	0.09	0.78
	(0.011)	(0.382)		

Standard errors are shown in brackets.

subtracting the results of equation (3.16) from observed values of inflation.

Another approach to the same problem is to say that today's inflation is equal to yesterday's inflation plus a shock term as follows:

$$\Delta_t = \Delta_{t-1} + e_t. \tag{3.17}$$

Regressing current values of inflation onto lagged values gives

$$\Delta_t = \alpha + \beta\Delta_{t-1} + e_t. \tag{3.18}$$

The fitted values and residuals from this regression can be used as estimates for expected and unexpected inflation.

It should be clear from this discussion that the debate concerning the appropriate method for estimating expected inflation is still open to discussion. Fama believes that Treasury Bill rates still remain the best single predictor of expected inflation.

3.5 UK studies on inflation hedging

The simplest test for a relationship between returns and inflation is to check the cross correlation coefficients between the rate of inflation and the returns on the property sector. Using continuous rates of return from a sample of 173 properties for monthly data over the period from January 1979 to December 1982 produced the results shown in Table 3.4. A comparison is also shown with the FTA All Share index.

These results show a high level of correlation between inflation and each sector of the property market. When combined into a portfolio, the relationship is even higher. By contrast the FTA All Share index shows little correlation with inflation.

Although these figures are uniformly high, a further question which needs to be addressed is whether the returns from property respond to

Table 3.4 Correlation between inflation and both property and the FTA index

Monthly returns		Industrial	Office	Retail	Portfolio	FTA
portfolio	EW	0.53	0.34	0.25	0.41	—
portfolio	VW	0.40	0.40	0.25	0.44	0.06

EW = Equally-weighted portfolio
VW = Value-weighted portfolio

current changes in inflation or whether they react more slowly. This can be examined by lagging the returns from the retail price index and measuring the effect on the coefficient of correlation. The results are shown in Table 3.5.

Table 3.5 Property returns and lagged inflation (January 1979–December 1982) using monthly returns

| Sector | | Lag in months | | | | | |
		0	1	3	6	9	12
Industrial	(EW)	0.53	0.25	0.31	−0.06	0.19	0.09
	(VW)	0.40	0.29	0.24	−0.04	0.11	0.05
Office	(EW)	0.34	0.03	0.41	0.06	0.24	0.48
	(VW)	0.40	−0.05	0.41	0.08	0.34	0.46
Retail	(EW)	0.25	0.18	0.41	0.08	−0.05	0.33
	(VW)	0.25	0.34	0.51	0.17	−0.03	0.26
Portfolio	(EW)	0.41	0.15	0.45	0.05	0.16	0.41
	(VW)	0.44	0.17	0.48	0.09	0.23	0.39

Although there is some evidence of strong positive association between property returns and lagged inflation, particularly after three months and twelve months, the relationship in the current month still remains very strong. This is also true when returns are calculated over longer holding periods, as shown in Table 3.6 for half-yearly returns. Again it will be seen that inflation twelve months ago has an impact on current returns but the effect of current inflation appears to be more significant.

This of course is not a direct test of inflation hedging as described

Table 3.6 Property returns and lagged inflation (January 1979–December 1982) using half-yearly returns

| Sector | | Lag in months | | |
		0	6	12
Industrial	(EW)	0.86	−0.21	0.35
	(VW)	0.87	−0.26	0.64
Office	(EW)	0.76	−0.09	0.73
	(VW)	0.86	0.11	0.63
Retail	(EW)	0.88	0.26	0.75
	(VW)	0.93	0.41	0.61
Portfolio	(EW)	0.87	−0.03	0.67
	(VW)	0.94	0.11	0.67

above. The model developed by Fama and Schwert, however, can be tested using the sample properties for the four-year period analysed above and estimating the values of expected and unexpected inflation from the regression model given in equation (3.18). The results of this analysis using monthly returns are as given in Table 3.7.

Table 3.7 Inflation analysis: January 1979–December 1982 (monthly returns)

$$r_t = \begin{matrix} 0.0046 \\ (0.005) \end{matrix} + \begin{matrix} 0.941\mathrm{E}(\Delta_t) \\ (0.563) \end{matrix} + \begin{matrix} 0.723[\Delta_t - \mathrm{E}(\Delta_t)] \\ (0.236) \end{matrix} \qquad \bar{R}^2 = 0.16$$

Standard errors are shown in brackets.

This regression model shows that the slope coefficients for both expected and unexpected inflation are statistically indistinguishable from unity implying that over the period analysed the returns from property were a complete hedge against inflation. However the intercept term is statistically indistinguishable from zero implying that the real rates of return earned over the period were on average equal to zero and so the nominal returns earned by the portfolio moved in line with changes in the retail price index. Note also that the $\bar{R}^2$ value, at 0.16, is quite low. Only 16% of the variation in returns on the property portfolio could be explained by changes in inflation. In other words, inflation is not the only factor which contributes to property returns.

This simple analysis provides some evidence to show that property is likely to be a complete hedge against inflation. The positive relationship between property returns and unexpected inflation implies that investors can expect returns to be higher in those periods when inflation is expected to be high.

For a more detailed analysis covering longer time periods we must now turn to the results of the limited number of published studies.

In the UK the only published study which has dealt with inflation hedging in an economically defensible manner is by Limmack and Ward (1988). Using a ten-year data sample of quarterly returns from the Jones Lang Wooton database they estimated the expected inflation rate by two methods. The first followed Fama's earlier approach, using the yield on three Treasury Bills calculated on the last day of the previous quarter to estimate the expected inflation rate for the following quarter. Subtracting this from the observed inflation rate, using the Retail Price index, gave an estimate of unexpected inflation. This was Approach A.

The alternative method, Approach B, used an autoregressive integrated moving-average model to estimate expected inflation on a rolling predictor basis using past data on quarterly inflation rates. Two versions of the model were used. The first took a 40-quarter data sample of inflation rates and used the model to estimate the expected inflation for the next quarter. Estimates for further quarters were obtained by substituting the actual inflation rate for the latest quarter and then re-estimating the model. Using this approach the data set increases by one observation for each subsequent forecast. The second version merely dropped the first observation whenever the actual inflation rate was obtained. Using this approach the data sample remained the same size.

The property sample consisted of quarterly continuous returns from January 1976 to March 1986 and was taken from institutional investment portfolios managed by Jones Lang Wooton. The number of properties included in the sample was not given.

Using Approach A they obtained the regression results in Table 3.8, which show that property was a hedge against expected inflation since the hypothesis that the regression coefficient is 1.00 cannot be rejected at the 5% level of significance. However the relationship with unexpected inflation is less encouraging. With the exception of the industrial sector they all differ significantly from 1.00.

The $\bar{R}^2$ values in all cases are low indicating that inflation only partly explains property returns. The intercept terms, representing the

Table 3.8 Quarterly inflation tests (Approach A) 1976–86 using T-bill rates as estimate of expected inflation

Sector	Expected inflation	Unexpected inflation	$\bar{R}^2$
Offices	$-0.003 + 1.45\mathrm{E}(\Delta_t) +$	$0.388[\Delta_t - \mathrm{E}(\Delta_t)]$	0.182
	(0.014) (0.517)	(0.225)	
Retail	$0.014 + 1.15\mathrm{E}(\Delta_t) +$	$0.363[\Delta_t - \mathrm{E}(\Delta_t)]$	0.052
	(0.019) (0.690)	(0.301)	
Industrial	$-0.002 + 1.68\mathrm{E}(\Delta_t) +$	$0.885[\Delta_t - \mathrm{E}(\Delta_t)]$	0.266
	(0.018) (0.650)	(0.283)	
Portfolio	$-0.000 + 1.47\mathrm{E}(\Delta_t) +$	$0.458[\Delta_t - \mathrm{E}(\Delta_t)]$	0.194
	(0.015) (0.530)	(0.231)	

Standard errors are shown in brackets.

real rate of return, are all insignificant implying that over the ten-year period 1976–86 real returns were on average equal to zero.

Subdividing the data sample into type and geographical location produced inconclusive results. Limmack and Ward argue that the low explanatory power of the model could be due to the fact that it is mis-specified and could be due to mis-identifying the variable representing expected and unexpected inflation or with the correlation between real rates of return and the expected rate of inflation. This would be consistent with the real rate of return over the period not being constant. It will be recalled that this was a precondition for using Treasury Bills as a measure of expected inflation. Over the period 1976–86 the observed rate of inflation was turbulent. During the early part, rates of 20% per annum could be observed. It is therefore quite possible that the real rate of return was not constant.

The alternative approach used by Limmack and Ward allows the real rate of return to vary. Version 2 of Approach B produced the results shown in Table 3.9 which are broadly in line with the previous regression concerning expected inflation except that the coefficient for the office sector is significantly different from 1.00. However, there is an improvement in relation to unexpected inflation. Each of the coefficients is statistically indistinguishable from unity implying that property has hedged against unexpected inflation.

The explanatory power of the model is still low but all of the intercept terms are significantly different from zero. The average real rate of return over the ten-year period was approximately 9.5% per annum at the total portfolio level.

Table 3.9 Quarterly inflation tests (Approach B, Version 2) 1976–86 using rolling predictor model to estimate expected inflation

Sector	Expected inflation	Unexpected inflation	$\bar{R}^2$
Offices	$0.021 + 0.52E(\Delta_t) +$ (0.006) (0.219)	$0.828[\Delta_t - E(\Delta_t)]$ (0.393)	0.119
Retail	$0.032 + 0.45E(\Delta_t) +$ (0.007) (0.285)	$0.739[\Delta_t - E(\Delta_t)]$ (0.511)	0.033
Industrial	$0.017 + 0.97E(\Delta_t) +$ (0.007) (0.268)	$1.310[\Delta_t - E(\Delta_t)]$ (0.481)	0.252
Portfolio	$0.023 + 0.58E(\Delta_t) +$ (0.006) (0.223)	$0.877[\Delta_t - E(\Delta_t)]$ (0.401)	0.141

Standard errors are shown in brackets.

Dividing the sample into sectors and geographical locations again produced inconclusive results concerning the inflation hedging properties.

In general the results of both tests imply that property is a hedge against expected inflation. There is some justification for believing that it is also a hedge against unexpected inflation. The interpretation of results depend on which measure is used for estimating expected inflation. Although the model which used Treasury Bills as the proxy did not confirm this hypothesis it should be noted that the regression coefficients are positive for all sectors. There is clearly some relationship between property returns and unexpected inflation. The more sophisticated model used for estimating expected inflation emphasizes this point and implies that property is a complete hedge against inflation.

Although more work needs to be done in identifying expected inflation and verifying property returns, these results suggest that investors can expect higher returns during periods of high inflation. Further work also needs to be carried out to identify sector factors which contribute to inflation hedging.

3.6 USA studies on inflation hedging

The classic study on inflation hedging was that undertaken by Fama and Schwert in the USA. Over a period 1953–71 they analysed the inflation hedging properties of Common Stocks, US Treasury Bills, longer-term US Government Bonds, Human Capital and Residential Real Estate using the model described in equation (3.10) with three-month Treasury Bills as a proxy for expected inflation.

The data used for property was the Home Purchase Price component of the Consumer Price index. The Purchase Price index was based on the purchase price of homes with mortgages newly issued by the Federal Housing Association. The index was expressed as a price per square foot and adjusted to take account of differences in quality between individual properties. It was however a three-month moving average because the price of a property was only reported at the time it was insured and so there was a lag of one to three months between the price being determined and the time it was reflected in the index. In addition the sample was not representative of all residential property.

A general picture of the inflation hedging properties of each of the assets, obtained by comparing inflation rates with average annualized returns for each asset, is shown in Table 3.10.

Table 3.10 Comparison of inflation and USA asset returns using average, annualized nominal rates of return

Asset	Years 1953–7	1958–62	1963–7	1968–71	1971–5
Inflation	1.3	1.3	2.3	5.1	7.1
Treasury Bills					
1 month	1.9	2.2	3.7	5.5	5.7
2 month	2.1	2.7	4.0	5.9	6.0
3 month	2.3	3.0	4.1	6.1	6.4
Government Bonds					
1 year	2.3	3.5	3.6	6.1	N/A
2 year	2.7	3.6	3.2	5.7	N/A
3 year	2.6	3.7	2.9	5.1	N/A
4 year	2.4	3.3	2.6	4.5	N/A
Real Estate	1.0	0.6	1.7	5.9	6.2
Human Capital	2.2	3.4	5.2	4.7	6.1
Common Stocks					
Value-wtd	12.3	12.8	12.5	3.0	1.6
Equal-wtd	10.5	14.4	18.5	3.3	−0.6

N/A: not available
All figures are in % per annum.

As the rate of inflation increases over each sub-period it will be seen that the returns on real estate and Treasury Bills correspond exactly to the ordering of average nominal returns. The same is true to a lesser extent with long-term government bonds and human capital. Common stocks however appear to be negatively related to changes in inflation and as such did not provide a good hedge. Despite this negative relationship the average returns on stocks were high and so observed real returns were positive although they did not move in line with inflation.

Using the model for relating nominal returns to both expected and unexpected inflation, derived in equation (3.10), Fama and Schwert obtained regressions for each of the assets. A summary of the results for real estate are given in Table 3.11 for monthly, quarterly and half-yearly returns.

These results show that irrespective of time period, residential property acts as a hedge against expected inflation. With regard to unexpected inflation it is only half-yearly returns which show a coefficient statistically indistinguishable from 1.00. However the coefficients for monthly and quarterly returns are significantly different from

Table 3.11 Monthly, quarterly and half-yearly returns for residential property (after Fama and Schwert)

Residential property	Expected inflation	Unexpected inflation	$\bar{R}^2$
Monthly	$-0.0012 + 1.19\text{E}(\Delta_t) + 0.31[\Delta_t - \text{E}(\Delta_t)]$ (0.0005) (0.16) (0.11)		0.21
Quarterly	$-0.0032 + 1.15\text{E}(\Delta_t) + 0.56[\Delta_t - \text{E}(\Delta_t)]$ (0.0019) (0.19) (0.20)		0.35
Half-yearly	$-0.0054 + 1.27\text{E}(\Delta_t) + 1.14[\Delta_t - \text{E}(\Delta_t)]$ (0.0073) (0.24) (0.49)		0.60

Standard errors are shown in brackets

zero which could imply that they are a better hedge against longer-term unexpected inflation. Fama and Schwert suggested that this result is probably due to measurement errors in the property data because returns are derived from a three-month moving average. The property transactions usually take place between one and three months prior to the date they are included in the index, and because of this, the correlation between the nominal return and the unexpected inflation component can be spread over a six month period. On the basis of this evidence they suggest property is a complete hedge against both expected and unexpected inflation even on a monthly basis. They verify this by using a technique developed by Scholes and Williams (1977) which involves regressing nominal rates of return on expected inflation as well as current and lagged values of unexpected inflation over a six-month period. The model they used was

$$r_t = \alpha + \beta\text{E}(\Delta_{1t}) + \sum_{i=0}^{6} \gamma_i[\Delta_{t-i} - \text{E}(\Delta_{1t-i})] + e_t \qquad (3.19)$$

where expected inflation is proxied using the Treasury Bill rate. The sum of the regression estimators for current and lagged values of unexpected inflation provides a consistent estimate of the relationship between the true return from property and the unexpected monthly inflation rate. Using this technique they found that the γ coefficient was 0.88 with a standard error of 0.29. Thus the coefficient for unexpected inflation was statistically indistinguishable from 1.00.

This result confirms the earlier studies described above and shows that property appears to be acting as a complete hedge against inflation and so the real return to property is unrelated to the inflation rate. This does not imply however that the real rate of return is certain. The $\bar{R}^2$ value given in Table 3.11 for half-yearly data shows that 60% of the variation in returns could be explained by inflation. The remaining 40% is still unexplained.

Of the other assets tested, all with the exception of stocks were a complete hedge against expected inflation. There was however less consistency with unexpected inflation. Over the period covered stocks were negatively related to both expected and unexpected inflation. Contrary to popular belief stocks did not appear to act as a hedge against inflation. This finding has been verified by other researchers in both the USA and UK and provides a good reason for including a proportion of property in a multi-asset portfolio as a means of protecting the investor from purchasing power risk due to inflation.

The Fama and Schwert study only covered residential property, while most institutional portfolios hold little if any residential property, preferring to build up substantial commercial property holdings. Although there have been other studies which have used returns calculated from an index, the only other published study in the USA which deals with actual returns from commercial property is that by Hartzell, Hekman and Miles. Using the methodology developed by Fama and Schwert they examined the inflation hedging ability of 300 commercial properties taken from a Commingled Real-estate Fund with quarterly holding period returns over a ten-year period 1973–83.

As described earlier Hartzell, Hekman and Miles estimated expected inflation using the alternative of Treasury Bill rates as well as an autoregressive integrated moving-average model. They constructed two samples from their data covering a 40-quarter and a 20-quarter period. Over the whole period 1973–83 the fund grew from 113 to 382 properties. Many of the acquisitions represented new rather than existing buildings and so the cash flow generated by many of the properties was low. The second half of the sample period however, was not influenced to the same degree by this and was felt to be more representative of the long-run income-producing ability of the portfolio.

In addition to running regression analyses to test for the ability to hedge against both expected and unexpected inflation Hartzell, Hekman and Miles also argued that the effectiveness of property in providing inflation protection is determined by the extent to which it can reduce the purchasing power risk of a portfolio. As default-free Treasury Bills are free of all risk except purchasing power risk the effectiveness of property as an inflation hedge can be measured by the percentage reduction in the variance of returns on Treasury Bills obtained by including property in a portfolio of bonds.

Two measures were used to determine the diversification benefits.

The first (W) represented the proportion of property needed to be held in a portfolio of property and government bonds in order to minimize the portfolio variance. The second (S) represented the percentage reduction in the variance of the portfolio gained by holding property in the portfolio. The ratio of W to S, i.e. W/S, is a measure of the efficiency of the inflation risk reduction; the lower the figure the higher the efficiency.

The first tests were carried out using the whole sample over the 40- and 20-quarter periods utilizing both the constant real return and moving-average real returns in the proxy for expected inflation.

The results are summarized in Table 3.12 and indicate that property provided a complete hedge against inflation over both periods. All the coefficients for expected inflation, with the exception of the 20-quarter sample which assumes a constant real return, are reliably greater than 1.00. The coefficients for unexpected inflation are also greater than 1.00 for the 20-quarter sample and within one standard error of 1.00 for the 40-quarter sample.

However the inflation efficiency measures do vary considerably over the sample periods. Property does appear to offer something in the region of a 20% reduction in inflation risk with about a 20% holding in the portfolio, the figures being significantly higher for the 20-quarter period.

Other tests were carried out to examine the inflation hedging properties of different sectors of the market. Briefly these showed that for the 40-quarter sample industrial and office properties provided a

Table 3.12 Commercial property inflation tests (Hartzell, Hekman and Miles)

	Expected inflation	Unexpected inflation	W	S	W/S	$\bar{R}^2$
40-quarter sample 1973–83						
Constant real return	1.44 (0.29)	0.76 (0.23)	32.7	19.1	1.71	0.40
Moving average real return	2.23 (0.58)	0.98 (0.49)	14.6	6.3	2.31	0.36
20-quarter sample 1978–83						
Constant real return	1.09 (0.27)	1.77 (0.38)	34.8	59.1	0.59	0.56
Moving average real return	1.65 (0.39)	1.63 (0.55)	20.7	24.8	0.84	0.53

Standard errors are shown in brackets.

complete hedge against expected inflation. The retail sector was much weaker although it provided a better hedge against unexpected inflation. The 20-quarter sample produced much stronger results with industrial and office properties showing complete protection against both expected and unexpected inflation. The retail sector was again weak in relation to expected inflation but provided better protection against unexpected inflation.

Another test which Hartzell, Hekman and Miles carried out was in relation to property size. They argued that property size may have an effect on inflation risk due to the nature of the tenant and type of lease. As properties increase in size, the proportion of single to multi-tenanted properties decreases. If inflation has an effect on individual firms then this will affect property returns through the demand for space. The results of the regressions showed that the coefficients for expected and unexpected inflation generally rise with property size, the implication being that portfolios comprising larger properties provided better protection against inflation.

3.7 Conclusion

The results of the empirical tests carried out in both the USA and UK seem to indicate that property is likely to be a complete hedge against inflation. Although much work still needs to be done on the assessment of expected inflation there can be little doubt that property plays an important rôle in protecting the purchasing power of multi-asset portfolios. This is particularly significant in relation to the fact that stocks do not appear to offer such protection.

Appendix 3A: A test for inflation hedging

This appendix presents a simple test for inflation hedging using monthly total returns provided by the Investment Property Databank (IPD) over the period from January 1987 to February 1990.

A simple plot of the total returns index and the retail price index, starting with 100 in December 1986, is shown in Figure 3A.1.

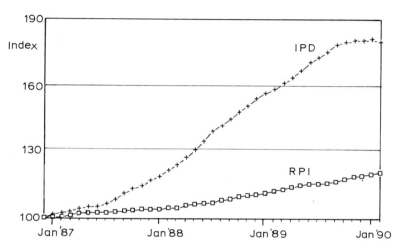

Figure 3A.1 IPD total returns index versus the retail price index (1987–90).

Over the three-year period it will be seen that the returns on property have considerably out-performed inflation. The obvious conclusion is that property has provided a hedge against inflation over this period. However, as shown in Chapter 3 it can be misleading to look at index numbers because they do not provide sufficient information concerning the hedging properties.

A more useful view of the situation can be seen by plotting the monthly returns on the property index and comparing these with similar figures for the retail price index. Using continuously compounded returns this information is shown in Figure 3A.2 which illustrates that in most months property has provided returns in excess of the retail price index although there does not appear to be a significant relationship between the two lines.

It will be recalled from Chapter 3 that a true test of whether an asset is a complete hedge against inflation requires an estimate of both expected and unexpected inflation. For the purposes of this analysis an

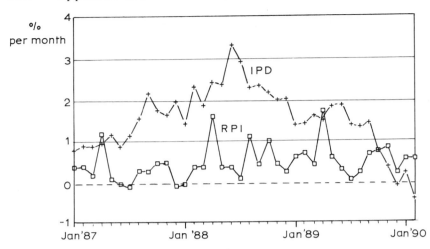

Figure 3A.2 Monthly property returns versus inflation.

estimate of expected inflation was obtained by taking the fitted values from a regression of current monthly inflation rates against similar figures for the previous month. The residuals from this regression represent unexpected inflation.

Given this information, it is then possible to regress the monthly property returns against both expected and unexpected inflation to test its hedging properties. The results of this analysis are shown in Table 3A.1, and a number of important points emerge from this regression.

1. The real return is positive and statistically significant. Over the three-year period analysed, the IPD index showed an average real rate of return of approximately 1.7% per month. This equates to 22.4% per annum.
2. The coefficient with regard to the expected inflation component is negative. Although it has a low absolute value it has a very large standard error. It is not significantly different from zero, nor is it

Table 3A.1 A test for inflation hedging using IPD monthly returns and the retail price index 1987–90

Dependent variable	Real return	Expected inflation	Unexpected inflation	$\bar{R}^2$
IPD returns	0.017	−0.357	0.000	0.00
	(0.007)	(1.38)	(0.001)	

Standard errors are shown in brackets.

significantly different from 1.00. In view of this, it is difficult to arrive at any positive conclusion with regard to property being a hedge against expected inflation. The fact that we cannot reject the hypothesis that the coefficient is significantly different from 1.00 lends some support to the belief that it may be a hedge against expected inflation. However the data may be obscuring the true facts.

3. The coefficient with regard to unexpected inflation is statistically insignificant implying that over the period analysed property did not respond at all, in relation to unexpected changes in the rate of inflation.

4. The R^2 value is zero implying that variations in both the expected and unexpected components of inflation do not explain any of the variation in property returns.

On the basis of the data used, this analysis implies that over the period 1987–90 property earned positive real rates of return although it cannot be guaranteed that if fully hedged against inflation.

To proceed any further with this analysis would need a better understanding of the property returns series. It can be shown that there is considerable serial correlation caused by smoothing. Although the inflation series is also smoothed, the transformation into expected and unexpected components removes this from the independent variables. As far as the regression results are concerned the presence of serial correlation in the dependent variable will cause the slope coefficients to be understated.

The principal point to be gained from this analysis is that using raw data can lead to misleading results unless care is taken in the interpretation. The serial correlation in the residuals from the regression shown in Table 3A.1 is in fact very high and is a clear indication that the property returns series needs to be transformed in order to eliminate the serial correlation. This aspect is covered in Appendix 5A to Chapter 5.

References

Fama, E. (1975) Short-term interest rates as predictors of inflation, *American Economic Review*, 65, June, 269–82.

Fama, E. and Gibbons, M. (1982) Inflation, real returns and capital investment, *Journal of Monetary Economics*, 9 (3), 297.

Fama, E. and Schwert, G. W. (1977) Asset returns and inflation, *Journal of Financial Economics*, 5, 115–46.

Fisher, I. (1930) *The theory of interest*, Macmillan, London.

Hartzell, D., Hekman, J. and Miles, M. (1986) Diversification categories in investment real estate, University of Texas, working paper.

Limmack, R. J. and Ward, C. W. R. (1988) Property returns and inflation, *Land Development Studies*, 5, 47–55.

Scholes, M. and Williams, J. (1977) Estimating betas with nonsynchronous data, University of Chicago, working paper.

4
Portfolio construction

In Chapter 1 the concept of constructing efficient portfolios was introduced in the context of assets which were infinitely divisible. In the absence of a regularly traded market in unitized property, the principles are unlikely to be adopted as the basis for advising on the construction of property portfolios. This is not to say however that the ideas have no validity within the framework of property investment. One of the most important aspects of understanding portfolio theory and asset pricing models is the insights this gives into investor behaviour and the rationale for making certain decisions.

One aspect of this will now be examined in more detail: what is of practical value to investors is to know how well diversified their portfolios are.

The principle of diversification is well known to investors in property although there are no empirical studies concerned with the reduction of risk and portfolio size. Assessments of diversification tend to be qualitative in nature with little quantitative content. The reason for this state of affairs is that good time-series data on a reliable sample of properties is extremely difficult to obtain. Consequently the developments in finance that have taken place over the last thirty years have, in the UK, generally ignored this major sector of the investment market. The position is similar in the USA although the amount of published material and research into the applications of modern portfolio theory to real estate are more extensive. See for example Findlay et al. (1979), Friedman (1970) and Hoag (1979; 1980).

Given the lack of empirical evidence, professional property advisors are unable to justify whether a proposed investment policy is worthwhile or whether diversification is worth pursuing. A central issue in this debate concerns the number of properties which investors should hold. This is important not only in terms of the property portfolio but also in a mixed-asset context.

4.1 Background

The problem of risk reduction and portfolio size related to stock portfolios has been well documented and several studies have been carried out to investigate the effect of increasing numbers on the standard deviation of portfolio returns, e.g. Elton and Gruber (1977) and Evans and Archer (1968). This work has been extended by Solnik (1974) to cover the impact of investing internationally.

One of the most quoted studies is by Evans and Archer. Recognizing that the total variation in portfolio returns can be split into two parts, i.e. systematic and unsystematic risk, they argued that the reduction in risk must be a function of the reduction of only the unsystematic portion of total variation. Thus as a portfolio increases in size and approaches the market, the expectation is that the variation in portfolio returns will approach the systematic level. Thus the relationship between portfolio size and standard deviation should be a declining asymptotic function. This was first identified by Markowitz (1959) in relation to stock portfolios and can be expressed as

$$\sigma_p{}^2 = \frac{1}{n}\,\bar{\sigma}^2 + \frac{n-1}{n}\,\overline{\text{cov}}(i,\,j) \qquad (4.1)$$

where

$$\sigma_p{}^2 = \text{portfolio variance;}$$
$$\bar{\sigma}^2 = \text{average variance of all stocks;}$$
$$\overline{\text{cov}}(i,\,j) = \text{average covariance between all stocks;}$$
$$n = \text{number of stocks.}$$

It will be seen from this that as n increases, the portfolio variance approaches the average covariance between all stocks. Empirical studies have shown that by maintaining equal levels of investment most of the reduction in risk occurs with portfolios consisting of between 15 and 20 stocks.

The method Evans and Archer adopted in their empirical studies was to randomly construct portfolios of increasing size and to calculate the average standard deviation of returns. Repeating the process many times enabled the relationship between portfolio risk and the number of stocks to be established.

Utilizing the same methodology to analyse the problem in property terms introduces two extra complications, the lack of data and the indivisibility of property.

Its indivisibility means that the weight of each property in a portfolio is a material consideration in terms of risk reduction. Although similar problems can exist in stock portfolios the choice of asset weights is generally within the control of the investor. Property investors however do not have this option without access to an investment trust specializing in property.

Nevertheless in trying to analyse the effectiveness of portfolio construction in relation to risk reduction, it is useful to construct a model based on the assumption of equal investment and compare this with the results obtained by simulating some value-weighted property portfolios.

The major problem however is the paucity of data coupled with the confidentiality which surrounds many of the figures relating to valuations and transactions. Although there is considerable interest in those matters which could result in a better understanding of the property market, there remains a great reluctance to release data. The climate is changing however and in time it is expected that our understanding of this important market will improve.

Despite these difficulties a database of property was established from the valuation records of a property unit trust. The properties within the portfolio were of differing age and quality and typical of commercial properties acquired by institutional investors. There was no attempt to bias the sample to include only prime quality property. The advantage of this sample of 135 properties was that it incorporated a time series of valuations which were prepared on a monthly basis running from January 1979 to December 1982. The data not only included changes in capital value but also income received together with expenditure incurred. From the resulting time series, continuously compounded monthly rates of return were computed. Although the time period covered was short it did have the advantage of being based on a verifiable sample of data.

All valuations were prepared on an open market basis and followed the principles laid down by the Royal Institution of Chartered Surveyors. It will be recalled that this requires

the best price at which an interest in property might reasonably be expected to be sold by private treaty at the date of the valuation assuming:

1. a willing seller;
2. a reasonable period within which to negotiate the sale, taking into account the nature of the property and the state of the market;
3. values will remain static throughout the period;

4. the property will be freely exposed to the market;
5. no account is to be taken of an additional bid by a special purchaser.

RICS Guidance Note No. 22 (2nd ed.)

The information subset is therefore clearly defined. Because of the infrequent nature of sales in the property market the analysis must be based on valuations. Indeed one of the features of an open market approach to valuation is that comparable data in the form of known transaction prices is frequently used as a reference point in order to establish a current valuation. Appendix 2A to Chapter 2 showed that given contemporaneous valuations and sales prices for the same group of properties valuations can serve as a good proxy for their equivalent sales price. This statement only holds true of course if sales prices and valuations both represent open market conditions. The effect of special factors, such as a forced sale or disposal to a tenant at a concessionary price, do not therefore form part of the information subset.

This is important for two reasons. Firstly, if valuations are a good proxy for prices then investment research undertaken using valuations will be equivalent to similar research using prices. Portfolio advice based on valuations will, therefore, be valid. Furthermore if there is a change in the information subset which enables a difference to be identified between a valuation and a potential transaction price this could lead to a position of profitable arbitrage assuming due allowance is made for both risk and trading costs.

Secondly, institutions holding property as part of a mixed-asset portfolio will endeavour to make asset allocation decisions on the basis of changes in valuation. Such decisions will hold true only if valuations and prices are a good proxy for each other.

4.2 Sample statistics

In view of the lack of reliable information concerning property returns it is worth examining some of the characteristics of the sample collected before considering the problem of portfolio construction.

Using monthly continuous returns over the period from January 1979 to December 1982, Table 4.1 presents the average distributional characteristics for individual properties within each sector of the market. (Although the data used in this analysis covers a relatively short period it does have the advantage that it is based on verifiable returns and is free from many of the problems associated with other

Table 4.1 Average monthly figures for individual properties (January 1979–December 1982)

Sector	Office	Retail	Industrial
Return	0.0134	0.0169	0.0136
Standard deviation	0.036	0.057	0.042
Skewness	1.682	2.049	1.122
Kurtosis	10.86	12.74	10.27
Studentized range	6.41	6.70	6.43
Number of properties	39	46	50
Number of properties >0.99 fractile of the studentized range:	33	25	37

0.99 fractile of studentized range for 47 observations = 5.77.

property samples. As long as the correlation structure between properties remains constant the findings presented here should have a general application.) In order to make a judgement concerning the effect of extreme observations on the assumption of normality the studentized range has also been included.

From this information it will be evident that the returns for each sector are positively skewed and leptokurtic relative to a Normal distribution. In other words there is a strong tendency for high positive returns and the distributions tend to be more peaked than Normal. Over the period analysed this was particularly marked in the retail sector. This would seem to rule out the proposition that the returns are drawn from a Normal distribution. Further confirmation of this can be seen by examining the studentized range. A high proportion of the properties in the sample exceeded the studentized range at the 99% level.

The assumption of non-Normality does, however, tend to be weakened if it is accepted that successive returns are affected to some degree by common factors which cause all properties to move together. In addition it can be shown (in Appendix 4A) that as the holding period increases the returns for each sector approach a Normal distribution.

Table 4.2 shows the same sample of properties combined into value-weighted portfolios and indicates that for monthly returns the data begin to approach a Normal distribution. This assumption becomes stronger as the holding period increases. The monthly data shown in Table 4.2 exhibit a considerable reduction in the standard deviation of returns confirming the effect of diversification.

Table 4.2 Average monthly figures for value-weighted portfolios (January 1979–December 1982)

Sector	Office	Retail	Industrial
Return	0.0138	0.0147	0.0121
Standard deviation	0.015	0.023	0.017
Skewness	1.172	0.886	0.276
Kurtosis	4.91	3.38	4.35
Studentized range*	5.43	4.42	5.77

0.99 fractile of studentized range for 47 observations = 5.77.

Given that the returns on all properties are affected to some degree by common market factors, the returns on individual properties cannot be regarded as independent. The degree to which these factors have an impact on the relative movement of returns can be seen by examining the zero-order correlation coefficients. Table 4.3 presents these results by taking a random sample of coefficients from the total population of properties within each sector. Each figure is significant at the 99% level.

In comparison with the return on stocks these coefficients are extremely low. Although market factors have an influence on the movement of property returns it is evident that there are other factors of considerable importance. Being a heterogeneous form of investment, the returns will reflect many factors including the type of tenant, the age of the property, its condition and location, the lease structure and so on. For these reasons it is not unusual to find evidence of low average correlation between individual properties.

Table 4.3 considers each sector separately, and only those factors which are important to individual sectors are revealed in the figures. Thus there are factors unique to the office sector which cause their

Table 4.3 Average correlation coefficients between properties within each sector, (January 1979–December 1982)

Sector	Correlation coefficient	Standard error	No. of observations
Office	0.12	0.01	235
Retail	0.06	0.01	205
Industrial	0.08	0.01	245

returns to move in a similar manner. Over the period analysed this sector had the highest coefficient of correlation. Although the returns from properties within the other sectors also tend to move together this co-movement is not as strong. The difference in co-movement between each of the sectors has implications in terms of the number of properties needed to diversify away most of the risk. This problem is addressed in the following sections.

4.3 Methodology

Although the low correlation between individual properties exhibited in Table 4.3 is advantageous in terms of risk reduction, it will be evident that this advantage can be eroded easily if there are considerable differences in the value weighting of individual properties. Although this is a material consideration in terms of risk reduction it is nevertheless useful to proceed on the basis of equal investment. Comparison of the theoretical results can then be made with those obtained by simulating the construction of a value-weighted portfolio.

Evans and Archer have shown that the reduction in risk on a portfolio is inversely proportional to the number of assets held. This can be expressed formally as

$$\sigma = A + B \left(\frac{1}{N} \right) \qquad (4.2)$$

where

$$\sigma = \text{standard deviation of the portfolio returns;}$$
$$N = \text{number of assets in the portfolio;}$$
$$A \text{ and } B = \text{constants.}$$

Assuming equal investment in each asset the values of A and B can be estimated by regression analysis after estimating the average risk on a sample of portfolios of increasing size. This was the procedure adopted by Evans and Archer. Trying to apply the same approach to the property market is not a practical proposition. Although the constraint of value-weighting can be dropped the limited sample available for analysis within each sector (between 39 and 50 properties) makes it impossible to estimate the average risk for properties of increasing size without double counting.

However, proxy values for A and B can be estimated by recognizing that as N approaches infinity the second term in equation (4.2) will approach zero and the value of A will approach the systematic risk level. Similarly when N is unity the standard deviation of returns for the portfolio $(A + B)$ will approach the average standard deviation of returns for the asset under consideration. This approach can be utilized to examine the risk reduction potential for each sector of the property market. In order to do this, however, it is necessary to estimate both the systematic and average risk for each sector of the market.

Clearly if sample sizes were large enough the standard deviation of returns on an equally-weighted portfolio constructed in each sector would approach its systematic risk level. However, bearing in mind the low correlations shown in Table 4.3 there is no guarantee that the sample sizes used are large enough to diversify away the residual risk. As a result it is likely that the total risk of the sector portfolios will be a poor proxy for their systematic risk. Estimates of systematic risk level using this procedure will be overstated. An alternative approach is to re-examine equation (4.1) and to recognize that as the portfolio increases in size its risk will approach the average covariance, so

$$\sigma_p{}^2 = \overline{\text{cov}}(i, j). \tag{4.3}$$

The covariance between two assets i and j can also be expressed in terms of their standard deviations and coefficients of correlation, i.e.

$$\text{cov}(i, j) = \rho_{ij}\sigma_i\sigma_j \tag{4.4}$$

where
ρ_{ij} = coefficient of correlation between i and j;
σ_j = standard deviation on asset j.

For very large samples, and given all possible combinations between i and j, it will be evident that the average value of σ_i and σ_j must be equal. Similarly the average coefficient of correlation between all pairs of assets must approach the average coefficient. Thus as N approaches infinity equation (4.4) will reduce to

$$\sigma_p{}^2 = \bar{\rho}\,\bar{\sigma}^2 \tag{4.5}$$

where
$\bar{\rho}$ = average coefficient of correlation;
$\bar{\sigma}^2$ = average variance of all assets.

Using monthly continuous returns data it was possible to estimate the average variance for each sector. These were multiplied by their average coefficients of correlation to provide an estimate of systematic risk. Table 4.4 presents these results together with a comparison of the empirical estimate of systematic risk obtained from equally-weighted portfolios within each sector.

Table 4.4 Systematic risk estimates for each sector of the property market based on monthly continuous returns (January 1979–December 1982)

Sector	Average variance $\bar{\sigma}^2$	Average correlation coefficient $\bar{\rho}$	Estimated systematic risk $\sqrt{\bar{\sigma}^2\,\bar{\rho}}$	Empirical sample risk	Sample size
Office	0.001549	0.12	0.01363	0.01423	50
Retail	0.003776	0.06	0.01505	0.01902	46
Industrial	0.00193	0.08	0.01237	0.01333	39
Total	0.002197	0.095	0.01445	0.01449	135

The total portfolio is value-weighted assuming the following proportions: 50% offices, 25% retail and 25% industrial property. This is broadly representative of institutional behaviour.

Table 4.4 clearly shows that the estimated systematic risk figures are below those obtained utilizing portfolios contructed from all the sample properties within each sector. At the total portfolio level the sample size has increased to 135 properties and the systematic risk level is almost identical to its theoretical counterpart.

The other piece of information required to estimate the parameters of equation (4.2) is the average risk level of each of the sectors, given in Table 4.5.

Table 4.5 Average risk levels (monthly returns)

Sector	Average risk $\bar{\sigma}$
Office	0.03687
Retail	0.05657
Industrial	0.04183
Portfolio	0.04540

Considering the information contained in Tables 4.4 and 4.5 and recognizing that the average property risk within each sector is equivalent to $(A + B)$ in equation (4.2), it is possible to estimate the equation parameters as shown in Table 4.6.

Figure 4.1 plots the equations for each of the sectors and shows the impact of increasing the number of properties in a portfolio on the standard deviation of returns. This illustration also shows that given equal levels of investment most of the risk reduction can be achieved

Table 4.6 Parameter estimates for equation (4.2)

Sector	A	B
Office	0.01363	0.02324
Retail	0.01505	0.04152
Industrial	0.01237	0.02946
Portfolio	0.01445	0.03095

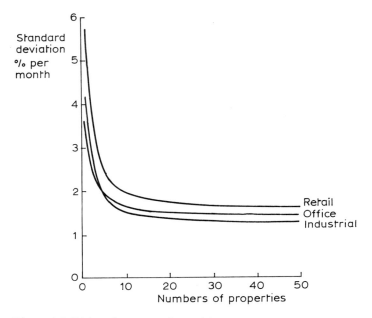

Figure 4.1 Risk reduction and portfolio size within each sector of the UK property market (January 1979–December 1982).

within the first five to ten properties. Table 4.7 shows the percentage reduction in risk that can be achieved.

During the period from January 1979 to December 1982 the greatest reduction in risk occurred within the retail sector followed by the industrial and office sectors. This is of course in line with the average correlation coefficients which showed that the retail sector exhibited the lowest correlation between individual properties and the office sector the highest correlation (see Table 4.3).

Assuming equal levels of investment in average properties it will also be evident from Table 4.7 that after about ten properties have been included in a portfolio the reduction in risk which can be achieved by

Table 4.7 Percentage reduction in risk assuming equal levels of investment in each sector

No. of properties	% reduction in risk			
	Retail	*Office*	*Industrial*	*Portfolio*
1	0	0	0	0
2	36	31	35	35
3	48	42	46	45
4	54	47	52	51
5	58	50	56	54
10	65	56	63	61
20	69	59	66	64
30	70	60	68	65
40	71	61	68	66
50	71	61	69	66
100	72	62	69	67
1000	73	63	70	68

holding more properties diminishes dramatically. The risk class of the portfolio will, therefore, be established very quickly. In this context however the choice of sector is important. It will be seen from Figure 4.1 that during the period analysed the systematic risk level of the retail sector is greater than both the office and industrial sectors when combined into portfolios. This fact can also be confirmed by regressing the returns from each sector onto a portfolio containing all properties within the sample. Table 4.8 presents these results assuming that the portfolios are both equally- and value-weighted. In both cases the retail sector is the most volatile having a beta coefficient which is reliably greater than 1.0.

Table 4.8 Regression results of sector returns versus portfolio returns (January 1979–December 1982)

Dependent variable		β	Standard error	$\bar{R}^2$
Industrial	(EW)	0.700	0.108	0.469
Office	(EW)	0.999	0.059	0.858
Retail	(EW)	1.300	0.092	0.811
Industrial	(VW)	0.849	0.148	0.408
Office	(VW)	0.936	0.077	0.764
Retail	(VW)	1.342	0.120	0.729

EW: equally-weighted portfolios
VW: value-weighted portfolios

Since the correlation structure and total risk of individual properties within a property portfolio will differ from the average it is evident that the risk of a value-weighted portfolio will be dominated by those properties which have the largest capital value. Depending on the return characteristics of individual properties, portfolio risk could be either increased or decreased. In the absence of any information concerning risk, portfolio managers will be unaware of the direction of change following the acquisition of each new property. The problem will be most acute with small-sized portfolios. As numbers increase, however, the effect of large-valued properties can be diversified away.

4.4 Empirical tests using value-weighted portfolios

The validity of the theoretical analysis given above has been tested by constructing value-weighted portfolios from the total sample of properties. This approach was intended to replicate the approach adopted by the fund manager in putting together a portfolio of properties. The only difference was that properties were chosen at random whereas the fund manager will follow some selection criterion and could well increase the capital value of successive acquisitions as the portfolio increases in capital value. The methodology employed in examining each sector was as follows.

A single property was chosen at random from the sample of available properties within each sector. This provided information for the first return and standard deviation. Another property was then randomly selected and the cash flows and capital values added to the first property. From the amalgamated cash flow the second mean and standard deviation of return was computed. The process was continued by randomly selecting portfolios and adding them to the portfolio until all properties within each sector were exhausted.

Because of the differences in capital value associated with each property a regression of standard deviation against increasing numbers will only approximately follow the theoretical estimates although they should be in the same order. This point is illustrated in the results of the analysis for the simulations for each sector given in Table 4.9.

The coefficients for *A* and *B* for each sector are significant at the 99% level. In addition it will be seen that the *A* coefficient in all cases is both higher than and statistically different from its theoretical value. In other words given the sample sizes used and bearing in mind the effect of different property values the portfolios have not diversified down to the systematic risk level for the sector. With the exception of

Table 4.9 Regression of standard deviation of returns against numbers of properties using value-weighted portfolios

$$\sigma = A + B\left(\frac{1}{N}\right)$$

Sector	A	Standard error	B	Standard error	$\bar{R}^2$	N
Office	0.0175	(0.0010)	0.0229	(0.0049)	0.35	39
(theoretical)	0.0136		0.0232			
Industrial	0.0203	(0.0004)	0.0379	(0.0023)	0.86	45
(theoretical)	0.0123		0.0295			
Retail	0.0288	(0.0011)	0.0200	(0.0056)	0.21	46
(theoretical)	0.0151		0.0415			

the office sector, where the B coefficient is statistically indistinguishable from its theoretical value, each of the other sectors have B coefficients which differ considerably from their theoretical values. This is probably due to the influence of large-valued properties on the average standard deviation of returns. It will also be noticed that there is considerable variation in the $\bar{R}^2$ values although they do indicate that increasing the numbers of properties within a value-weighted property portfolio does explain a reasonable proportion of the reduction in risk. The fact that the $\bar{R}^2$ values are not high does however indicate that the portfolios are poorly diversified even though they have achieved significant reductions in risk. This aspect is covered in section 4.6.

4.5 Investment in all sectors

It is unusual for property managers to concentrate their funds in one sector, since they generally argue that a portfolio is better diversified by spreading funds across each sector of the market. It is appropriate therefore to undertake the same analysis as above but to construct portfolios randomly combined from each sector. The methodology employed to examine the problem is as previously described with the exception that the portfolio sizes were limited to a maximum of 40 properties. Three value-weighted portfolios were simulated and the regression results of standard deviation versus increasing numbers is given in Table 4.10.

With the exception of simulation 2, each of the A coefficients differs statistically from its theoretical value. The B coefficients for all

Table 4.10 Regression of standard deviation of returns versus numbers of properties using (value-weighted portfolios)

$$\sigma = A + B\left(\frac{1}{N}\right)$$

Portfolio	A	Standard error	B	Standard error	$\bar{R}^2$	N
Simulation 1	0.0184	(0.0001)	0.0118	(0.0004)	0.95	40
Simulation 2	0.0139	(0.0005)	0.0534	(0.0027)	0.91	40
Simulation 3	0.0191	(0.0004)	0.0230	(0.0026)	0.58	40
(theoretical)	0.0145		0.0309			

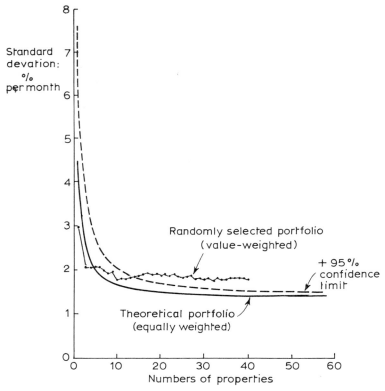

Figure 4.2 Simulation 1: randomly constructed value-weighted portfolio compared with mean and +95% confidence limits for a theoretical equally-weighted portfolio.

simulations differ from their theoretical value. This is to be expected bearing in mind that a comparison is being made between value-weighted portfolios and an equally-weighted theoretical line. Generally speaking the value order of the coefficients is in line with the theoretical counterpart.

The results of these simulations are plotted in Figures 4.2 to 4.4. They clearly illustrate that the risk reduction potential is quite significant although the profile followed by each portfolio is being influenced by large-valued properties. Clearly for a portfolio which has a large variation in property size its risk reduction is likely to be influenced by the effect of the largest properties. The exposure of the portfolio to the performance of these properties can only be minimized by adding a large number of small properties or a smaller number of large properties. In all cases by the time the portfolio consists of about 20 to 30 properties it is approaching its systematic risk level.

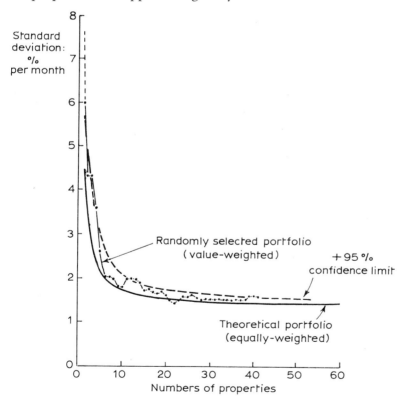

Figure 4.3 Simulation 2: randomly constructed value-weighted portfolio compared with mean and +95% confidence limits for a theoretical equally-weighted portfolio.

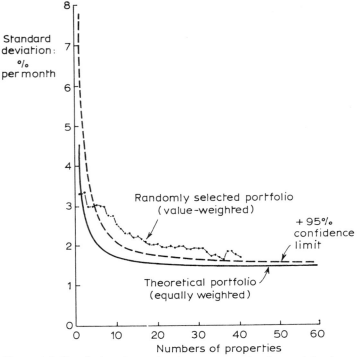

Figure 4.4 Simulation 3: randomly constructed value-weighted portfolio compared with mean and +95% confidence limits for a theoretical equally-weighted portfolio.

Bearing in mind that these results are based on single simulations of value-weighted portfolios it is nevertheless encouraging to see that the theoretical profile can be regarded as a valid approximation.

4.6 Portfolio diversification

The foregoing sections have been primarily concerned with reduction in risk. It has been shown that by holding about 30 properties and assuming that the portfolio is not unduly influenced by large-valued properties it is possible to diversify down to the systematic risk level. Assuming average properties and equal-weighting the degree of risk reduction has been shown to be in the region of 62–73% depending on sector and about 68% at the portfolio level. Comparable figures in the UK stock market are in the region of 50%.

The high levels of risk reduction shown here are due entirely to the low correlation of returns that exists between individual properties.

Although this is useful in terms of reducing portfolio risk the unequal weights and small numbers generally associated with property portfolios does mean that their performance from period to period will be heavily influenced by factors specific to individual properties as opposed to market-wide factors. The only way that the market can significantly affect portfolio performance is by holding very large numbers of properties.

Given the correlation structure shown in Table 4.3, it is possible for a portfolio to hold a relatively high number of properties but for it still to be poorly diversified in an economic sense so that the periodic variation in returns has a significant impact on performance.

This process can be formalized by recognizing that as a portfolio increases in size the coefficient of determination, R^2, between the returns on the portfolio and the property market will be an increasing function which is asymptotic to 1.0. Therefore the coefficient of determination is taken as a measure of diversification.

Assuming equal investment in each property the relationship between R^2 and the number of properties can be expressed in the form of a declining asymptotic function as follows.

$$\frac{1}{R^2} = X + Y\left(\frac{1}{N}\right) \tag{4.6}$$

where

R^2 = coefficient of determination between portfolio
returns and the market;
N = number of properties.

As the number of properties in a portfolio increases the ratio $1/N$ will become smaller. As N approaches infinity, $1/N$ disappears. At this point the portfolio is completely diversified with the market explaining all of its variation in returns, so that R^2 is unity. For the equality in equation (4.6) to hold it will be evident that X must also equal unity.

In addition when the portfolio consists of a single property, N will be unity and $1/(R^2)$ will approach its average value for the sector or for all properties. Thus given the average R^2 value for each sector of the market and the total portfolio it is possible to derive general equations relating portfolio size to diversification.

Values for R^2 can be obtained by regressing portfolio returns against a portfolio of property representing the market. The sample of R^2 figures can then be used to estimate the average for each sector. Alternatively the average value for a single property in each sector can be obtained from the parameters of equation (4.2) by recognizing that the average proportion of total risk which is explained by the market is equal to the systematic risk divided by total risk when $N = 1$. In terms of equation (4.2) this is equivalent to

$$R^2 = \frac{A^2}{(A + B)^2}. \tag{4.7}$$

Estimates for R^2 together with the parameters for equation (4.5) were derived using the figures given in Table 4.6, and are shown in Table 4.11.

Table 4.11 Average R^2 values and equation (4.6) parameters for each sector and the total portfolio

$$\frac{1}{R^2} = X + Y\left(\frac{1}{N}\right)$$

Sector	Average R^2	$X + Y/N$
Office	0.1367	$1.0 + 6.315/N$
Retail	0.0708	$1.0 + 13.124/N$
Industrial	0.0875	$1.0 + 10.429/N$
Portfolio	0.1013	$1.0 + 8.872/N$

Examination of the R^2 figures clearly show that the property market explains a relatively small proportion of the variation in returns for the average property within each sector. At the total portfolio level the market explains only about 10% of the variation in returns of the average property. A similar figure for the stock market would be in the order of 30%. It follows from this that it is easier to create highly diversified portfolios within the stock market than it is within the property market.

Increasing portfolio size does of course increase diversification and this fact is demonstrated in Table 4.12.

Again the validity and effect of value-weighting can be examined by building portfolios of increasing size and estimating the change in R^2 value measured relative to the market sample. Two portfolios were simulated and a regression analysis based on equation (4.5) was then run. The results are presented in Table 4.13.

The X coefficients in both cases are above 1.0 reflecting the small samples used. As the number of properties increases however this figure will approach 1.0. The value of Y by contrast varies depending on the value-weighting of the properties. The higher the value the

Table 4.12 Diversification and portfolio size: the percentage of variation in returns explained by the market

No. of properties	% diversification (R^2)			
	Office	*Retail*	*Industrial*	*Portfolio*
1	0.137	0.071	0.087	0.101
2	0.241	0.132	0.161	0.184
3	0.322	0.186	0.223	0.253
4	0.388	0.233	0.277	0.311
5	0.442	0.276	0.324	0.360
10	0.613	0.432	0.489	0.529
20	0.760	0.603	0.657	0.693
30	0.826	0.696	0.742	0.772
40	0.864	0.753	0.793	0.818
50	0.888	0.792	0.827	0.849
100	0.941	0.884	0.906	0.919
200	0.969	0.938	0.950	0.958
1000	0.994	0.987	0.989	0.991

Table 4.13 Regression of $1/R^2$ versus number of properties

Portfolio	$1/R^2 = X + Y(1/N) + e$					
	X	*Standard error*	Y	*Standard error*	R^2	N
Simulation 1	1.253	(0.069)	5.432	(0.348)	0.86	40
Simulation 2	2.192	(0.459)	11.050	(2.278)	0.37	40
(theoretical)	1.000		8.872			

The theoretical estimate is based on a portfolio with 50% of funds in offices and 25% each in retail and industrial property. The distribution of funds in the simulated portfolio differed from these figures. Nevertheless the X coefficient should still be close to 1.0 if the portfolio is well diversified. Differences in the distribution of funds will be reflected in the Y coefficient.

greater the influence of large-valued properties reducing the level of diversification. This is clearly seen in Table 4.13 where the explanatory power of the second simulation is 0.37 and the Y coefficient is 11.050 with a high standard error. These simulations are plotted in Figure 4.5.

If it is assumed that a portfolio can be constructed with properties of equal value it will be evident that in order to be highly diversified, with the market explaining over 95% of the variation in returns, it will be necessary to hold about 200 properties. The majority of UK property portfolios tend to hold less than 30 properties which indicates that they

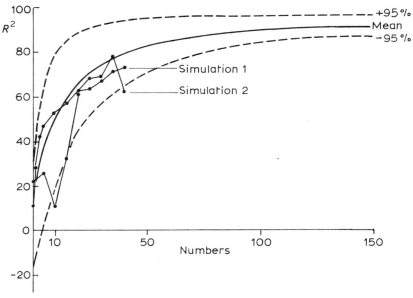

Figure 4.5 R^2 values for simulations 1 and 2 plotted against increasing portfolio size. Mean and confidence limits also shown for an equally-weighted portfolio.

must be poorly diversified. Those few which hold close to 200 properties will still find that the effect of value-weighting could cause significant differences in the level of diversification unless a number of properties are highly correlated with the market.

The effect of numbers and diversification in the property market can be contrasted with the stock market. On average the market explains about 30% of the variation in returns of the average stock. Using comparable stock market data and applying similar reasoning to that given above, a regression model should have the following parameters.

$$\frac{1}{R^2} = 1.0 + 2.349\left(\frac{1}{N}\right) + e. \tag{4.8}$$

Using a sample of 14 observations each representing the average of portfolios of 1 to 100 assets a regression of $1/R^2$ against N produced the results shown in Table 4.14.

Table 4.14 Regression of $1/R^2$ versus number of stocks in a UK portfolio

X	Standard error	Y	Standard error	$\bar{R}^2$
0.999	(0.0022)	2.342	(0.0067)	0.999

The coefficients are statistically indistinguishable from their theoretical values and show that equal investment in only 45 stocks is all that is required to explain about 95% of the variation in market returns. It is therefore much easier to build highly diversified portfolios using stocks than using property. It also follows that it is much easier to track an index with a stock portfolio than it is with a property portfolio. This is due entirely to the difference in correlation structure of the assets returns with the market.

Property portfolios can therefore show rapid reductions in risk with relatively few properties but require large numbers of properties in order to be highly diversified. The implications of this will be discussed in the next chapter on strategy. This characteristic can be seen in Table 4.15 which shows the total risk of a portfolio split into its component parts, market and specific risk. For the purposes of illustration the market risk is assumed to be constant at 5% per annum.

To get a reasonable balance between diversification and risk reduction it will be seen from the above that by holding about 30 properties it should be possible to achieve a level of risk reduction of about 64% and for the market to explain about 77% of the variation in portfolio returns. This of course assumes properties of equal value. But even with this constraint, and assuming a market risk level of 5% per annum, it will be seen that there is still 2.72% of specific risk per annum which could be diversified away. This will clearly have an effect on the performance of the portfolio on an annual basis.

Table 4.15 Risk reduction and diversification for a property portfolio with constant market risk (% per annum)

No. of properties	Total risk	Market risk	Specific risk	% risk reduction	% R^2 diversification
1	15.73	5.00	14.91	00.00	10.10
2	11.66	5.00	10.53	25.87	18.40
3	9.94	5.00	8.59	36.81	25.30
4	8.97	5.00	7.45	43.17	31.10
5	8.33	5.00	6.66	47.04	36.00
10	6.87	5.00	4.71	56.63	52.90
20	6.01	5.00	3.34	61.79	69.30
30	5.69	5.00	2.72	63.83	77.20
40	5.53	5.00	2.36	64.84	81.80
50	5.43	5.00	2.12	65.48	84.90
100	5.22	5.00	1.50	66.82	91.90
200	5.11	5.00	1.05	67.51	95.80
1000	5.02	5.00	0.45	68.09	99.10

As more properties are added to the portfolio it is possible that its risk class will change. The extent of the change will be affected by the value-weighting of its component properties.

4.7 Systematic risk of existing portfolios

Although additional simulations are required to provide further confirmation of the results given above the findings are nevertheless sufficiently encouraging to utilize the analysis to estimate the systematic risk of some existing portfolios.

The validity of the procedure can then be tested by regressing the empirical values of β onto their estimated values. If the foregoing analysis is valid the intercept term should be close to zero and the slope coefficient should be statistically indistinguishable from 1.0.

It will be recalled that the total risk on a portfolio can be expressed in terms of its market risk and specific risk as follows.

$$\sigma_p{}^2 = \beta_p{}^2 \sigma_m{}^2 + \sigma_s{}^2 \tag{4.9}$$

where

$$\sigma_p = \text{portfolio total risk;}$$
$$\beta_p = \text{portfolio market risk;}$$
$$\sigma_m = \text{standard deviation of market returns;}$$
$$\sigma_s = \text{specific risk.}$$

Dividing equation (4.9) by the portfolio variance $(\sigma_p{}^2)$ it can be redefined in terms of the amount of portfolio variance which can be explained by the market (i.e. R^2) together with the residue, which cannot be explained by the market. Considering only the market portion it will be evident that

$$R^2 = \frac{\text{market risk}}{\text{total risk}}. \tag{4.10}$$

Substituting from equation (4.9) gives

$$R^2 = \frac{\beta_p{}^2 \sigma_m{}^2}{\sigma_p{}^2} \tag{4.11}$$

which transformed gives the portfolio beta as follows.

$$\beta_p = \sqrt{\left(\frac{R^2 \sigma_p{}^2}{\sigma_m{}^2}\right)}. \tag{4.12}$$

Given a sample of portfolios with R^2 values and variances it is possible to obtain estimates of their systematic risk. To test the validity of this procedure annual returns data on seven portfolios of differing size were collected over the period 1979–83 and regressed onto the returns from the Richard Ellis Property Market Indicators over the same period. This provided empirical estimates of the portfolio beta coefficients. Estimated values of β were then computed from equation (4.12) utilizing the standard deviation of returns for each portfolio and the market together with an estimate of R^2 based on the portfolio size, the results of which are shown in Table 4.16.

Table 4.16 Empirical and estimated beta coefficients

Port- folio	*Empirical* % pa values standard deviation	N	β	Standard error	*Estimated values* Mean values β_{mean}	$\bar{R}^2$	Confidence limits $\beta_{+95\%}$	$\bar{R}^2$	$\beta_{-95\%}$	$\bar{R}^2$
1	8.72	200	1.36	(0.16)	1.34	0.95	1.37	0.99	1.31	0.91
2	5.29	8	0.78	(0.21)	0.55	0.44	0.73	0.76	0.28	0.11
3	12.06	30	1.68	(0.63)	1.64	0.74	1.82	0.92	1.42	0.56
4	10.49	17	1.21	(0.85)	1.30	0.62	1.54	0.87	1.01	0.37
5	11.19	13	1.53	(0.68)	1.32	0.56	1.62	0.84	0.92	0.27
6	10.29	15	1.50	(0.44)	1.25	0.59	1.50	0.85	0.84	0.32
7	8.87	11	1.35	(0.19)	1.00	0.51	1.26	0.81	0.64	0.21
Index	6.34									

The empirical values of β were regressed against their estimated values giving the results shown in Table 4.17.

Although the sample sizes are extremely small the values for α_0 in all cases are close to zero. None is statistically significant. In addition the α_1 coefficients are all statistically indistinguishable from 1.00. Both these findings are consistent with the hypothesis that the procedure can be used to obtain proxy values for β. Alternatively an estimate of the diversification value of a portfolio can be readily obtained from information concerning the number of properties in a portfolio and

Table 4.17 Empirical versus estimated betas

$\beta_{emp} = \alpha_0 + \alpha_1 \beta_{est} + e$	α_0	Standard error	α_1	Standard error	R^2
β_{mean}	−0.208	0.33	1.047	0.239	0.75
$\beta_{+95\%}$	−0.064	0.29	1.093	0.214	0.81
$\beta_{-95\%}$	−0.429	0.54	1.002	0.394	0.48

making an adjustment for differential property values. It will also be seen from these figures that the regression with the greatest explanatory power utilized the +95% confidence value for R^2 in equation (4.12). This is also consistent with the findings shown in simulations 1 and 2.

At the sector level the reasoning outlined above can be used to estimate sector betas. In essence this means using equation (4.12) redrafted for each sector, thus

$$\beta_s = \sqrt{\left(\frac{R_s^2 \sigma_s^2}{\sigma_m^2}\right)}. \tag{4.13}$$

Assuming R^2 values of 1.00 for each sector together with the systematic risk estimates from Table 4.4, the estimated betas for each sector measured relative to the property market are as given in Table 4.18.

Table 4.18 Estimated betas for each sector measured relative to the property market based on available data (January 1979–December 1982)

Sector	β
Office	0.943
Retail	1.041
Industrial	0.855

This shows the retail sector as being the most risky with the industrial sector being the least risky. In other words during the period from January 1979 to December 1982 investors expected higher returns from the retail sector than from the industrial sector. There is no guarantee of course that the standard deviation of returns for each sector will remain constant over time. Changes in demand for each sector will cause the standard deviation of returns to vary over time so that the estimates of β will also change. As the standard deviation of returns for a sector changes it will not be unusual to see the ranking of market risk change in anticipation of differing expectations.

This can be directly translated into differences in risk premia. Examples of the changes in risk premia can be seen in Appendix 2H where the estimates of systematic risk were derived in a completely different way.

4.8 Conclusion

If the above analysis concerning risk reduction and portfolio size holds true in all periods it indicates that it is extremely difficult to achieve portfolios which are highly diversified. This becomes more acute when the effect of large-sized properties are taken into consideration. As a result investors will find it virtually impossible to produce a portfolio which is capable of tracking an index. Assuming that the average-sized portfolio consists of about 30 properties the amount of residual risk still to be diversified away can be quite substantial and will have a significant affect on periodic performance. Two portfolios which are following identical policies in terms of buying strategy and sector weightings might find that their returns differ considerably on a period by period basis purely because of differences in specific risk.

Applying the same logic to the analysis of property indices reveals that it would be necessary to hold many thousands of properties in order to achieve a portfolio which is a good proxy for market movements. Many of the commercially available indices utilize only a few hundred properties. The foregoing discussion would indicate that there is likely to be a considerable amount of residual risk remaining in these indices. In addition to this there is the problem caused by smoothing. This arises because the infrequent nature of valuations causes properties which do not have synchronous values to be included in the index.

One of the most important factors arising from the above is that the performance of individual properties are affected to a large degree by the unsystematic components of risk. Property market effects play a relatively small part in explaining periodic returns. If however the average holding period for property tends to be long then it is likely that the effect of intermediate variations in returns can be diversified away. Unless individual properties become marginal, one of the consequences of long holding periods is that as properties age they will suffer a decline in systematic risk. Thus if a portfolio is inactively managed its expected return will decline over time.

Although much work remains to be done in this area the unsystematic components are probably dominated by locational factors which are specific to each property. These tend to produce low correlation coefficients between properties which are helpful in terms of reducing risk. If these are constant over time then Table 4.7 would seem to indicate that there is little advantage to be gained by diversifying across sectors. Similar levels of risk reduction can be achieved merely by diversifying within a single sector. If investors can successfully forecast positive abnormal returns for an individual sector then they would achieve a better trade-off between risk and return by diversifying solely within that sector. Diversification across sectors is probably motivated by the long holding periods associated with property and the difficulty of switching between sectors as prospects change.

Whether it is possible for investors to successfully forecast positive abnormal returns is of course an empirical matter. If perfect forecasting ability does not exist then it suggests that investors should pursue some policy of diversification. The findings presented above show however that the common beliefs concerning diversification followed by many property investment funds are not as effective as imagined.

Appendix 4A: The characteristics of property returns

Despite the high institutional commitment to property surprisingly little is known about the distributional characteristics of property returns. Research in this area has been considerably hampered by the lack of reliable returns data on individual properties. Nevertheless an examination of the distributional characteristics of returns is important because they are a major factor in determining the risk of investment in property.

The analysis given here has been based on the monthly returns series generated over the period from January 1979 to December 1982. As the data are free from the problems of smoothing it is suggested that an examination of the distributional characteristics should provide a good indication of property in general.

Background

The earliest work on the distribution of returns related to stock market prices and was carried out in 1900 by Bachelier (1900). However his work was largely ignored until it was subsequently derived independently by Kendall (1953) and Osborne (1959). Both researchers assumed that changes in price were drawn randomly from the same distribution. In other words they assumed that price changes were independently distributed. Utilizing the Central Limit Theorem they argued that the sum of many independent identically distributed drawings would approach a Normal distribution as the sample size increased.

Examining this aspect in property terms it will be evident that the same type of information is not generally available on transactions prices. Valuations have to be substituted for prices although as indicated in Appendix 2A to Chapter 2 the use of valuations appears to be a good proxy for traded prices. A further problem exists, however, in obtaining valuations at frequent enough intervals to enable an anlysis to be carried out.

It has been common in the past for property portfolios to be valued infrequently, but this trend is disappearing and many funds now have their property holding valued annually in order to provide the basic information needed for performance measurement. Relying solely on annual valuations as the basis for understanding the distributional characteristics would produce very small sample sizes. In fact anything before 1978 must be regarded with caution as the need for keeping accurate records of valuations on a time-series basis was not considered essential then. The emergence of Property Unit Trusts and Property Bonds, providing a vehicle for investment by individuals, has also brought with them the need for more frequent valuations, so these are often carried out on a monthly basis.

Valuations are determined by reference to transactions taking place in the market. Each property is considered separately and adjustments made to reflect the latest market conditions. In addition a physical inspection of each property is carried out once a year. The introduction of computers into the valuation process has meant that the valuation of each property can be considered monthly by making adjustments for any changes that may have taken place in yields or rental value. The routine process of estimating the value can then be undertaken by the computer. Prior to this facility being available a random sample of properties from the portfolio were valued monthly and the change in value used as a means of adjusting the whole portfolio. (This process is by no means universal. Valuation by sample is still undertaken.)

Analysis of distributional characteristics

The following analysis has therefore been based on monthly valuations taken from the portfolio of a Property Bond. Continuously compounded returns were calculated using the following expression:

$$\ln(1 + r_t) = \ln\left(\frac{V_t + a}{V_{t-1}}\right) \tag{4A.1}$$

where

$$r_t = \text{rate of return in period } t;$$
$$V_t = \text{value of property in period } t;$$
$$V_{t-1} = \text{value of property in period } t - 1;$$
$$a = \text{income received during period } t - 1 \text{ to } t.$$

Valuation and cash flows were collected on a monthly basis from January 1979 to December 1982 covering a sample of 135 properties, which comprised 46 retail properties, 39 offices and 50 industrial properties. Using continuously compounded returns gave the added advantage that returns for periods longer than a month could be obtained by addition. For independent returns Fama (1965) has shown that since 'the log of a product is the sum of the logs' then for intervals where the number of sub-periods is large the Central Limit Theorem would indicate that for longer holding periods the returns would be approximately Normal. This can be expressed as follows.

$$\ln(1 + R_t) = \ln(1 + r_1) + \ln(1 + r_2) + \ldots + \ln(1 + r_N)$$
$$= \sum_{n=1}^{N} \ln(1 + r_n). \tag{4A.2}$$

If N is large then $\ln(1 + R_t)$ should be approximately Normal.

The above assumes that as the time interval increases the sample size also increases. Unfortunately the analysed sample is quite small. The four-year period from January 1979 to December 1982 gave rise to 48 valuations and thus 47 continuously compounded returns. Adding the monthly returns together to give returns over longer periods dramatically reduces the number of observations. The longest holding period analysed using the sample was six months and was thus based on only seven observations. Although the results cannot be regarded as conclusive they are the best that can be achieved within the data limitations. However the methodology is valid for all holding periods and can easily be repeated when larger samples of reliable data become available.

The basic analysis proceeds by estimating the following statistics for each property:

1. the average return;
2. the standard deviation of returns;
3. the skewness;
4. the kurtosis.

In order to make a judgement concerning the effect of extreme observations and their likely impact on the assumption of normality, the studentized range has also been calculated. The average of each of these figures is shown in Table 4A.1.

The returns for each sector are positively skewed and leptokurtic, relative to a Normal distribution. In other words there is a strong

Table 4A.1 Average statistics for individual properties using monthly returns

Sector	Average return	Standard deviation	Skewness	Kurtosis	Studentized range	* No. of observations > 0.99 fractile
Industrial	1.36	4.20	1.12	10.27	6.43	33 out of 50
Office	1.34	3.60	1.68	10.86	6.41	25 out of 39
Retail	1.69	5.70	2.05	12.74	6.70	37 out of 46

Sample size = 47 observations.
*0.99 fractile of studentized range for 47 observations = 5.77 (approximately).

tendency for high positive returns but the distribution is more peaked than Normal. This would seem to rule out the proposition that the returns are drawn from a Normal distribution. Further confirmation of this can be seen by examining the studentized range. For a sample of approximately 47 from a Normal distribution the probability that the studentized range will be less than 5.77 is 0.99. It will be seen from the last column of Table 4A.1 that over half of the observations exceed this limit. On this basis the hypothesis that monthly returns from property are derived from a Normal distribution is rejected.

Two factors are important however. Firstly, successive returns generated by individual properties in a portfolio will be affected to some degree by common market factors which will cause all properties to move together. The sample of properties from each sector therefore cannot be regarded as independent and so there will be some similarity between the results for individual properties. Any departure from Normality would be expected to appear in all properties. This weakens the assumption of non-Normality.

Secondly, although property bonds and unit trusts provide returns on a monthly basis their financial structure is such that the unit price returns will only imperfectly correlate with the underlying property. (The liquidity of property bonds and unit trusts can vary quite considerably and in some cases can be up to 25–30% of total capital value.) Although investors may choose to adjust their holdings in any of these vehicles their decisions, because they are motivated by the unit price changes, may only partially reflect underlying property movements. Equity investors in property however will be reluctant to alter their holdings in any sector purely as a result of short-term changes in the market. Transaction costs are usually so high (approximately $3\frac{1}{2}$–4% on both buying and selling) and legal negotiations so lengthy that this militates against frequent revision of property portfolios. Investors will therefore be more interested in the distributional characteristics of property returns over longer holding periods.

This information is provided in Tables 4A.2 and 4A.3 using quarterly and half-yearly returns, and from these tables it will be seen that as the holding period gets longer the distribution of returns for individual properties tends towards a Normal distribution. The maximum holding period was of course only six months. The assumption of Normality is probably even greater with annual returns. Recall also that the data have been drafted in terms of continuous returns by taking natural logs. Raw returns are therefore log Normally distributed. This is consistent with the observation of returns from other investment media.

Table 4A.2 Average statistics for individual properties using quarterly returns

Sector	Average return	Standard deviation	Skewness	Kurtosis	Studentized range	* No. of observations > 0.99 fractile
Industrial	4.00	6.80	0.59	4.60	4.15	13 out of 50
Office	4.10	6.20	0.82	4.50	3.90	7 out of 39
Retail	5.20	9.70	1.11	4.63	4.03	10 out of 46

Sample size = 15 observations.
*0.99 fractile of studentized range for 15 observations = 4.5 (approximately).

Table 4A.3 Average statistics for individual properties using half-yearly returns

Sector	Average return	Standard deviation	Skewness	Kurtosis	Studentized range	* No. of observations > 0.99 fractile
Industrial	7.10	9.70	0.36	2.72	3.14	11 out of 50
Office	7.40	8.20	0.32	2.59	3.03	6 out of 39
Retail	9.10	12.60	0.57	2.57	3.02	6 out of 46

Sample size = 7 observations.
*0.99 fractile of studentized range for 7 observations = 3.34 (approximately).

The average returns and standard deviations given in the table reflect conditions which prevailed at the time of the analysis. The high average returns and standard deviations in the retail sector cannot always be expected to occur.

Institutional investors tend not to hold individual properties but combine them into portfolios. Tables 4A.4–6 show the distributional characteristics for each sector over different holding periods, and Table 4A.7 shows the result of combining all the properties into a single portfolio.

Table 4A.4 Average statistics for value-weighted portfolios using monthly returns

Sector	Average return	Standard deviation	Skewness	Kurtosis	Studentized range*
Industrial	1.21	1.80	0.28	4.35	5.77
Office	1.38	1.50	1.17	4.91	5.43
Retail	1.47	2.20	0.89	3.38	4.42

Sample size = 47 observations.
*0.99 fractile of studentized range for 47 observations = 5.77 (approximately).

Table 4A.5 Average statistics for value-weighted portfolios using quarterly returns

Sector	Average return	Standard deviation	Skewness	Kurtosis	Studentized range*
Industrial	3.46	3.80	0.29	2.35	3.72
Office	4.25	3.30	1.10	2.87	3.32
Retail	4.47	4.70	0.38	2.30	3.35

Sample size = 15 observations.
*0.99 fractile of studentized range for 15 observations = 4.5 (approximately).

Table 4A.6 Average statistics for value-weighted portfolio using half-yearly returns

Sector	Average return	Standard deviation	Skewness	Kurtosis	Studentized range*
Industrial	5.81	5.60	0.13	1.20	2.44
Office	7.49	3.80	0.40	1.74	2.83
Retail	7.78	7.10	−0.14	1.72	2.93

Sample size = 7 observations.
*0.99 fractile of studentized range for 7 observations = 3.34 (approximately).

Table 4A.7 Average statistics for value-weighted portfolio comprising each sector

Holding period	Average return	Standard deviation	Skewness	Kurtosis	Studentized range*	0.99 fractile
Monthly	1.40	1.40	0.93	3.40	4.52	5.77
Quarterly	4.10	3.30	0.95	2.89	3.59	4.50
Half-yearly	7.10	4.60	0.23	1.45	2.76	3.34

Each of these tables shows that when combined into portfolios, the distributional characteristics of property for each sector are closer to Normality than the average for each sector. This is the case irrespective of the holding period. It will also be seen that the returns for each sector portfolio are similar to the average returns although the standard deviation at the portfolio level has been approximately halved.

The highest return is in the retail sector and this occurs uniformly at both the portfolio and individual property level. This is consistent with the conditions prevailing in the market over the period from January 1979 to December 1982. Both the return and variance increase proportionally over longer holding periods. The skewness, being a pure index number, should however remain invariant to scaling. It will be seen from the tables showing average figures that the retail sector has the greatest positive skewness. This is uniform over all holding periods. When combined into portfolios the office sector shows the greatest skewness. This may be caused by the influence of some large-valued properties or alternatively it is a reflection of the fact that the office sector has the potential for earning high positive returns. Further research in this area is needed.

The correlation structure of returns

It will be recalled that the returns on all properties will be affected to some degree by common market factors. Returns on individual properties are not, therefore, independent.

The degree to which these factors have an impact on the returns within each sector can be seen by examining the zero-order correlation coefficients between individual properties. The average correlation between individual properties is given in Table 4A.8.

Table 4A.8 Average correlation coefficients between properties within individual sectors

Sector	Monthly returns	Quarterly returns	Half-yearly returns	No. of observations
Office	0.12 (0.01)	0.23 (0.02)	0.23 (0.03)	235
Industrial	0.08 (0.01)	0.13 (0.02)	0.18 (0.02)	245
Retail	0.06 (0.01)	0.14 (0.02)	0.14 (0.03)	205

Standard errors are shown in brackets.

These figures have been calculated by taking a random sample of coefficients from the total population covered. Each figure is significant at the 99% level. For all holding periods it will be seen that the office sector exhibits the highest correlation between property returns. The average figure in each case is relatively low although the standard error increases with the longer holding periods. This is more likely to be the result of the reduction in sample size over the longer holding periods.

By comparison with the return on stocks these coefficients are extremely low. Although market factors have an influence on the movement of property returns it is evident that there are other factors which are of considerable importance. Being a heterogeneous form of investment the returns on property are influenced to a large degree by factors specific to individual properties. Thus the return on a property in any period will be a reflection of many factors and will be influenced by the type of tenant, the age of the property, its condition and location, the lease structure and so on. For these reasons it is not unusual to find such low correlation figures.

Table 4A.8 considers each sector independently, and only those factors which are important to individual sectors are revealed in the figures. Thus there are factors unique to the office sector which cause all office returns to move together to some degree. Although the properties in each of the other sectors move together the factors which cause this co-movement are not as strong as the office sector. It was shown in Chapter 4 that this has implications in terms of the number of properties needed to diversify most of the risk.

The correlation of property with other assets

So far this analysis has concentrated on property in isolation. However we are also concerned with the way property responds to the returns from other investments because this has an influence on the contribution that property can make to a mixed-asset portfolio.

An analysis over the period from January 1979 to December 1982 was carried out to establish the cross-correlation coefficients between property and the following investments:

1. FT All Gilts index;
2. FT over 15-year Gilts index;
3. $2\frac{1}{2}$ Consols index;
4. FT Property Share index;
5. FT All Share index;
6. Retail Price index.

The results are summarized in Tables 4A.9 and 4A.10 for equally- and value-weighted portfolios.

Over the period from January 1979 to December 1982 both equally- and value-weighted portfolios exhibited low, and in many cases negative, correlation with the gilt (FT–G), the over 15-year gilts index

Table 4A.9 Zero-order correlation coefficients between property and other investments (equally-weighted portfolio)

	Monthly			Quarterly			Half-yearly		
	Industrial	Office	Retail	Industrial	Office	Retail	Industrial	Office	Retail
FT–G	−0.19	0.01	−0.23	−0.39	−0.09	−0.38	−0.53	−0.40	−0.66
FT15	−0.20	0.01	−0.23	−0.39	−0.09	−0.37	−0.56	−0.46	−0.70
CONS	−0.06	0.07	−0.10	−0.35	−0.17	−0.36	−0.57	−0.69	−0.78
FT–P	−0.10	0.10	−0.11	−0.29	−0.00	−0.24	−0.22	0.10	−0.14
FT–A	−0.08	0.17	−0.05	−0.06	0.31	0.08	0.21	0.52	0.46
RPI	0.53	0.34	0.25	0.71	0.48	0.51	0.86	0.76	0.88

Table 4A.10 Zero-order correlation coefficients between property and other investments (value-weighted portfolio)

	Monthly			Quarterly			Half-yearly		
	Industrial	Office	Retail	Industrial	Office	Retail	Industrial	Office	Retail
FT–G	−0.08	−0.01	−0.23	−0.26	−0.09	−0.40	−0.33	−0.39	−0.61
FT15	−0.10	−0.02	−0.23	−0.26	−0.09	−0.40	−0.37	−0.45	−0.65
CONS	0.03	0.07	−0.10	−0.23	−0.15	−0.41	−0.40	−0.70	−0.79
FT–P	0.03	0.23	−0.10	0.05	0.33	0.12	0.30	0.62	0.51
FT–A	0.01	0.15	−0.18	−0.12	−0.07	−0.24	0.13	0.13	−0.13
RPI	0.40	0.40	0.25	0.70	0.43	0.65	0.87	0.86	0.93

(FT15) and consols (CONS) index. As the holding periods increased the correlation coefficients also increased.

There is a very poor relationship between property and the FT All Share index (FT–A), and this is consistent irrespective of holding period. The relationship with the Property Share index (FT–P) is much higher and increases with holding period. This is no doubt a reflection on the fact that property is a constituent part of the Property Share index.

The one consistent factor emerging from these tables is the high correlation between property and the Retail Price index (RPI). This is further confirmation of the ability of property to provide a hedge against inflation.

Conclusion

Examination of a random sample of property from each sector of the market has shown that the returns follow a distribution which is approximately log Normal. Thus with finite compounding this research suggests that one-period rates of return are derived from positively skewed probability distributions.

The low correlation between individual returns confirmed the belief that property responds more to specific factors rather than general market movements. At the portfolio level, property showed low correlation with a number of other assets but was highly correlated with the Retail Price index.

This evidence suggests that property has an important rôle to play in the construction of mixed-asset portfolios where a long-term passive strategy not only implies diversification but also hedging against unexpected changes in the rate of inflation.

Appendix 4B: Risk reduction, correlation and average property risk

Appendix 4A has shown that the correlation structure of returns between individual properties is likely to depend on a number of specific factors such as the type of tenant, the lease structure, the location of the property, its age, type of construction, quality and so on. As yet little is known about how the returns generating structure is affected by changes in each of these factors. What is certain however is that they form a unique combination for each property and it is this uniqueness which contributes to the low correlation of returns with other properties and also with the market.

Unless the fundamental characteristics of individual properties change radically it is possible that the correlation structure for each sector of the market either will remain constant or will vary within a narrow band. It is clear that this is an area which requires further research, and what is needed is a large sample of properties which have a time-series of returns free from the problems of serial correlation. The creation of better databases will, in time, enable this information to be verified.

This appendix makes the assumption that the correlation structure remains constant and shows how the average risk of a property can be derived from information concerning market risk.

The total risk of the average property, P, can be expressed as

$$\sigma_p^2 = \beta_p^2 \sigma_m^2 + \sigma_e^2. \tag{4B.1}$$

When combined into a portfolio the residual risk, σ_e^2, gradually decreases until it reaches zero. At this point the portfolio has diversified down to its systematic risk level, σ_s^2. That is,

$$\sigma_p^2 = \beta_p^2 \sigma_m^2 = \sigma_s^2 \text{ when } \sigma_e^2 = 0. \tag{4B.2}$$

Figure 4B.1 illustrates the procedure involved.

The level of risk reduction in a portfolio can be expressed as a percentage of the change in standard deviation from the average to the systematic risk level. If the risk reduction is defined as RR,

$$RR = \frac{\sigma_p - \sigma_s}{\sigma_p} \tag{4B.3}$$

$$= 1 - \frac{\sigma_s}{\sigma_p} \tag{4B.4}$$

By substituting $\sigma_s = \beta_p \sigma_m$ from (4B.2)

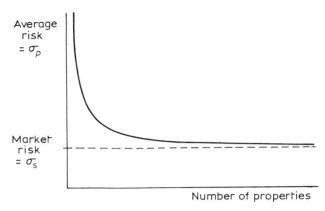

Figure 4B.1 Risk reduction down to the systematic level.

$$RR = 1 - \frac{\beta_p \sigma_m}{\sigma_p} \tag{4B.5}$$

We also know that β_p can be expressed in the following standard form:

$$\beta_p = \frac{\text{Cov}(r_p, r_m)}{\sigma_m^2} = \frac{\rho_{pm}\sigma_p\sigma_m}{\sigma_m^2} \tag{4B.6}$$

$$\beta_p = \frac{\rho_{pm}\sigma_p}{\sigma_m}. \tag{4B.7}$$

Substituting into equation (4B.5) gives:

$$RR = 1 - \rho_{pm}. \tag{4B.8}$$

This confirms that the risk reduction in a portfolio is a function of the correlation structure alone, that exists between a property and the market.

Values for the average correlation with the market can be derived from Table 4.12 in Chapter 4 which shows the average R^2 values for each sector of the market. It will be recalled that the correlation coefficient is merely the square root of this figure. Given this information the risk reduction for each sector can be simply derived. It will be seen that the risk reduction figures, shown in Table 4B.1, are identical to those contained in Table 4.7 in Chapter 4.

Knowing the level of risk reduction it is therefore a simple matter to reverse the procedure to find the average property risk. This can be found from equation (4B.3) by rearranging as follows.

Table 4B.1 Estimates of risk reduction derived from equation (4B.8) using average diversification figures given in Table 4.12

Sector	Average R^2	ρ_{pm}	Reduction in risk (RR%)
Office	0.137	0.37	0.63
Retail	0.071	0.27	0.73
Industrial	0.087	0.29	0.70
Portfolio	0.101	0.32	0.68

$$\sigma_p = \frac{\sigma_s}{1 - RR}. \tag{4B.9}$$

Assuming that we are able to estimate the market risk level it is then a simple matter to estimate the average property risk. If for example the current market risk level is assumed to be 8.8% per annum then the average risk for properties within each sector can be calculated using equation (4B.9) as shown in Table 4B.2.

The high levels of average property risk are determined by the high market risk. The latter is probably the most difficult to estimate as it needs to be representative of current market risk. Estimating it by reference to the returns on a property index will result in the figure being grossly understated because index returns tend to be highly smoothed. Nevertheless it will be recalled from Figure 2D.2 in Appendix 2D of Chapter 2 that the standard deviation of returns for the property market can vary considerably over time. (The data used in this illustration has been derived from the Jones Lang Wooton index. The annual returns series is relatively free of serial correlation. It is however based on a small sample size and probably carries a reasonable amount of residual risk.) The range given in Figure 2D.2 was

Table 4B.2 Estimates of average property risk for each sector

Sector	% RR	Average property risk (% per annum)
Office	0.63	23.78
Retail	0.73	32.59
Industrial	0.70	29.33
Portfolio	0.68	27.50

Market risk = 8.8% per annum.

between 5% and 15%. On this basis, average property risk is likely to vary between 15% and 47% per annum depending on market conditions.

When average risk levels are high it follows that development and investment in property will be restricted. This aspect is exacerbated when the high level of gearing common in property is taken into consideration.

Table 4B.2 has shown that the current average risk level is about 28% per annum. For those who find this level of risk hard to believe, it should be recognized that if the level is lower this implies that the correlation of returns of property with the market must be increasing as market risk increases. For example instead of taking 28% per annum it is assumed that the true average risk level is only 15% per annum it can easily be shown that the correlation between property and the market must therefore be about 0.59. (By substituting equation (4B.8) into (4B.9) the average correlation can be found by dividing the market risk by the average risk. In this example the market risk is estimated at 8.8% per annum and it is assumed that the total risk is 15% per annum. The quotient is therefore 0.59.) This implies that the market explains about 35% (i.e. $R^2 = 0.59$) of the variation in property returns on an annual basis.

If the average risk is assumed to be constant the correlation structure will increase significantly as market risk increases. It will be self evident that if the market risk is equal to the average risk a correlation coefficient of 1.00 is implied. As this state of affairs is extremely unlikely we can be safe in assuming that average property risk is likely to vary over time.

References

Bachelier, L. (1900) *Théorie de la spéculation*, Paris Gauthier-Villars.

Elton, E. J. and Gruber, M. J. (1977) Risk reduction and portfolio size, *Journal of Business*, 50, (4), 415–37.

Evans, E. J. and Archer, S. H. (1968) Diversification and the reduction of dispersion: an empirical analysis, *Journal of Finance*, 761–7

Fama, E. (1965) *Foundations of finance*, Basic Books, New York.

Findlay, M., Hamilton, C. W., Messner, S. D. and Yormark, J. S. (1979) Optimal real estate portfolio, *AREUEA Journal*, 7, (3), 298–317.

Friedman, H. C. (1970) Real estate investment and portfolio theory, *Journal of Financial and Quantitative Analysis*, December, 861–74.

Hoag, J. W. (1979) *A new real estate return index: measurement of risk and return*, proceedings of the seminar on the analysis of security prices, University of Chicago, 24, (1), May, 223–59.

Hoag, J. W. (1980) Towards indices of real estate value and return, *Journal of Finance*, XXXV, (2), May.

Kendall, M. (1953) The analysis of economic time series, part 1, *Journal of the Royal Statistical Society*, 11–25.

Markowitz, H. (1959) *Portfolio selection: efficient diversification of investments*, Yale University Press.

Osborne, M. F. M. (1959) Brownian motion in the stock market, *Operations Research*, 7, 145–73

Solnik, B. (1974) Why not diversify internationally rather than domestically?, *Financial Analysts Journal*, (5) July–August.

5
Portfolio strategy and asset allocation

The foregoing chapters have discussed a number of current investment issues and considered them in relation to the property sector. Through research of other investment sectors our knowledge of areas such as inflation hedging, market efficiency and portfolio theory is fairly comprehensive, and by extension it is possible to gain some insights into the way the property sector is likely to operate.

However, currently there is no established theory of investment strategy which brings all these aspects together, and this is not surprising. The property market tends to be deal-oriented with considerable emphasis being placed on the ability of advisors to identify and select those properties which are believed to be under-priced and are thus expected to perform well.

Clearly there is nothing wrong with this approach although there are two questions which need to be asked.

1. Can professional advisors utilize costly information in such a way that under-priced properties can be selected?
2. Is professional advice sufficiently good that positive abnormal returns can be earned consistently from period to period?

The first question deals with strategy and the second with performance measurement. This chapter looks at the strategies which are possible given the investment characteristics of property. It also deals with the problem of asset allocation. The analysis of performance is discussed in Chapter 6.

5.1 Portfolio strategy

Although no formal theory of property strategy exists it is possible to examine the problem in relation to the work which has been undertaken in the stock market. An understanding of portfolio strategy therefore depends on the implications of the efficient market hypothesis.

Chapter 2 examined the efficient market hypothesis in the context of property investment and concluded that at the weak form level the market could be regarded as being efficient. In other words merely tracking the way property has moved in the past will give no guide as to the way it will move in the future and as such it is not possible to develop a profitable strategy by examining market trends. This result is not unexpected. To the vast majority of investors, if they have no access to inside information or exceptional forecasting ability, most markets will appear to be highly competitive and efficient. Prices, or open market valuations for property, will tend to reflect available information and respond rapidly to any changes in market sentiment. The way the market responds depends on the quality and cost of available information. The property market will therefore become more efficient as the cost of producing information decreases.

The principles of market efficiency are believable but the investment community has argued vociferously for some time concerning its implications for investor behaviour. There can be few theories which cut across conventional market advice which have such a profound effect on investment practice. Two areas which are worthy of discussion are technical analysis and fundamental analysis.

5.2 Technical analysis

The principle behind technical analysis is that by plotting past trends, particularly in stock market prices, it is possible to predict future trends. Consequently if there is an upturn in the market this could be taken as a signal to acquire an investment at below its true market price thus giving rise to abnormal returns. The efficient market approach to this argument is to say that past data represents publicly available information and any implications about the future are already impounded into the current price. A significant increase in price is merely a reflection of the riskiness of that asset. The returns that an investor achieves from the price rise cannot generally be regarded as being abnormal but merely compensation for the risk of that asset.

There is a growing trend to produce graphs which plot movements in the property market and it is tempting to use this as the basis for developing an investment strategy. The concept of buying low and selling high should not be considered as being without risk.

The fact that there appear to be discernable trends in price movements does not mean that they are predictable. Random price movements plotted over time appear to exhibit all the characteristics of a pattern, (Roberts, 1959) although this does not mean that they are following any predictable trend.

As explained in Chapter 2 the efficient market hypothesis implies that the net present value of any investment must be zero if it is correctly priced, and market prices are the best estimate of present value.

Although there is a considerable amount of empirical evidence to support this view it is very easy to misunderstand the implications of the efficient market hypothesis. It does not imply that it is impossible to earn abnormal returns by studying charts and trend analyses. What it does imply however is that it is impossible to do this consistently over long periods. Appendix 5B analyses the returns from a group of property bonds to see whether abnormal returns were discernible or not. What the results show is that over the period analysed abnormal returns were achievable but they could not be sustained over the whole period.

This is an important finding and one which is common in other investment sectors. It appears that it is extremely difficult to earn consistent abnormal returns on a risk-adjusted basis. This is particularly interesting in the property sector where it is frequently reported that the market is inefficient! As property information becomes more available and less costly it will become more difficult to seek out and earn abnormal returns.

5.3 Fundamental analysis

A more defensible approach to investment strategy is through fundamental analysis which tends to look at specific factors which contribute to the value of an asset. If these can be correctly identified and their impact incorporated into a valuation it may be possible to identify an asset which is mispriced, and then secure an abnormal return.

This approach implies that the market is mistaken and that through research it is possible to identify under-priced assets. Although in principle this may be possible, in practice it is necessary to ensure that the cost of research does not erode any of the possible gains. The implication is that markets are not completely efficient and so there is sufficient room to earn abnormal returns as long as those assets can be identified.

It will be recalled that abnormal returns refer to the difference between the returns actually achieved and the expected returns implied by the security market line after making an adjustment for risk.

5.4 Active/passive strategies

In Chapter 4 it was shown that property portfolios tend to be poorly diversified. One of the criticisms frequently levelled at the efficient market hypothesis is that investors do not diversify efficiently. In other words they do not believe the efficient market hypothesis. Despite the fact that individuals may not diversify efficiently, it is the tendency of market to be competitive that creates efficiency. To put this another way, the more people believe that the market is not efficient the more competitive it is likely to become. This in turn makes it more efficient.

Abnormal returns can then be obtained only through three sources:

1. luck;
2. inside information;
3. superior forecasting ability.

This of course is an interesting notion for it has a direct bearing on the type of strategies which can be developed.

In essence portfolio strategy depends on the degree of forecasting ability which investors possess. This can be considered in relation to two extremes, perfect forecasting ability and no forecasting ability.

If, for example, an investor possesses perfect forecasting ability he will be able to predict with complete accuracy those investments which will show superior performance. The strategy he should adopt in this case is to invest as much as possible in those assets which he knows to be under-priced because he can be guaranteed that they will provide abnormal performance.

At the other end of the spectrum is the investor who has no forecasting ability whatsoever. Here again the strategy to adopt is also straightforward. All he has to do is follow the herd and construct a diversified portfolio which tracks an index. Because he is tracking an index there will be no abnormal performance but the investor will at least have the comfort of knowing that he is performing no better nor worse than average.

The problem really comes when investors have some forecasting ability. Recognizing the differences in degree of forecasting ability has led to a widely recognized approach to investment known as the active–passive strategy. In essence it suggests that the investment process can be split in two parts. The first part is to create a portfolio which tracks an index. All specific risk is eliminated through diversification so that the returns move in line with an index. The penalty for doing this, as mentioned above, is that it is not possible to outperform the index. The second part reserves a proportion of funds which can be used to back investors' beliefs concerning forecasts of performance for individual assets. If they invest this part successfully then over time the performance of the portfolio should be better than a managed portfolio carrying the same level of market risk. If of course they invest it badly then the performance of the portfolio will be below that of the managed equivalent.

The active strategy is to try and identify those assets which have an intrinsic value which is different to their current value. This requires some knowledge of the risk class of the asset in order to determine whether it is under- or over-priced. The type of asset which should be selected is shown in Figure 5.1.

Market timing can easily be incorporated by gearing up the returns on the index funds if the market is rising or by investing a higher proportion of funds in gilts if the market is falling. In this way the market risk of the portfolio is altered in relation to market expectations.

In the property market the situation is interesting in that most advisors believe they have perfect forecasting ability but behave as if they have none. In other words every property recommended for purchase is believed to be under-priced but the strategy which many investors try to pursue is to track an index.

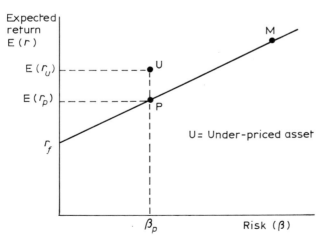

Figure 5.1 Selection of under-priced assets.

This raises two questions. Firstly, is it possible to track an index with a property portfolio, and secondly is this a viable strategy to pursue?

5.5 Tracking an index with a property portfolio

The two requirements for a portfolio to track an index are that it should have a high R^2 value and have a beta coefficient equal to 1.0. In other words a high proportion of the variance in returns of the portfolio should be explained by the market and it should be similar in composition to the market.

It will be recalled from Chapter 4 that it is very difficult to achieve a property portfolio with a high R^2 value. Table 4.12 showed that for an equally-weighted portfolio approximately 200 properties would be needed to achieve an R^2 value of 95%. If the effect of value-weighting is taken into consideration then the figure is likely to be much higher unless there are some properties which are highly correlated with the market.

It is useful to make a similar comparison with the equity market. Table 5.1 shows that it is much easier to achieve highly diversified portfolios with equities than with property. Since very few property portfolios hold over 170 properties it is almost impossible to achieve a portfolio which will track an index.

Table 5.1 Diversification of property and equity markets compared

% diversification	Number of properties	Number of equities
95	171	44
99	891	228

Although there may be a desire for property investors to try to track an index, the practicalities of the situation make this impossible. This does not mean however that the rationale for following this type of strategy is unrealistic; it hinges on two factors, market timing and differences in borrowing and lending rates.

Market timing

In an ideal world if it were possible to predict the slope of the security market line investors would buy all the high beta properties when the market was rising and shift into the low beta properties when the market was falling. This way they could minimize their exposure to fluctuations in market conditions. However due to liquidity problems in the property market it is almost impossible to switch in and out of different risk categories without sustaining substantial losses. For this reason it would make sense to maintain the market risk of a portfolio as close to 1.0 as possible. There may however be differential tax influences which will cause the investor to prefer one type of property to another, i.e. high income as opposed to high growth. This merely means selecting a different risk class for the portfolio which meets these criteria. If there is no evidence of superior ability in picking under-priced properties then in the long run the return on the portfolio will be in line with its expectations. On average we would expect the portfolio to do no better nor worse than the market after having made an adjustment for risk.

Different borrowing and lending rates

It was shown in Chapter 1 that the security market line is not straight due to differences in borrowing and lending rates. When this occurs the security market line will kink at the market portfolio. This kink will occur irrespective of whether the market is rising or falling, as shown in Figure 5.2.

The best trade-off between risk and return will be achieved when the portfolio has a beta coefficient of 1.0. This can easily be seen by inspection of the Figure 5.2. As investors do not like to change risk class there are good reasons for trying to maintain the beta coefficient of the portfolio close to 1.0.

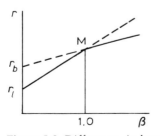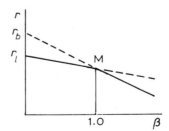

Figure 5.2 Differences in borrowing and lending rates.

5.6 Consistent and inconsistent strategies

This discussion naturally leads on to what can be considered consistent and inconsistent strategies (Brealey, 1983).

If a portfolio is highly diversified with a very high R^2 value then it should reduce the turnover in its assets in order to minimize management charges. The aim of the portfolio should be to track an index. This is a consistent strategy. If however the portfolio is poorly diversified then it should be actively managed with the emphasis being placed on forecasting abnormal returns. This too is a consistent strategy. In both cases the strategy pursued follows from an understanding of the partitioning of the variance of returns into the systematic and non-systematic components.

An inconsistent strategy would be to have a highly diversified portfolio which is actively managed or a poorly diversified portfolio which is inactively managed.

It is probable that many property investors in the past have been pursuing an inconsistent strategy. It was common practice a number of years ago to build up a small property portfolio which was then left to produce income and capital growth. Because the portfolio was small it was poorly diversified. The inactive management policy was however consistent with a highly diversified portfolio. The performance of the portfolio was almost certainly due to non-market factors and probably owed more to chance than good management.

It cannot be assumed that this strategy would produce poor results as in some periods the returns may be spectacularly good. Providing a convincing explanation for the results against a predetermined policy may however be more difficult to justify. This would be more marked during a downturn in the property market.

A simple examination of the performance of property portfolios shows that this state of affairs is economically indefensible. The trend these days is to actively manage portfolios in order to achieve the best possible returns. This means that although the active-passive strategy, in the form used in the equity market, cannot be pursued in the property market it can nevertheless be interpreted in the sense of tracking the expectations of an index and using research to select those properties which are under-priced.

5.7 Tracking expectations

It has already been shown that for most portfolios it is unlikely that the market will have a major part to play in explaining performance on a period by period basis. Nevertheless tracking the expectations of the market is important because there may well be no significant skill in identifying under-priced properties. In this case return in the long run will depend upon the market risk of the portfolio.

It is suggested that the certainty equivalent expectations model derived in Appendix 2F can be used to determine the market risk of a property portfolio, which can then be tracked over time and compared with the index. Although this model is not suggested as being the complete truth concerning risk and return, it nevertheless will give a consistent indication of changes in risk.

Merely tracking the equivalent yield will not provide correct answers as each yield is assumed to carry the same weight even though there may well be forecasting differences which affected the estimate.

If the market risk of the portfolio is agreed in advance it is important to ensure that the buying decisions maintain it at the same level. If the portfolio is inactively managed then our expectation is that over time its expected return will decline as the properties get older. In this case the market risk of the portfolio will also decline. This is illustrated in Figure 5.3.

It is therefore useful to know the average age of the portfolio as well as the index being used for comparison. There is a danger that some professional indices may in part be tracking changes in age as well as market movements if there is little change in the constituent properties. The danger here is that if an inactively managed portfolio is compared with an inactively managed index the portfolio may not show any

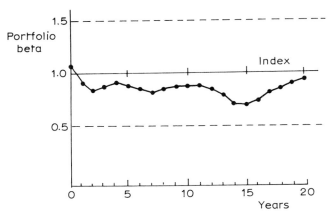

Figure 5.3 Market risk of a portfolio compared with an index.

change in market risk because it is declining at the same rate as the market. Whether this is a problem in reality has yet to be determined.

5.8 Property selection

Identifying individual properties which are under-priced in an economic sense is more difficult to achieve. At present there is no consensus view as to how properties should be defined in terms of being under- or over-priced. There is of course plenty of research and advice concerning the prospects for individual properties but whether this can be converted into information which is profitable is open to debate. If the information is widely available then there is every likelihood that it will already be impounded in values. Unless the professional advisor or investor has access to information which is not widely known or is contemplating the purchase of a property where the information set differs significantly from that used for open market valuations then it is unlikely that he will be able to consistently acquire under-priced properties. In addition the high cost of research could well erode any potential gains which have been identified.

This has significant implications for property research departments, for without a formal theory of market equilibrium it is doubtful whether the research function can identify under-priced properties other than by chance.

The starting point for developing this area is to recognize that property is part of a much larger investment market and that the theories of risk, return and equilibrium apply as much to property as any other investment sector. Although much has been written about property there is nothing in the literature which substantiates the view that property is so different from all other markets that it requires a whole new theory of investment. Pursuing this logic the next step is to accept that the market only rewards investors for taking on that part of risk which cannot be diversified away, i.e. systematic or market risk. This is the basic form of the capital asset pricing model.

Whether the model is true or not does not really matter. What is important is that it provides a good framework within which to develop an economically sound approach to selecting under-priced properties. Having developed an approach it can then be refined to deal with any inconsistencies.

The purpose of the analysis is to identify abnormal returns on an ex-ante basis. This is the rôle of property analysis, the results of which can then be fed into a system of recommendations for buying, selling or holding the property. In terms of the net present value criteria discussed earlier this can be considered as shown in Table 5.2.

Table 5.2 Property recommendations and net present value

Recommendation	Net present value	Abnormal return
Buy	Positive	Positive
Sell	Negative	Negative
Hold	Zero	Zero

If this type of analysis is carried out against a specific time-horizon the results represent an economically defensible approach to the problem of property selection. Whether the selection process proves to be worthwhile or not is the subject of performance measurement, and this is discussed in Chapter 6.

In identifying whether a property is under- or over-priced all available information concerning that property has to be processed in a better than average way. If the property market is believed to be inefficient then there should ample opportunity to earn abnormal returns. Due however to the lack of a central market-place where properties can be bought and sold the presence of agents, with a wide network of contacts, tend to fill the information void which then leads to an increase in efficiency. This would also occur if the proposals for a unitized market were accepted and commercial properties became more frequently traded.

5.9 Processing information

The ability to identify under-priced properties depends on how well information can be processed. If all research departments are reviewing the same markets in the same way then there could be a consensus view concerning future prospects. In this scenario it is only the unconventional approach which will achieve the greatest rewards. Recommendations for purchase currently make no reference to the potential abnormal returns that could be achieved. References are more frequently made by a comparison of yields and what this implies in terms of growth. However, as discussed earlier this type of analysis is only likely to identify under-priced properties merely by chance. Forecasts of future performance will be of little use unless they include information which is different from the consensus. The approach suggested here is based on an ex-ante technique suggested by Rudd and Clasing (1982) for analysing equities.

The principal problem in trying to analyse whether a property is under- or over-priced in the economic sense discussed earlier is that there is unlikely to be sufficient historic information to enable a judgement to be made of its risk class. Where a new property is involved this is of course impossible. It would then be necessary to make reference to similar properties where such data are available. At best this would still provide an historic estimate of beta where what is needed is an expected beta. Using the certainty equivalent expectations model described in Appendix 2F it is however possible to overcome this problem and arrive at an expected beta for an individual property based on information concerning that property. It is an ex-ante estimate and with suitable corrections for valuation error is likely to be our best estimate of market risk.

With this information together with the riskless rate of return it is possible to estimate the expected return for a property. If we have some knowledge of the slope of the security market line it is then possible to determine whether the property it is under- or over-priced. Graphically this can be represented in Figure 5.4.

This process can be more usefully developed by analysing a large sample of properties at a single point in time. By plotting expected return against risk and analysing the results using regression analysis it should be possible to identify those properties which are under- or over-priced.

The technique for arriving at this information is as follows. As explained in Chapter 2 valuations are a reflection on the quality of information available. Some property values will be good, others will

Figure 5.4 Identification of under- and over-priced properties.

be poor. Even though they may all be based on the same general belief that they are open market valuations they will nevertheless contain some random error, or noise. The important point to note however is that valuations contain valuable information which can be analysed using the equated yield model.

The standard version of this model assuming that a property is valued part-way through a review period is

$$V_0 = \frac{a[1 - (1 + r)^{-n}]}{r} + \frac{R(1 + g)^n}{r(1 + r)^n}\left[\frac{(1 + r)^p - 1}{(1 + r)^p - (1 + g)^p}\right]. \quad (5.1)$$

Assuming that the value of the property is known it can be substituted into this equation together with details of the lease structure and the growth rate and solved for the expected rate of return.

The certainty equivalent model can also be used to provide an estimate of systematic risk. An alternative approach to estimating the rate of return is to tabulate the projected cash flows over say a twenty-year period so that they include both rental income and projected expenditure. The rate of return of the net cash flow can then easily be determined by iteration.

If this process is repeated for a large enough sample of properties it is possible to plot rates of return against beta on a graph as shown in Figure 5.5.

The regression line through this data then represents the security market line for the property market at the time of the analysis. The slope of the line is also significant. It will change over time and will represent the aggregate risk aversion in the property market. Because it is drafted in terms of expectations it may provide valuable information concerning the future direction of market movements.

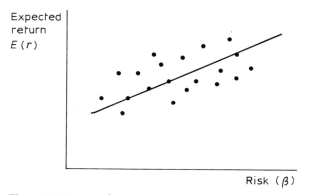

Figure 5.5 Rates of return versus beta.

Having established this relationship it is then a straightforward matter to identify those properties which are under- or over-valued by establishing whether they lie above or below the line.

It is unreasonable however to assume that all valuations contain the same level of information. Some valuations may be better than others because the information set used to assess the value is more complete. In these cases the assessment of abnormal returns will be better. If this fact is not recognized it will be evident that by altering the cash flows for a property it is easy to generate positive abnormal returns which will give the impression that the property shows greater potential than actually exists. In order to make use of this technique the assessments of abnormal return need to be adjusted within a Bayesian framework.

The adjustment suggested by Rudd and Clasing is to recognize that the average abnormal return, i.e. the difference between the expected and actual return, should be zero. The prior prediction for the abnormal return is therefore zero. We do however have a predicted value (PA) for the abnormal return which should be combined with the prior prediction.

$$\text{Estimated abnormal return} = \alpha$$
$$\text{Predicted abnormal return} = \text{PA}$$
$$\text{Prior estimated abnormal return} = 0$$

Thus

$$\alpha = (1 - \text{BA})(\text{prior estimate}) + \text{BA} \times (\text{predicted value})$$

$$= (1 - \text{BA})(0) + \text{BA} \times \text{PA}$$

$$= \text{BA} \times \text{PA} \tag{5.2}$$

where BA is the Bayesian adjustment factor representing the degree of confidence placed on the estimate. Using this adjustment, the estimated abnormal return is therefore moved closer to or further away from zero by an amount which captures the information content of the valuer.

If we assume that the valuer's confidence in his forecast is constant through time it is possible to derive a simple regression model for arriving at the adjustment factor. The assumption given here implies that it is no easier to forecast returns at one point in time than in another. Although this may sound unrealistic there is no reason to believe that a valuer is capable of assessing what the return will be on a property in twelve months' time with any better accuracy than he could in five years' time. If he were able to do this in practice then he could guarantee to make money and would very easily create a money machine. The fact that this does not happen provides some evidence for accepting this assumption.

The regression model used for estimating the adjustment factor relates the realized abnormal return (RA) to the forecast abnormal return (PA).

$$RA = a + b(PA) + e. \tag{5.3}$$

Taking expectations and recognizing that the expected value of the error term is zero gives the following:

$$E(RA) = \alpha = a + bE(PA). \tag{5.4}$$

Having estimated a and b they can then be used to obtain an unbiased estimate of the abnormal return for each property. This procedure corrects each raw abnormal return (PA) for the information content in the valuations and provides an estimate representing the pure information in the forecast.

In order to implement this procedure it would be necessary for professional advisors to undertake an analysis of their forecasting skills by collecting data on abnormal returns and risk. This information is not as yet available. As a starting point however it would not be unreasonable to ask valuers to forecast the valuation in the next period whenever a current valuation is being made. If they have any forecasting ability then a regression analysis of realized returns versus forecast returns would produce a positive slope coefficient. It is interesting to note that similar tests undertaken on UK equities (Dimson and Marsh, 1985) has shown that there does seem to be a relationship between a forecast and subsequent price movements although it is not very strong. Whether a stronger relationship can be found in the property market remains to be seen.

A further piece of information can be gleaned from the regression analysis. The $\bar{R}^2$ of the regression can be regarded as the information coefficient. If it is high (or low) then we can say that a high (or low) proportion of the variation in the realized abnormal returns can be explained by the forecast.

Appendix 5B presents an analysis of a group of property bonds and shows that over a nine-year period there was considerable variation in observed abnormal returns so that on average they were statistically indistinguishable from zero. This would seem to imply that selection skills may well be poor and so evidence of superior forecasting ability may be weak. On this basis it is probable that corrected abnormal returns will produce results much closer to zero. Selection of under-priced properties will therefore fall within a much narrower band.

This approach to property selection has the advantage of focusing attention on the calculation of abnormal returns which are central to the concept of added value. The use of yields as the basis for selecting properties has not been considered because it has no bearing on the identification of abnormal returns and will only create added value merely by chance.

The process described also concentrates on forecasts of rental income for individual properties. A by-product of this is that the regression of expected return versus beta may convey some information about a market forecast. It may well be easier to forecast market movements using this approach than through direct forecasting of the market itself.

5.10 Asset allocation and sector allocation

The selection of individual properties is part of a much larger problem concerning the allocation of funds. This should really be seen at two levels: firstly what proportion of funds should be invested in property relative to other investment media and secondly what proportion of funds should be invested in each sector of the property market.

Asset allocation

The problem of asset allocation between different financial sectors has received considerable coverage in the literature. In general terms the problem is a straightforward application of the Markowitz model to determine the proportion of funds which should be invested in each sector in order to identify the efficient frontier. Chapter 2 described the procedure involved and showed that once the investor has chosen where on the efficient frontier he wishes to lie it is then a simple matter to identify the proportion of funds to invest in each of the sectors which will help him achieve his expected return for minimum risk.

In terms of asset allocation what we are really concerned with is the proportion of funds which should be invested in relation to future expectations. Historic time-series information is useful in terms of giving an indication of the past variability of returns but this must be adjusted to provide a forecast of expected returns and variances over some agreed time-horizon.

The key to the asset allocation problem is the correlation structure that exists between each of the financial sectors. The problem with property is that the data samples available in the past for this type of analysis have been very poor. This aspect is being addressed and will improve over time. The data sample referred to in Chapter 4 does not have the same problems normally encountered with property and can therefore be used to provide valid correlation coefficients.

Using monthly data, the figures are as shown in Table 5.3. The most significant feature of this table is that property exhibits low correlation with every sector with the exception of the Retail Price index, and this is in line with the findings concerning inflation hedging discussed in Chapter 3. The fact that property portfolio exhibits low correlation with the FT Property Share index is largely due to the fact that property shares tend to be highly geared so that the equity returns are more likely to move in line with the FT All Share index. It will be seen from Table 5.3 that the correlation coefficient relating property shares to equity shares is 0.79. There will be little diversification benefit to be achieved by incorporating property shares into a portfolio consisting of equities on the pretext that property shares represent a holding in direct property.

The low correlation between direct property and all other assets does mean however that property has an important part to play in creating efficiently diversified portfolios. This is also reinforced by the fact that property is highly correlated with the Retail Price index and so the inclusion of property in a mixed-asset portfolio will enhance the inflation protection properties of the portfolio.

There have been a number of studies which have examined the allocation of assets between different sectors of the market. Each of these has concluded that the proportion of funds currently held in property by investing institutions is much lower than is desirable to maximize the trade-off between risk and return. The final allocation however depends on the needs of the investing institution. If for

Table 5.3 Correlation coefficients between financial sectors (January 1979–December 1982) for value-weighted portfolios

		PP	FTG	15G	Cons	FT–P	FT–A	RPI
Property portfolio:	PP	1.00						
FT All Gilts index:	FTG	−0.11	1.00					
>15 year Gilts index:	15G	−0.12	0.98	1.00				
2.5% Consols:	Cons	0.01	0.82	0.80	1.00			
FT Property index:	FT–P	0.11	0.63	0.61	0.52	1.00		
FT All Share index:	FT–A	0.03	0.57	0.53	0.51	0.79	1.00	
Retail price index:	RPI	0.44	−0.03	−0.06	0.16	0.16	0.07	1.00

example liquidity is important then the decision will tend towards those assets which are more easily marketed and are thus out of property. Therefore there can be no definitive answer to the allocation problem, only a series of choices.

In all these analyses a major problem which keeps recurring is that the standard deviation of returns on the property portfolio is likely to be understated if the underlying returns series is smoothed. Property will therefore appear to be less risky that it is in reality. However this is a statistical problem which can be overcome by transformation of the data. The process involved is described in Appendix 5A. Even when the standard deviation increases significantly there appears to be little change in the allocation of resources between sectors. It is also assumed that the correlation structure between property and the other sectors remains unchanged by the transformation.

In any event it would appear that a core holding of property should represent about 20% of total funds (Fogler, 1984). This would represent a long-term position which could vary from period to period depending on changes in expectations.

Sector allocation

With regard to sector allocation, the principles concerning the analysis of the correlation structure remain the same. It is unlikely however that property advisors would even consider the correlation structure that exists between properties when trying to put together a portfolio. The more realistic option as mentioned above is to maintain the risk class of the portfolio at a desired level. In the absence of any strong proposals to the contrary this means maintaining the portfolio beta as close to 1.00 as possible. In pursuing this policy there does not appear to be any significant advantage to diversifying across sectors as opposed to within sectors. The risk reduction profiles identified in the previous chapter confirm that the reduction in risk for a portfolio consisting of offices, shops and industrial property is not significantly different from the risk reduction within each sector. This is a fact which has also been verified by Jones Lang Wooton in analysing the portfolios they manage (Jones Lang Wooton, 1987). The reason for diversifying across sectors is probably a hedging strategy to take advantage of any potential changes in the market and to cope with the problem of liquidity. For example, abnormal growth in the retail market could lead to abnormal returns for properties held within that sector. An investor trying to buy retail property may find that the

abnormal returns have been arbitraged away if they have been correctly priced. Maintaining a constant risk class by diversifying across
sectors means that in the long run the portfolio will perform on
average no better nor worse than the market.

It has also been pointed out that property portfolios are likely to be
poorly diversified due to the small numbers held and so they carry a
considerable amount of residual risk. Being poorly diversified means
that on a period by period basis, the returns will not track an index
but it does give the opportunity to capitalize on any abnormal returns
which can be identified particularly if one of the sectors becomes
marginal.

In order to exploit this in a way which is potentially useful, expected
returns for each sector can be compared with actual returns achieved.
If there is a difference between the two then it may mean that the
direction of movement of a sector could be forecast in advance. The
hypothesis being pursued here is that observed returns still contain
residual risk which has not been diversified away. The expected return
by contrast only tracks market returns and has no residual risk. If a
sector has become marginal and is exhibiting excess demand then a
number of properties may well be showing abnormal returns. These
would show up as a difference between observed and expected return
during periods of upside potential or downside risk depending on the
whether the abnormal return was positive or negative.

If this is correct then it could create opportunities for improving
portfolio performance. This type of analysis is as yet in its infancy but
the following three graphs provide a plot of expected returns calculated
using the certainty equivalent market risk model compared with actual
returns. It will be seen that definite trends can be observed with each
sector exhibiting periods when they appear to be under- or over-
valued.

These illustrations also help to explain one of the results in *Property
Investment Performance Over 20 Years* (Jones Lang Wooton, 1982).
Using returns data for the period 1961–81, they calculated the average
returns and risk levels shown in Table 5.4. Over the 20-year period the

Table 5.4 Average returns and risk for property (1961–81)

Sector	Average return	Standard deviation
Industrial	17.40%	9.50%
Retail	14.60%	11.80%
Office	14.10%	11.00%

Source: Jones Lang Wooton, *Property Investment Performance over 20 Years.*

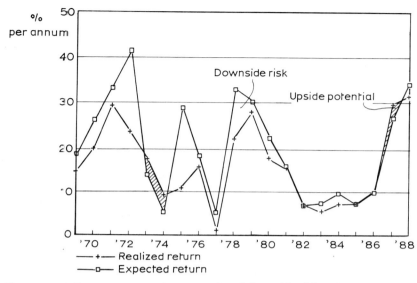

Figure 5.6 Office sector: Upside potential and downside risk.

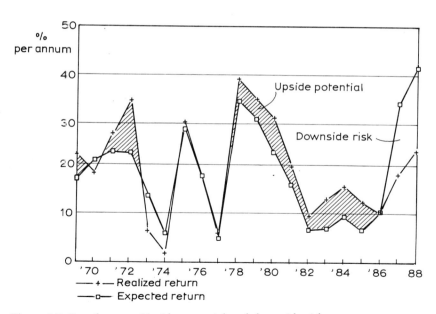

Figure 5.7 Retail sector: Upside potential and downside risk.

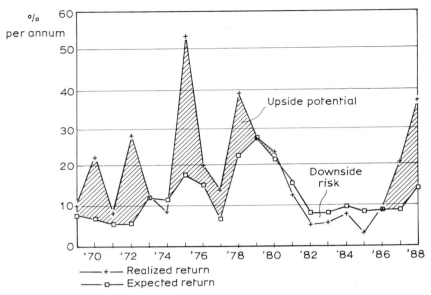

Figure 5.8 Industrial sector: Upside potential and downside risk.

industrial sector exhibited the highest return with the lowest risk. Although the report pointed out that the trade-off between risk and return was better for the industrial sector than either retail or office it was unable to provide an explanation for this result.

The first point to notice from Table 5.4 is that it confirms the ranking of market risk which has already been identified in previous chapters. The second point is that from the plot of expected and actual returns shown in Figure 5.8 there are a number of periods when actual returns were in excess of expected returns. In fact during the 1960s and 1970s there was considerable activity in the industrial sector which probably contributed to high abnormal returns. It is not unreasonable therefore to see such high average returns during this period in a sector which is characterized by low market risk.

Having said this it must be acknowledged that the data used in the graphs for the period prior to 1978 is open to considerable interpretation. It was not until about 1978 that the need to collect data and publish property returns was considered to be sufficiently important. Nevertheless the difference between actual and expected returns as shown in these illustrations does go some way to improving our interpretation of underlying trends.

5.11 Conclusion

This chapter has shown that in order to strive for improved property performance the research function ought to be directed to utilizing information in a way which will help to identify abnormal returns. This requires a better understanding of the returns generating process and the factors contributing to risk and return. Merely tracking indices in the hope that the trend will give some indication of future performance is unlikely to produce positive abnormal returns in the long run unless there is some better understanding of expectations.

The information content of valuations is clearly important and with better analysis, valuations may well provide information which could lead to the identification of abnormal returns.

At the moment this area of research has received little formal treatment in the property literature. Strategy decisions are frequently based on naïve or ill-informed judgement. It is probable that this situation will change, but it may take some time before risk analysis and tracking becomes a routine part of property analysis.

Appendix 5A: Eliminating smoothing in property indices

This appendix follows the derivation proposed by Blundell and Ward (1987) for removing the serial correlation which exists in a time series of returns created from property valuations. This is a major problem with property indices which can seriously restrict their use in such areas as performance measurement and the development of portfolio models.

Smoothing in a return series can be introduced through two effects.

1. Valuers may not respond fully to the impact of new information on the valuation of a property. This may be caused by the fact that information may be sparse and could take some time to be incorporated. Other valuers may be over-optimistic in their interpretation of available information. In either case the information set used by the valuer differs from the true information set affecting the open market valuation of the property.
2. The valuations included within an index are unlikely to be carried out at exactly the same time. Depending on the quality of the index and the frequency of the reporting date they may well include a number of valuations which have been undertaken both before and after the reporting date. For example an index which is published in March representing the movements of the market in December may include valuations prepared in both November and January. The resulting index number is therefore a moving average and this causes a smoothed returns series.

The principal problem with these effects is that the standard deviation of returns calculated from the smoothed series will be understated and imply that the property market carries considerably less risk than it does in reality.

Blundell and Ward have suggested the following model which identifies current valuations as being a weighted average of the true market valuation and the valuation in the previous period.

$$V_t = (1 - A)P_t + AV_{t-1} \qquad (5A.1)$$

where

V_t = valuation at time t;
P_t = true market valuation at time t;
A = constant lying in the range from 0 to 1.

The greater the value of A, the more weight is attached to the previous valuation.

A similar expression can be derived for the previous period as follows:

$$V_{t-1} = (1 - A)P_{t-1} + AV_{t-2}. \qquad (5A.2)$$

Subtracting this from equation (5A.1) gives the following:

$$V_t - V_{t-1} = (1 - A)(P_t - P_{t-1}) + A(V_{t-1} - V_{t-2}). \qquad (5A.3)$$

Assuming that all the valuations are expressed in terms of natural logs the difference between the valuations represents continously compounded rates of return over the period $(t - 1)$ to t. Equation (5A.3) can therefore be drafted in returns form as follows:

$$r_t = (1 - A)rm_t + Ar_{t-1} \qquad (5A.4)$$

where

$$r_t = \text{return derived from the valuation series;}$$
$$rm_t = \text{return which would be observed if market prices were correctly captured by valuations.}$$

In order to proceed further it is necessary to assume that like other markets the true property returns series is weak form efficient and follows a random walk process. This would also be the case if valuations were present values. The underlying process for rm can therefore be expressed as

$$rm_t = B + e_t \qquad (5A.5)$$

where B is a constant and e_t is a Normally distributed random variable with an expected value of zero and is serially uncorrelated for all lags. Applying the expectations operator:

$$E(rm_t) = B. \qquad (5A.6)$$

It will be seen that the expected value of the true return series is a constant with a variance given by

$$\text{Var}(rm) = \text{Var}(e). \qquad (5A.7)$$

By substituting equation (5A.5) into equation (5A.4) we have

$$r_t = (1 - A)(B + e_t) + Ar_{t-1} \qquad (5A.8)$$

$$r_t = B(1 - A) + Ar_{t-1} + (1 - A)e_t \qquad (5A.9)$$

and applying the expectations operator to equation (5A.9) gives

$$E(r_t) = B(1 - A) + AE(r_{t-1}) + (1 - A)E(e_t). \qquad (5A.10)$$

If the time series $r_t, r_{t-1}, \ldots$ etc. is stationary then there will be no change in the expected value of the mean return and so $E(r_t)$ is equal to $E(r_{t-1})$. Similarly the expected value of the error term is zero. Taking these factors into consideration equation (5A.10) can be redrafted as:

$$E(r)(1 - A) = B(1 - A) \qquad (5A.11)$$

$$E(r) = B = E(rm). \qquad (5A.12)$$

The expected return of the observed series is therefore equal to the underlying true market return. What will differ however is the variance of the true return series. This can be shown by taking the variance of equation (5A.9).

$$\text{Var}(r_t) = A^2 \, \text{Var}(r_{t-1}) + (1 - A)^2 \, \text{Var}(e_t). \qquad (5A.13)$$

Again assuming that the series has been transformed so that it is stationary the variance of the returns will be constant. Hence $\text{Var}(r_t)$ will equal $\text{Var}(r_{t-1})$ so equation (5A.13) can be redrafted as

$$\text{Var}(r) = \frac{(1 - A)^2}{1 - A^2} \, \text{Var}(e_t). \qquad (5A.14)$$

Substituting from equation (5A.7) gives

$$\text{Var}(r) = \frac{(1 - A)^2}{1 - A^2} \, \text{Var}(rm). \qquad (5A.15)$$

The variance of the true returns series can be found by rearranging as follows.

$$\text{Var}(rm) = \frac{1 - A^2}{(1 - A)^2} \, \text{Var}(r). \qquad (5A.16)$$

Similarly the true returns series can be transformed from equation (5A.4) as follows:

$$rm_t = \frac{r_t}{1 - A} - \frac{A}{1 - A} \, r_{t-1}. \qquad (5A.17)$$

This series will have the same mean as the observed return series but will have a greater variance. Whether the variance of this adjusted series represents the true systematic risk of the underlying portfolio will depend on the number of properties used to construct the index.

Appendix 5B: The performance of property bonds

An interesting feature of the property market is that investment decisions are almost universally based on measures of yield. Differences in the quality of individual properties are taken into consideration by either adding or subtracting fractions of a percentage point from yield information which has been derived from comparable properties.

Clearly there is nothing wrong with this approach as long as the derived figure is correct. By this I mean that the yield can be used as a means of advising investors that the potential purchase price of a property is lower than its true market value. If this condition holds then the investor will receive a higher rate of return than expected, and will therefore be able to show superior performance.

In the long run, of course, it is returns that count and not yields. If professional advisers use the latter as the basis for making investment decisions then it implies that they have some foresight concerning the prospects of individual properties which they are able to justify from an examination of the yields. In fact every property recommended for purchase is almost certainly suggested on the basis that it has a good yield, implying that it is under-priced. Coupled with this is the belief that the market is grossly inefficient so that prices do not reflect true market value. Such beliefs, however, are frequently based on opinion derived from one or two transactions, with little if any proper empirical support.

The implications are clear. The market is inefficient; professional advisors know that it is inefficient and are able to exploit that fact to the advantage of their clients. All relevant information is then impounded into the yield so that under-priced properties can be selected from period to period.

If this is true the annual results of property investment funds should, on the basis of professional advice and the strategy pursued, always show positive superior performance. Whether this is in fact the case can only be satisfactorily determined by empirical analysis.

What follows consists of the results of a study into the performance of a group of property bonds over a nine-year period 1973–82. Property bonds are important because they provide a publicly available record of their performance. In addition they represent a wide range of professionally managed property portfolios so their results can be considered typical of investment management practice.

If property portfolios are poorly diversified they should offer the opportunity for abnormal returns. The methodology for testing this proposition is that suggested by Jensen (1968) in the analysis of mutual funds in the USA.

The approach he adopted was to assume that the capital market is in equilibrium so that the expected return on any asset can be expressed as

$$E(r_p) = r_f + \beta_p[E(r_m) - r_f] \qquad (5B.1)$$

where

$E(r_p)$ = expected return on the asset;
r_f = risk-free rate of return;
$E(r_m)$ = expected return on the market portfolio;
β_p = systematic risk of the asset.

In risk premium form this can be redrafted as

$$E(r_p) - r_f = \beta_p[E(r_m) - r_f]. \qquad (5B.2)$$

In terms of expectations this equation will yield no abnormal performance. Ex-post, however, the record may show that realized returns have differed from expectations, in which case the empirical counterpart of equation (5B.2) can be written as the following regression model.

$$r_p - r_f = \alpha + \beta_p[r_m - r_f] + e \qquad (5B.3)$$

where

r_p = realized return on the asset;
r_m = realized return on the market portfolio;
α = abnormal performance;
β_p = systematic risk of the asset.

Expressing the model in risk premium form overcomes the problem of non-stationarity in the risk-less rate of return. Table 5B.1 shows the results of this analysis using continuously compounded quarterly returns for a sample of nine property bonds from the second quarter of 1973 to the fourth quarter of 1982. The return on the Money Management equally-weighted bond index was used as a proxy for the market portfolio and cash on deposit was used as the risk-free rate of return.

The fact that each bond includes different levels of liquidity is reflected in differences in systematic risk. Any values for α which were statistically significant would correspond solely to the performance of the underlying property.

There are two most important facts to note from Table 5B.1. Firstly,

Table 5B.1 Property bond performance using quarterly returns (1973–82)

Property bond	α	Standard error	β	Standard error	$\bar{R}^2$	Durbin–Watson
Abbey	−0.0049	(0.008)	1.47	(0.228)	0.52	2.24
M&G	0.0003	(0.004)	1.02	(0.141)	0.58	2.31
Guardian	0.0008	(0.003)	0.96	(0.095)	0.73	1.65
Cannon	0.0013	(0.003)	0.71	(0.086)	0.65	1.97
Hambro	0.0022	(0.002)	0.72	(0.049)	0.85	2.04
Hill Samuel	−0.0001	(0.003)	1.21	(0.082)	0.85	2.36
Merchant Investors	−0.0013	(0.001)	1.28	(0.122)	0.75	2.13
Tyndall	−0.0115	(0.009)	1.51	(0.153)	0.72	2.56
S&P	0.0027	(0.004)	0.95	(0.114)	0.65	2.26
Averages	−0.0012		1.09		0.70	

all the $\bar{R}^2$ figures are low in comparison with portfolios which would generally be considered well diversified. This latter figure is normally in the region of 0.95. The average of the portfolios examined is only 0.7, confirming the result given in Chapter 4 that property portfolios tend to be poorly diversified.

The second fact is that none of the α values is statistically significant and all are close to zero. It would appear that although there is the possibility for the portfolios to earn abnormal returns this was not achieved consistently over the nine-year period analysed. As a result the long-term returns on the bonds are likely to be heavily influenced by the risk class of the bond. Of the nine bonds analysed only Abbey, Hill Samuel, Merchant Investors and Tyndall had levels of market risk which were statistically greater than 1.00. It would appear that these bonds are pursuing a growth policy.

The Durbin–Watson statistic shows that in 7 out of the 9 portfolios examined there is some evidence of negative serial correlation in the residuals implying that over the periods analysed the values of most of the portfolios were falling.

Another way of examining this problem is to decompose the portfolio abnormal returns in the manner suggested by Fama (1972) as illustrated in Figure 5B.1.

The abnormal return (α) on a portfolio can be expressed as

$$\alpha = r_p - [r_f + \beta_p(r_m - r_f)]. \tag{5B.4}$$

This can be decomposed into a portion due to diversification and the remainder due to the ability to pick under-priced properties.

The portion of abnormal return due to diversification can be

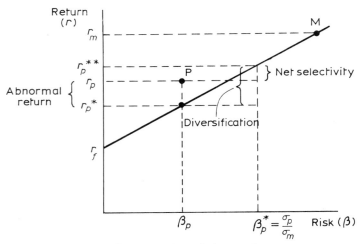

Figure 5B.1 Fama's decomposition of abnormal returns.

compared with a portfolio which is perfectly correlated with the market. It can be expressed as follows.

$$r_p^{**} - r_p^* = r_f + \beta_p^*(r_m - r_f) - [r_f + \beta_p(r_m - r_f)]$$
$$= (r_m - r_f)(\beta_p^* - \beta_p). \qquad (5B.5)$$

Similarly the component of abnormal return due to the ability to select properties is given by the difference between the abnormal return and the contribution from diversification. This can be expressed as

$$(r_p - r_p^*) - (r_p^{**} - r_p^*) = r_p - [r_f + \beta_p^*(r_m - r_f)]. \qquad (5B.6)$$

The abnormal return and its decomposition for each portfolio is given in Table 5B.2 from which it will be seen that the proportion of abnormal return due to diversification is negative and the remainder, due to selection is generally positive. This confirms the proposition that the portfolios are poorly diversified but have the potential for picking under-priced properties. The magnitude of the numbers involved however show that the selection ability could not be maintained on a consistent basis.

The information on systematic risk available from an analysis of bond returns can also be used to determine whether investors have some preference for a specified risk class. If there is a significant preference then a portfolio in a high risk class in one period should also exhibit the same risk preference in the following period. Table 5B.3 shows the systematic risk of each of the portfolios calculated over two non-overlapping four-year periods.

Table 5B.2 The decomposition of quarterly abnormal returns

Property bond	Abnormal return	Diversification	Selection
Abbey	−0.440	−0.034	−0.407
M&G	0.061	−0.019	0.080
Guardian	0.058	−0.022	0.080
Cannon	0.150	−0.011	0.161
Hambro	0.232	−0.004	0.235
Hill Samuel	0.028	−0.007	0.035
Merchant Investors	−0.085	−0.013	−0.073
Tyndall	−1.098	−0.015	−1.083
S&P	0.295	−0.014	0.309
Averages	−0.046	−0.015	−0.072

Table 5B.3 Systematic risk over two non-overlapping periods

Property bond	1973–77	1978–82
Abbey	1.52	1.11
M&G	1.13	0.67
Guardian	0.94	0.97
Cannon	0.74	0.47
Hambro	0.69	0.92
Hill Samuel	1.21	1.09
Merchant Investors	1.31	1.09
Tyndall	1.49	0.89
S&P	1.02	0.59
Averages	1.12	0.86

It will be seen that there is a considerable change in a number of the beta estimates for each of the periods. The second, more recent period, shows a lower average systematic risk which could be due partly to an increase in the average level of liquidity or a change in management policy concerning the type of properties being held. Comparison with Figure 2D.3 shows that the latter period covered a time when the systematic risk of property companies was declining. This was probably due to an increase in liquidity.

As the cost of managing property portfolios tends to be high, the risk class of the underlying property should remain fairly constant from period to period. This will be more significant for portfolios holding large numbers of properties. Changes in systematic risk of property bonds will, therefore, be influenced more by changes in liquidity. Thus the figures in Table 5B.3 are a reflection of investors' perceived attitude to risk.

The rank order coefficient of correlation between the two sets of figures is 0.546 ($t = 1.72$). Although this is not high the relationship is however positive. Thus the underlying property is likely to stay within the same risk class although portfolio managers can change this relationship by altering the liquidity. This will be influenced by the realized performance of individual bonds.

To summarize, the performance of property bonds gives rise to the following conclusions.

1. Probably all property portfolios are poorly diversified.
2. On average no property bond showed better performance than a market-based portfolio with the same risk.
3. Although there is some evidence to suggest that portfolio managers can pick under-priced properties they are not able to do this consistently from period to period.
4. There is a positive relationship between risk class in non-overlapping periods although this is not very strong and is influenced by the liquidity policy.
5. Returns measured in the long run are more likely to be influenced by the market risk of the portfolio.

References

Blundell, G. and Ward, C. W. R. (1987) Property portfolio allocation: a multi-factor model. *Land Development Studies*, 4, 145–56.

Brealey, R. (1983) *An introduction to risk and return from common stocks*, 2nd edn, Basil Blackwell, Oxford.

Dimson, E. and Marsh, P. (1985) Stock pickers: Chumps, champs or chimps?, *The Investment Analyst*, (75), January, 26–36.

Fama, E. (1972) Components of investment performance, *Journal of Finance*.

Fogler, R. H. (1984) 20% in real estate: can theory justify it?, *The Journal of Portfolio Management*, Winter, 6–13.

Jensen, M. (1968) The performance of mutual funds in the period 1945–64, *Journal of Finance*, **XXIII** (2), 389–416.

Jones Lang Wooton (1987) *The Property Review*, 1 (1), Winter.

Roberts, H. (1959) Stock market patterns and financial analysis: Methodological suggestions, *Journal of Finance*, March, 1–10.

Rudd, A. and Clasing, H. K. (1982) *Modern portfolio theory: The principles of investment management*, Dow Jones–Irwin, Homewood, Illinois.

6
Performance measurement

If investors are prepared to pay a premium for bearing risk then risk must play an important part in explaining performance. This has been the basic premise of this book and underlies how performance measurement should be carried out. This chapter places performance measurement in an economic context, examines the problems and proposes a methodology which takes account of the factors involved.

The reason for developing a system which is economically valid is because the achievement of returns is likely to be a requirement of future property investment. Although the development of investment advice at this level is slow the general intention can be summed up in the following comment by Patrick Hall (1985)

> ... certain funds are now making achievement of target returns a condition of appointment of their advisors. The advisors have obviously made an actual or implicit acceptance of the risk involved when agreeing to act on that basis.

This is of course a loaded statement. If an advisor accepts that he or she is appointed to achieve a target return then it is essential to have some understanding of the risks and returns involved. If a portfolio fails to meet a specific target then it may still be possible to show that for the risk taken it has earned an abnormal return. Without knowledge of the risks involved this is unlikely to be possible.

Some commentators would argue that this approach is over-sophisticated bearing in mind the nature of the market. Hager and Lord (1985) for example published a paper on the property investment market which seriously questioned the ability of valuers to arrive at similar views concerning the market value of a property and to draw meaningful conclusions concerning the performance of portfolios based on those valuations. These are serious issues which need to be addressed by the profession because they attack the very basis on which the market operates. If it is not possible to estimate the value of a property in a meaningful way then the whole basis of performance measurement is invalid and professional advice concerning the selection of properties is a waste of time. An investor need only select properties on a random basis as professional advice has no rational basis.

This contention must of course be invalid. The underlying basis of valuations is economically defensible and there is nothing wrong in extending this into the area of performance measurement. Appendix 2A examined the evidence in support of the belief that valuations acted as a good proxy for prices. In order to develop this area however it is worth considering the common problems frequently raised as they draw together many of the issues raised in this book.

6.1 The valuation process

Although there are a number of different valuation models used throughout the profession the accuracy of the valuations produced does not depend on the sophistication of the model used. It has been shown that the correct rôle of valuation models is to define the economic relationship between the relevant variables in order to arrive at values which would establish a market in equilibrium, in other words, one in which the market would clear if a group of properties were offered for sale at prices which were equal to their equilibrium values. The principal function of valuation models in this context therefore is to establish whether individual properties offered for sale are either under- or over-priced relative to their equilibrium market values. Although the market never remains in equilibrium for very long this view of the market is central to the determination of prices.

Allied to this is the fact that each valuation is drafted in terms of expectations and is a reflection on the quality and amount of information available.

Irrespective of the type of model they can all be expressed in either of the following forms:

$$E(V_t) = f[E(a, r, g)]|\phi_t \tag{6.1}$$

or

$$E(V_t) = f[E(a, y)]|\phi_t \tag{6.2}$$

where

$E(V_t)$ = expected value at time t;
  a = income;
  r = required return;

g = expected growth rate;
y = yield;
ϕ_t = information subset available at time t.

In other words the expected value of a property is a function of expected income, expected return and growth, or alternatively the latter two combined to give a yield, all subject to a subset of information. This will depend on location, lease structure, tenant, reversions, quality of building, voids and so on. There is therefore a distribution of valuations which will depend on the probabilities assigned to each variable.

Faced with the problem of valuing a property a valuer will determine the expected income, return and growth and adjust the figures depending on the subset of available information.

If a group of valuers is asked to value a property each will have different views concerning the relevant subset of information and the weight they wish to assign to each factor and will therefore arrive at different values. There is no correct answer in this case as each value will reflect the interpretation placed on the subset of information. The variation in values could be quite wide if the size of the information subset is restricted. For example, failure to inspect the property will restrict the amount of available information as will access to a limited data base concerning comparable market transactions and investment yields.

There will therefore be a distribution of values, and the sales price achieved should be a random drawing from that distribution if the market is using the same subset of information.

Given this scenario it is more likely that the average of a group of values will approach the market consensus as random variations in the subset of information will tend to cancel out. This can be seen in the Hager and Lord paper where control valuations were obtained. The two properties, A and B had average values of £722 000 and £590 000 respectively. Both were statistically significant at the 99% level. The corresponding control valuations of £725 000 and £605 000 are both within one standard error of the sample averages.

A valuer with intimate knowledge of a particular property and its location is more likely to arrive at a figure which represents the consensus of market opinion. In the case of property A the control value is within 0.4% of the average value and for property B the figure is 2.5%. This order of variation should not cause investors a problem if over time they can be shown to be random. A more serious problem would be caused by bias and would result if in the example quoted the control valuations consistently occurred at either end of the range of values.

6.2 Valuations versus prices

Allied to the joint problem of valuation and performance measurement is the question of whether valuations act as a good proxy for prices. Information on this is important because the basis of open market valuations rests on this assumption. If they are not a good proxy for each other in an open market context then carrying out performance measurement is likely to be suspect. In addition constructing property indices on the basis of valuations is unlikely to be representative of true market conditions and revising portfolios on the basis of valuations would be invalid. This aspect was examined in some detail in Appendix 2A where it was shown that current evidence would appear to confirm that valuations are a good proxy for prices.

6.3 Valuations versus valuations

If valuations are a good proxy for prices it is also reasonable to assume that valuations prepared by one firm are a good proxy for valuations prepared by another firm. If both firms have access to the same set of information, although they may interpret the information differently, at the portfolio level there should be a high degree of correlation.

This hypothesis was also tested in Appendix 2A to Chapter 2 by taking a group of properties which are regularly valued by two different firms. By regressing the valuations of one firm it is possible to test whether inter-firm valuations were a good proxy for each other.

Table 6.1 summarizes the results and shows that over the four-year period analysed the slope coefficients were all statistically indistinguishable from 1.00 and the intercept terms were indistinguishable from

Table 6.1 Regression results of inter-firm valuations

	a_0	Standard error	a_1	Standard error	$\bar{R}^2$
1981	0.108	(0.14)	0.985	(0.034)	0.98
1982	0.071	(0.12)	0.993	(0.030)	0.98
1983	−0.002	(0.10)	1.003	(0.029)	0.98
1984	0.000	(0.00)	1.006	(0.025)	0.99

zero. A plot of these results can be reviewed in Figure 2A.2 in Chapter 2.

Given that this analysis has been based on a sample of average properties and if, in addition, it can be assumed that the results are representative of the whole market then valuations prepared by different firms should be good substitutes for each other. Underlying this is the principle that both firms have access to the same or similar databases of comparable information. Although this sample is small it is anticipated that this general result should hold for much larger samples.

The above also suggests that there is no evidence of any significant bias between valuations prepared by different firms. In other words one firm does not appear to be consistently conservative relative to the other. Although there may be examples of this from time to time the bias should not be consistent if professional valuation standards are being maintained.

One of the rôles of the RICS is to strive to ensure that the standards used in ascertaining valuations are maintained consistently. If they are successful in maintaining high professional valuation standards then by assessing relevant information it should not be possible for firms to compete with each other purely on the quality of their valuations.

6.4 Valuation whim

If valuers are doing a good job of impounding relevant information into values, they should be responding to the information which is available to them at the time of the valuation. If they are responding to new information, changes in value should be independent of each other irrespective of the period over which the changes are measured.

This proposition was examined in some detail in Chapter 2 where it was shown that given the assumption that open market valuations conform to the recommendations of the RICS guidelines, valuers appear to be responding to new information. The implications for investors are two-fold.

1. At the level of open market valuations for individual properties, because there is little evidence of serial correlation, changes in value follow some form of random process implying that property values are properly discounted present values. The market therefore follows the requirements of a fair game.

2. On average investors will be compensated for the level of risk they take on. In other words properties with high systematic risk should be expected in the long run to offer higher rates of return than low risk properties.

These results follow from the assumption that all are open market valuations, having an equivalent open market price. There are many cases however where the price paid for a property differs considerably from its open market value due to special circumstances such as the sale to a tenant or a forced sale. In these situations it is possible to earn rewards which are higher (or lower) than implied by the risk class of the property. This is not inconsistent with the results presented above because the sales prices merely reflect a change in the subset of information available at the time of the original valuation. What is important however is that this evidence suggests that changes in value are less likely to be the result of whim than is generally imagined.

The fact that changes in valuation follow some form of random process should not be misinterpreted as confirmation of whim. Such a process is essential for an efficiently operating market. For example if the first-order serial correlation coefficients were large this would imply that valuers were merely changing valuations by a given percentage with little regard for any change in information. If this were true at the level of transaction prices it would mean that it would be possible to construct trading strategies to guarantee abnormal returns. Although abnormal returns can be observed in the property market there is no evidence to suggest that they can be sustained consistently from period to period. This is the crux of the matter, and the following extract from Franks and Broyles (1979) summarizes the position.

If securities are priced efficiently, their prices reflect forecasts of expected benefits from owning future cash flows capitalized at appropriate discount rates. Of course, individuals can disagree, and it is this disagreement which results in transactions. The aggregation and resolution of expectations in the transaction process produces an unbiased valuation in an efficient market. Fama (1965) describes such a market as a 'fair game' in which all participants have an equal opportunity for gains. Information emerging subsequent to transactions may prove the market valuation to have been incorrect, and some investors may be seen with hindsight to have experienced unusual gains or losses. However, no individual relying only on foresight can expect exceptional gains (or losses) on average if the market is a fair game.

Because no market is completely efficient there is sufficient incentive for investors to acquire costly information in order to earn abnormal returns.

This then is the framework within which performance measurement should take place. Performance measurement is concerned with the compensation achieved for the level of risk taken on and any additional return obtained through the ability to select and manage properties. This principle applies irrespective of the time period over which returns are measured and so performance measurement over a one-year period is a legitimate exercise.

This last point is important. Hager and Lord argued that because they believe valuations to be suspect, performance measurement must also be suspect. This is the view taken by Sykes (1983) also. Both these commentators however are incorrect in their interpretation of the evidence. The truth of the matter is that abnormal performance varies randomly and depends on changing prospects for individual properties. Performance measurement would be suspect in this case only if abnormal performance was not random but biased.

Like Hager and Lord, Sykes believes that performance measurement over periods greater than one year are likely to produce better results. Continuing this line of argument would imply that performance measurement over an infinitely long period would provide definitive results. Both however fall into the time−diversification trap which means that the variance of returns for an asset or portfolio will diminish the longer the period over which the returns are measured. Adopting this approach it is possible to reduce the variance of returns to zero by measuring returns over very long periods. This may sound attractive, tying in with the common belief that property is a long-term investment, and so intermediate changes do not matter, but it presupposes that investors have an infinitely long investment horizon and can afford to wait for their expectations to be realized. The reality however is far from this. Investment horizons have been getting shorter. It is not unusual to have a time-horizon of less than one year and for investors to readjust their allocation of funds between different assets at frequent intervals in order to maximize returns in the light of changing expectations. Given short time-horizons it is essential to be able to develop performance measurement systems which help with strategic investment decisions.

The above discussion has presented the background against which performance measurement should be undertaken. Before proceeding further however it is useful to examine the reasons for undertaking performance measurement as this will influence the type of information required from performance measurements systems.

6.5 Communication, accountability and research

There are three main reasons for undertaking performance measurement: communication, accountability and research.

Communication is important because portfolio results must be conveyed to the trustees or shareholders of a fund to show that targets are being met, to review existing and future strategies and to advise on any changes that need to be made. Without this reporting function it is impossible to make any valid decisions concerning the portfolio.

Because investment decisions are made on behalf of other people, accountability is likely to become more important as professional advisors are called upon to justify their advice. If precise terms of reference concerning expected rates of return are being specified as part of professional appointments, then it is likely there will be a greater awareness of the risk factors involved since this will be the only way investment decisions can be justified. Even though this may not be happening at present it is only a matter of time before accountability achieves greater importance.

The investor has two main objectives when making investments. He is trying to maximize his wealth position in addition to efficiently allocating his resources. Performance measurement looks at these aspects in a way which should make professional advisors accountable for their actions.

As a specialist field, performance measurement is relatively new. In the equity area it began in the early 1970s but did not have an impact on property until the late 1970s. Performance measurement systems for equities are also available which take risk into consideration. As yet this is not available commercially for property, and the principal reason here is the lack of education. The understanding of risk in property is relatively new and it has to be accepted that much of the data made available for analysis is often of poor quality thus giving rise to poor measures of risk. However it should not be assumed from this that the process of measuring performance is invalid. An understanding of the problems involved can only improve the interpretation of the results. In addition if the problems associated with the data are more widely known then there is a better chance of them being overcome, and the recording of information may well become more accurate.

The third reason for undertaking performance measurement is to provide information which can then be used for future research. Performance measurement of individual properties provides the basis for developing databases which can be used to carry out empirical analysis. It is only in this way that a better understanding of the property sector as an investment medium can be established.

6.6 Objectives of a performance measurement system

There are two main objectives for performance measurement:

1. External
   This covers such aspects as the measurement of performance against preset targets. These may be set in the market-place or by the trustees of a fund.

   In addition the system should be able to compare the performance of the portfolio against other funds as well as with other investments. It is at this level that the need to make an assessment of the riskiness of property relative to other funds or investments is important because the direct comparison of returns in different risk classes will give rise to an invalid intepretation.

2. Internal
   This aspect covers the comparison of returns of individual properties and tries to explain why one has performed better than another. It also leads directly to the balancing of the portfolio so that one sector of the market is not over-invested and therefore giving rise to poor performance.

   Adjustment of the portfolio weights is one way of trying to maximize the performance of the portfolio in the long-term and is part of the development of a strategy. It will be seen therefore that portfolio strategy and performance measurement go hand in hand with each other. This of course reinforces the need for a valid system of measuring performance.

Bearing in mind that professional advice is not free it makes sense to monitor whether it is good or bad. It is very difficult however to determine whether investment performance is due to skill or just good luck. It is not sufficient to just measure performance. It is essential to give some weight to the measures achieved and to establish where the performance is coming from. A good performance measurement system will therefore try to answer a number of important questions, such as those listed below.

1. What returns have been achieved?
2. How do the returns compare with other portfolios and assets?
3. Has the timing of purchases been good, i.e. have properties been acquired in full knowledge that the market was going to rise in the future?
4. Has the selection ability been good, i.e. have properties been acquired which were under-priced in an economic sense?
5. Can good performance be achieved consistently?
6. What is the risk profile of the portfolio?
7. How well-diversified is the portfolio?
8. Where are the returns coming from, i.e. is it skill or is it chance?

Given this background there are three aspects to performance measurement which need to be addressed, namely, measuring rates of return, choosing a bench-mark against which to make a comparison, and analysing the results.

6.7 Measuring returns

Although measuring the rate of return on a property or portfolio may seem relatively simple it is fraught with problems. For example should the return be 'money-weighted' or 'time-weighted'? Each has a specific part to play but it should be borne in mind that performance measurement is concerned with the relative skill of managers in the way they have utilized resources.

As relative skill is being measured it is not necessary to allow for the effect of general economic conditions. For example it is easy to earn high returns in a rising market but should the manager be congratulated for this? Similarly should he be blamed if the returns on the portfolio go down when the market is falling? These are general market influences which affect all players to a similar degree. Nevertheless if the manager is successful in the way he selects properties or manages the portfolio it should still be possible to identify relative skill. It is important therefore to use the correct calculation for the rate of return.

6.8 Money-weighted and time-weighted rates of return

The difference between these two rates of return arises when there are cash flows into and out of a portfolio and can be highlighted with some simple examples.

Consider for example an asset which has a present value of £100 which is invested for five years and revalued at the end of each year. Over the five-year period the value of the asset changes as the market rises and falls as shown in Table 6.2.

The time-weighted rate of return (TWRR) is the geometric mean rate of return and is calculated by taking the root of the product of all intermediate rates of return. Using the five-year period given above the TWRR can be calculated as:

$$TWRR = \sqrt[5]{(1.05 \times 1.10 \times 1.20 \times 1.02 \times 1.04)} - 1$$

$$= 0.08014$$

$$= 8.014\%$$

The money-weighted rate of return (MWRR) is the internal rate of return and is calculated by finding the rate of return which makes the terminal value of the portfolio together with any intermediate cash flows equal to the initial value. In the example given above, where there are no intermediate cash flows, the solution can be found as follows:

$$100.00 = \frac{147.00}{(1 + MWRR)^5}$$

$$MWRR = 0.08014$$

$$= 8.014\%$$

Because there are no intermediate cash flows the TWRR and the MWRR are identical and this will be the case irrespective of the period

Table 6.2 Changes in asset value

Periods	Market growth	Asset value
		£100.00
Year 0 to 1	5%	£105.00
Year 1 to 2	10%	£115.00
Year 2 to 3	20%	£138.60
Year 3 to 4	2%	£141.37
Year 4 to 5	4%	£147.02

over which the returns are measured. Differences between the two measures will occur however when intermediate cash flows are involved. This can be illustrated using a simple example of a cash flow spread over two years in both a rising and falling market.

Case 1: rising market

Assume that an individual has £200 to invest. The market is rising so he decides to invest £100 in some stocks. At the end of the first year the market has moved up by 15% and the reported forecast is that it will continue to rise. Our investor is encouraged by this and decides to invest the remainder of his money. During the second year his investment increases by 35%. What rate of return has he achieved?

The cash flows involved can be set out as shown in Table 6.3, and calculating the TWRR as before gives

$$\text{TWRR} = \sqrt{(1.15 \times 1.35)} - 1$$

$$= 0.2459$$

$$= 24.59\% \text{ per annum.}$$

In continuous returns format this is equal to 21.99% per annum.

Calculating the MWRR is more complicated because there are intermediate cash flows. The final value of the investment is £290.25 and has been created by an initial investment of £100.00 followed by a further investment of £100.00 one year later.

$$100.00 = \frac{-100.00}{(1 + \text{MWRR})} + \frac{290.25}{(1 + \text{MWRR})^2}$$

$$\text{MWRR} = 0.2755$$

$$= 27.55\% \text{ per annum.}$$

In continuous returns format this is equal to 24.33% per annum.

Table 6.3 Cash flows in a rising market

Years	Growth	First investment	Second investment	Totals
		£100.00		£100.00
Year 0 to 1	15%	£115.00	£100.00	£215.00
Year 1 to 2	35%	£155.25	£135.00	£290.25

Case 2: falling market

Assume now that the market conditions are reversed. The initial investment of £100 at the end of the first year has grown by 35% and this encourages our investor to make a similar deposit on the prospect of achieving a similar return in the second year. Unfortunately the market takes a turn for the worse and he only earns 15% during the second year. What rate of return has he earned overall? Again the position can be laid out in the form of a cash flow as in Table 6.4.

Table 6.4 Cash flows in a falling market

Years	Growth	First investment	Second investment	Totals
		£100.00		£100.00
Year 0 to 1	35%	£135.00	£100.00	£235.00
Year 1 to 2	15%	£155.25	£115.00	£270.25

The calculation of TWRR is exactly the same as before, and the fact that the returns have been reversed makes no difference to the calculation.

$$\text{TWRR} = \sqrt{(1.35 \times 1.15)} - 1$$

$$= 0.2459$$

$$= 24.59\% \text{ per annum}$$

In continuous returns format this is equal to 21.99% per annum.

Similarly the basis of computing the MWRR is exactly the same although the intermediate cash flows alter the end result.

$$100.00 = \frac{-100.00}{(1 + \text{MWRR})} + \frac{270.25}{(1 + \text{MWRR})^2}$$

$$\text{MWRR} = 0.2183$$

$$= 21.83\% \text{ per annum}$$

In continuous returns this is equal to 19.75% per annum.

We now summarize the results of this brief analysis in Table 6.5, and inspection reveals that the money-weighted rate of return (MWRR) is sensitive to the timing of cash into and out of the investment so that relative skill is not being measured. In other words we cannot tell from the MWRR whether the investor has been successful in picking under-priced assets. The time-weighted rate of return (TWRR) by

Table 6.5 Return comparisons in a rising and falling market

Market	Return	Type of return	
		Discrete	*Continuous*
Rising	TWRR	24.59%	21.99%
	MWRR	27.55%	24.33%
Falling	TWRR	24.59%	21.99%
	MWRR	21.83%	19.75%

contrast neutralizes the effects of timing so that relative skill can be measured. This is the more appropriate return to use for performance measurement purposes.

If we accurately determine cash flows for a portfolio and can time them carefully it is possible to calculate both the MWRR and TWRR and make a comparison between them. With this information we can draw the following conclusion.

If MWRR > TWRR then the timing of investment into and out of the fund has been good.
If MWRR < TWRR then the timing of investment into and out of the fund has been poor.

This finding can be verified by examining the example given above. By tracking both rates of return over a number of years it is possible to see how well a portfolio is performing in relation to its timing.

The time-weighted rate of return is the favoured method for use in performance measurement.

6.9 Calculating time-weighted rates of return

There are two common methods used for calculating time-weighted rates of return: the exact method discussed here and the linked internal rate of return, discussed in the next section.

The exact method highlights the main problem associated with calculating time-weighted rates of return because it requires a valuation every time there is a cash flow. Each of these has to be precisely dated in order to produce accurate measures. The calculation of money-weighted rates of return also requires the precise dating of cash flows but has the advantage that it requires only two valuations: one at the beginning and one at the end of the period.

The formula proposed by the Bank Administration Institute (1968) for calculating the exact time-weighted rate of return is as follows.

$$\text{TWRR} = \frac{1}{t_f - t_0} - \left[\ln\left(\frac{V_f}{V_0}\right) - \sum \ln\left(\frac{V_j + C_j}{V_j}\right) \right] \qquad (6.3)$$

where

C_j = net amount of jth cash flow;
V_0 = initial value of the fund;
V_f = final value of the fund;
V_j = value of fund immediately before jth cash flow;
$t_f - t_0$ = time in years from beginning to end of period under consideration;
TWRR = continuous time-weighted rate of return.

Using the cash flows and returns for the falling market situation given in Table 6.4, equation (6.3) can be used to calculate the TWRR as follows.

$$\text{TWRR} = \frac{1}{2}\left\{ \ln\left(\frac{270.25}{100.00}\right) - \left[\ln\left(\frac{135.00 + 100.00}{135.00}\right) + \ln\left(\frac{270.25}{270.25}\right) \right] \right\}$$

$$= \tfrac{1}{2}[0.9941 - (0.5543 + 0)]$$

$$= 0.2199$$

$$= 21.99\% \text{ compounded continuously.}$$

This procedure is equivalent to calculating continuous internal rates of return (MWRR) for each sub-period when a cash flow occurs and then taking the average by weighting each return by the length of its corresponding sub-period.

It will be seen from this that difficulties can arise because the dating of cash flows may not be exact. For example, the rent from a property under the terms of a lease may be expected quarterly in advance. Even though there may be a delay in receiving payment the date at which it is recorded may well be taken so that it is in line with the terms of the lease. In addition it is unlikely that there will be a valuation at the time of the cash flow so that an estimation of value would be needed. Errors of this nature can give rise to substantial variation in the calculation of time-weighted rates of return.

In general if cash flows are quarterly it is important that valuations are quarterly. Similarly if cash flows are monthly, valuations must also be undertaken monthly. This immediately introduces a further problem as the precise valuation of a property will be expensive and will reduce its return. However valuations at less frequent intervals will introduce errors into the return calculation.

The technique proposed for getting over this problem is to use what is known as the linked internal rate of return method.

6.10 The linked internal rate of return

This method divides the time-span over which the time-weighted rate of return is estimated into sub-periods. Knowing the value of the fund at the beginning and end of each period together with the timing and amount of each of the cash flows into or out of the fund it is possible to compute the internal rate of return for each sub-period. The time-weighted rate of return is then calculated by taking an average of the internal rates of return assuming they are continuously compounded on an annual basis. The weight used for each sub-period is equal to the length of the period.

This approach is an approximation and does of course produce some errors in the estimation of returns. Table 6.6 for example which is adapted from the BAI (1968) report shows typical mean absolute percentage errors which are likely to be experienced in a stock portfolio during periods of moderate growth.

It will be seen from this that even during periods of moderate growth there are likely to be significant errors in the measurement of returns if there is a wide variation in the dating of cash flows and the frequency of valuations.

These are the problems confronted when calculating time-weighted rates of return for property portfolios. The most frequently used method in commercial performance measurement systems for calculating rates of return is the mean fund concept.

Table 6.6 Mean absolute errors for time-weighted rates of return calculated using the linked internal rate of return method, after BAI (1968)

Dating precision of cash flows	Frequency of valuations			
	Monthly	Quarterly	Half-yearly	Annually
Daily	0.04	0.45	0.56	0.60
Monthly	0.12	0.48	0.59	0.62
Quarterly		0.51	0.61	0.64
Half-yearly			0.67	0.62
Annually				0.69

6.11 The mean fund concept

This has many similarities to the linked internal rate of return method described above. It is based on the assumption that a value for a property is known at both the beginning and end of each period but there are no valuations at the time of any intermediate cash flows. The principle involved is to measure the internal rate of return adjusted for the average capital employed during the period. The formula frequently used is as follows:

$$r = \sum_i \frac{[M_{i_n} - M_{i_{n-1}} - C_{i_n} + I_{i_n}]}{[M_{i_{n-1}} + C_{i_n}(1 - t_i)]} \tag{6.4}$$

where

M_{i_n} = capital value of property i at period n;
$M_{i_{n-1}}$ = capital value of property i at period $(n - 1)$;
C_{i_n} = capital expenditure on property i at period n;
I_{i_n} = income received from property i at period n;
t_i = timing of expenditure C_i as a proportion of total period from $(n - 1)$ to n.

An alternative to this is to substitute half the capital expenditure in the denominator rather than weight each expenditure by the time period involved:

$$r = \sum_i \frac{[M_{i_n} - M_{i_{n-1}} - C_{i_n} + I_{i_n}]}{[M_{i_{n-1}} + \frac{1}{2}(C_{i_n})]} \tag{6.5}$$

Both methods provide a money-weighted internal rate of return which can be used as a proxy for the time-weighted rate of return. The system can be applied to both individual properties and portfolios. The accuracy of the results depends on the dating accuracy of valuations and whether individual cash flows are weighted by time or whether the alternative of taking half the costs is used. Another important aspect concerning accuracy is whether an accurate open market valuation is available at the date of the return calculation. If this is not the case an interpolated value may be used although linear interpolation between two other values could miss important intertemporal changes. Linear interpolation could also introduce serial correlation into the return series.

Currently there are no empirical tests to compare the accuracy of conventional return calculations with exact methods. It is likely however that reported returns could have mean absolute errors in the region of $\frac{1}{2}\%$ per annum. This clearly points to the need to develop better estimation techniques for calculating returns. One approach which may produce better results would be to use regression methods. This analysis would specify those factors important in explaining known values at a particular point in time. The regression model could then be used to identify the value of all non-valued properties at the same time. When used in the analysis of equity portfolios this approach has been shown to reduce the error in estimating returns by a factor of about three. Considering that conventional return calculations could have absolute errors in the region of $\frac{1}{2}$% the regression approach is certainly worth developing.

6.12 Choosing a bench-mark

It is at this point that it is important to address the issue of risk. Current commercial systems assume that all properties lie within the same risk class, which is the same as the market, and so a direct comparison of returns is adequate for ranking performance. This is illustrated in Figure 6.1 on the basis of the security market line discussed earlier. It will also be seen from this illustration that the ranking of returns is independent of market conditions.

As it is unlikely that each property carries the same level of market risk, obviously this type of comparison will have economic meaning only when the return on the property market is the same as the risk-free rate of return, in which case the security market line will be horizontal.

The more usual situation is for the security market line to be either upward or downward sloping. If risk is taken into consideration it

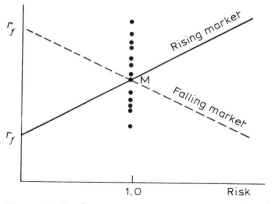

Figure 6.1 Performance measurement assuming that all properties lie within the same risk class.

would not be unusual to find two properties with the same total returns differing in terms of abnormal performance because of differences in risk class, as illustrated in Figure 6.2.

This is the method of identifying abnormal performance which has been one of the central themes of this book. However it is not without its critics. One of the principal problems concerns the return on the property market which is usually calculated from an index. If we have an ex-ante securities market line based on the risk-free rate of return and the expected return on a property index, it could be argued that the residual return on a portfolio can be considered abnormal if it is in excess of the predicted risk adjusted return.

Richard Roll (1977) has argued that any ranking of performance is possible if measurement is made relative to an ex-ante inefficient index. We also know that all property indices are inefficient because they contain residual risk. However, if performance is measured relative to an ex-ante efficient index then no security or property will have abnormal performance.

If it were possible to identify an ex-ante efficient index then it would also be possible to identify expected returns and variances in advance. Performance measurement would not therefore be needed because the expected risks and rewards would be known in advance. By using an efficient index there would be no winners or losers.

Performance measurement does not however take place in an ex-ante world. Markets never remain permanently in equilibrium and it is because of this dis-equilibrium that investors can obtain abnormal returns. Since it is not possible to locate an ex-ante efficient index an inefficient index will be able to designate winners and losers. If we

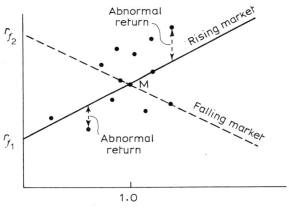

Figure 6.2 Abnormal performance when differences in market risk are taken into consideration.

therefore consider performance measurement to be like a race then a sensible index should be chosen in advance and retained for future comparison. What constitutes a sensible index however is still open to debate.

The question of the appropriate risk measure is also debatable. Investors do not generally hold highly diversified portfolios nor do they confine themselves to a single asset. The appropriate risk measure is neither beta nor total risk but somewhere between the two. A composite risk measure is difficult to achieve and the argument for using beta is that it acts as a proxy for the true risk when measured against an index which is representative of market trends. The same argument holds true with the valuation of properties. Although individual investors hold poorly diversified portfolios, the open market valuation of a property will be estimated as if it were part of highly diversified portfolio. This ensures consistency in the valuation process and also helps to explain why the expected risk premium is generally in the region of 2.0%. The actual price achieved depends on an individual investor's perception of the added value that a particular property can offer.

The whole exercise of performance measurement is concerned with identifying relative skill and seeing whether the managers are able to add value to the portfolio. If managers have some skill in identifying under-priced assets then they should be able to do this on an ex-ante basis. As ex-post realization is the only way of measuring the existence of abnormal returns it is likely to be subject to considerable noise which will obscure any true managerial skill.

A major part of this exercise is to estimate the risk class of the properties and portfolio under consideration. Here we are up against a major problem because the standard approach for estimating beta is to use regression analysis to relate the returns on the property or portfolio to the market. In applying this to property there are three problems which present themselves.

1. Performance measurement is usually carried out over periods of one year whereas risk measures using regression analysis needs to be based on five years of monthly data in order to provide reliable estimates. The resulting betas relate only to the period for which data are available. They are historic measures and adjustments are usually made to derive expected values based on the assumption that there is a tendency for all betas to regress towards the grand mean of one. Although a simple average can be employed it is more common to employ a Bayesian adjustment.

2. If regression analysis were used in a property context for estimating betas, the resulting values would be understated because of the high levels of serial correlation which exist in property indices, although with sufficient time-series data this problem can be overcome. Considerable work has been undertaken on the intervaling effect and Dimson (1978) has proposed a method which derives efficient estimates for beta when individual assets are infrequently traded.

3. It is unlikely that there would be sufficient time-series data available on many properties to estimate risk levels. This would be particularly true for new properties which would have no time-series data at all.

As performance measurement is concerned with the difference between what was expected and what is actually achieved, it would seem to make sense to make use of the model described in Appendix 2F for estimating the expected market risk at the beginning of the measurement period. Using this as the basic risk measure it is then possible to establish the appropriate risk-adjusted rate of return which can then be compared with the realized return on the portfolio.

The risk-adjusted return calculated in this way is the bench-mark return. The implication of this is that a fund manager could have achieved the bench-mark return merely by investing a proportion of funds in a riskless asset and the remainder in the index. The exact proportion of funds would be related to the market risk. For example if the portfolio had a beta of 0.6 then 60% of funds invested in the index with the remaining 40% being invested at the risk-free rate of return would have produced a return equal to the bench-mark return. This is a passive strategy, while by investing in a risky portfolio the fund manager has exercised his skill in trying to perform better than the bench-mark. The difference between the two is an estimate of the abnormal return. This can be either positive or negative depending on whether the performance is superior or inferior. The abnormal return can also be redrafted in terms of net present value so that the abnormal return is expressed in absolute terms.

6.13 Analysing the results

This then is the basic measure of performance. It is a significant improvement on a straight comparison of returns because it recognizes that risk is an important aspect of the returns generating process.

There is a lot of noise however associated with this measure so that despite its added advantages the abnormal return is not a useful statistic on its own. It does not necessarily identify skill as the return achieved could be due entirely to chance. A measure of skill can be determined however by calculating what is known as the information ratio. This is merely the abnormal return divided by the residual standard deviation of the portfolio. This would imply that a low abnormal return which is accompanied by a high information ratio is better than a high abnormal return with a low information ratio. Conventional performance measurement systems are unable to produce this level of interpretation.

The main aim of performance measurement is to see whether the manager of a portfolio has some skill. It is therefore useful to further analyse the abnormal return to see how it is made up. This is known as performance attribution. Conventional systems quite often include an analysis of performance attribution although it is based on the assumption that all properties carry the same level of market risk. The validity of such attribution analysis must therefore be questioned.

The basis of performance attribution is to analyse the sources of abnormal return to see whether they match the intentions of the manager. This aspect was considered briefly in the analysis of property bonds covered in Appendix 5B.

A formal definition of abnormal return can be written as follows.

$$\text{Abnormal return} = \text{actual return} - \text{expected return}$$

$$= r_p - [r_f + \beta_p(r_m - r_f)]. \tag{6.6}$$

The abnormal return only arises because the portfolio has not diversified down to the systematic risk level. The investor is therefore exposed to the total risk of the portfolio and not just to systematic risk. The total risk can be expressed as

$$\sigma_p{}^2 = \beta_p{}^2 \sigma_m{}^2 + \sigma_e{}^2 \tag{6.7}$$

As the residual risk, $\sigma_e{}^2$, has not been diversified away it is necessary to ask whether the additional return has compensated for the extra risk taken on as a result of the reduction in diversification. This can be determined by estimating the hypothetical beta that would result if the residual risk were zero. From equation (6.7)

$$\sigma_p{}^2 = \beta_p{}^2 \sigma_m{}^2$$

so

$$\beta_h = \frac{\sigma_p}{\sigma_m}. \tag{6.8}$$

Using this measure of beta gives rise to an expected return due to diversification, $E(r_b)$. The abnormal return can therefore be considered as a return due to selectivity which can be split into two components, part due to diversification and the remainder due to net selectivity.

$$r_p - E(r) = \quad [E(\hat{r}) - E(r)] + [r - E(\hat{r})] \qquad (6.9)$$

| Return due to selectivity | Return due to diversification | Return due to net selectivity |

The portion of return due to **diversification** is what the investor would get if only systematic risk were taken into consideration, in other words if the portfolio were highly diversified. The return due to **net selectivity** measures performance adjusted for poor diversification. It can be either negative or positive depending on whether the investor is under- or over-compensated for taking on the additional risk.

A simple example will serve to illustrate the principles involved. Assume that over a five-year period a portfolio has the following data.

Average rate of return: 25.5%
Standard deviation: 15.5%
Systematic risk: 1.15

The market data over the same period is estimated as

Average rate of return: 12.5%
Standard deviation: 10.5%.

Assume also that the risk-free rate of return over the period was 6.5%. From this information it is possible to derive the following:

1. The abnormal return
   To calculate the abnormal return we first need to calculate the expected return, from equation (6.6).

   $$E(r) = 6.5\% + 1.15(12.5\% - 6.5\%)$$
   $$= 13.4\%.$$

   The abnormal return is then the difference between the actual and expected return, so

   $$r - E(r) = 25.5\% - 13.4\%$$
   $$= 12.1\%.$$

2. Estimation of market risk of portfolio with same total risk, from equation (6.8) gives

$$\beta_h = \frac{\sigma_p}{\sigma_m} = \frac{15.5}{10.5} = 1.48.$$

3. Expected return of portfolio for this level of market risk, from equation (6.6) again, gives

$$E(r_h) = 6.5\% + 1.48(12.5\% - 6.5\%)$$

$$= 15.38\%.$$

This is the expected return on the portfolio assuming that all its risk is systematic.

4. Excess return due to diversification

$$E(r_h) - E(r) = 15.38\% - 13.40\%$$

$$= 1.98\%$$

This represents the extra return that could have been achieved had the portfolio consisted only of systematic risk. The fact that there is an excess return indicates that the portfolio is poorly diversified. The figure can be either positive or negative and will depend on the total risk of the portfolio and the slope of the market line.

5. Net selectivity

As the abnormal return measures total selectivity, the net selectivity effect can be found by removing the excess return due to diversification.

$$[r - E(r)] - [E(r_h) - E(r)] = r - E(r_h)$$

$$= 25.50\% - 15.38\%$$

$$= 10.12\%$$

As this figure is positive it indicates that the portfolio has adequately compensated the investor for the additional risk taken on due to the fact that the portfolio is poorly diversified.

The results of this analysis are shown in Fig 6.3.

In this example most of the abnormal return can be attributed to net selectivity. This is what we would expect from an analysis of a property portfolio. As Chapter 4 has shown most property portfolios tend to be poorly diversified so that most of the return is dependent on selection ability or creative management.

A detailed analysis of a property portfolio using the technique described above is contained in Appendix 6B.

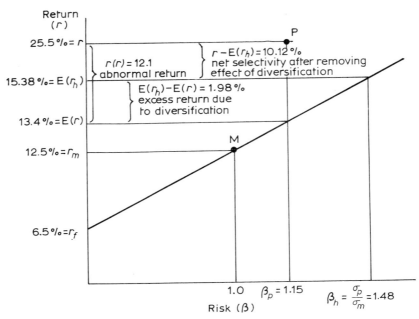

Figure 6.3 Portfolio analysis and performance attribution.

6.14 Conclusion

This chapter has shown that it is possible to utilize the principles of portfolio theory to undertake an analysis of performance which can give a better interpretation of the way a portfolio is performing. The measures used are relatively easy to calculate and represent an improvement over the direct comparison of returns. They also recognize that risk is an important part of performance and as such should not be ignored. Some of the measures, such as the comparison between money-weighted and time-weighted rates of return, require a reasonable time-series of data so that they can be interpreted properly.

As these techniques become more established our interpretation of performance will be enhanced. This has a direct bearing on investment strategy as it is only through a better understanding of the underlying processes that investment performance can be improved.

Other more sophisticated measures are available which reveal more detailed aspects of performance. Their use depends on much better data than is available at present. At this stage however it is felt that the measures described here act as a good starting point. Much remains to be done in terms of quantifying portfolio risk and achieving better measures of market risk.

Appendix 6A: Performance measurement of a property portfolio

This appendix uses the principles discussed throughout this book to analyse a portfolio on a risk-return basis. In adopting this approach the belief is that it will provide greater insight into the underlying performance of the portfolio and offer evidence, if it exists, of management skill.

The portfolio chosen for analysis has been randomly put together from properties taken from a number of different portfolios. It consists of 36 properties, which is about the average size of most portfolios, but has not involved any management skill in terms of the selection of individual properties or sector weighting. On this evidence the analysis should expose the presence of poor management skill.

The analysis which follows does not provide the usual regional breakdown of rental income, capital growth or total returns as these aspects are generally statements of fact. Although they are important, the emphasis here is on investment performance.

It has been shown that the performance of portfolios depends on the ability of investors or their advisors to select properties which are under-priced or to manage a portfolio in such a way that its net present value is maximized. Net present value is not a measure frequently used in performance analysis but it is useful because it provides a measure of absolute rather than relative value. In terms of the discussion in Chapter 1 it confirms whether management skill has contributed any added value to the portfolio. The function of performance measurement is to detect whether there is any evidence of superior performance which results in added value. Commercially available systems are unable to do this in an economically defensible way because they suffer from three basic problems.

1. The index used for comparison purposes usually has a high level of serial correlation in its returns. This is generally introduced by the averaging of property values round the publication date of the index. Property indices are therefore moving averages. When used in performance measurement it is difficult to attribute abnormal performance to superior skill or the fact that the index number is not a true reflection of the underlying market.

   Serial correlation is a major problem and can be very high for property indices. A by-product of high serial correlation is that it is possible to forecast with a high degree of accuracy the return for the next period. Given this information it would then be possible to construct a trading strategy which could capitalize on this information. (For example if the first-order serial correlation coefficient in a property index is 0.8 this implies that it is possible to explain 64% (i.e. 0.8×0.8) of the return in the next period. This would provide better than average odds on which to earn above average returns, if they really existed.)

The reason this does not happen in practice is because the high levels of correlation are caused by statistical problems in the way the index is calculated.

2. The index used almost certainly carries some specific risk which could be diversified away. The index return may not therefore be the true market return.
3. The risk of the portfolio under consideration is assumed to be exactly the same as the market. Observed abnormal performance based on this assumption may therefore be due to differences in risk class and not due to management skill.

The combination of these factors means that commercial property performance measurement systems probably say very little about real performance and it is doubtful whether the reported output provides useful information in guiding future investment strategy. This position is unlikely to change unless there is greater emphasis on justifying investment decisions. There is some evidence to suggest that this is beginning to happen and it will of course accelerate as institutions become more accountable for their actions.

The following analysis is an attempt to overcome some of these problems by trying to solve them in a way which is economically valid. The output from the analysis aims to provide the following information for each property as well as the portfolio:

1. an estimate of market risk;
2. an estimate of abnormal return in terms of rates of return as well as net present value;
3. an estimate of risk-adjusted required rates of return;
4. an estimate of expected growth;
5. an analysis of the abnormal return in terms of diversification and selection ability;
6. an estimate of specific risk;
7. an estimate of the reduction in risk.

Analysis period

The period used in this analysis covers one year from December 1988. This was a time when the market showed a considerable downturn with a significant fall in total returns. Irrespective of market conditions if there is any management skill evident in the portfolio then it should still be possible for the portfolio to exhibit evidence of positive abnormal return even during the downturn.

In order to proceed with the analysis in a structured way additional information on the risk of individual properties together with details of the market are required. These are considered below.

Risk assessment

The following analysis recognizes that risk is important in explaining performance. This has been discussed at length in earlier chapters and has identified that estimates are required for both market risk and total risk.

Market risk

The measure of market risk used in this analysis is based on the system described in Appendix 2F by relating individual property data to similar information obtained for the market. The reference portfolio used in this case is the IPD Monthly Property Index and the technique provides an estimate of the volatility of each property in terms of the beta coefficient (β) relative to that index. Using a different index would of course produce a different set of volatilities. It is therefore important to maintain the same reference index when performance measurement is being carried out from period to period.

The principle being followed is to determine the expected risk for each property at the beginning of the analysis period based on information available at that time. This information is then used to determine the expected return over the year. The outcome at the end of the period is related to what was expected to happen at the beginning of the period. The analysis therefore relates ex-post performance to ex-ante expectations.

Total risk

To consider risk in more detail an assessment needs to be made of the total risk of both the market and each property. This is measured in terms of the standard deviation of returns.

As far as the market is concerned the standard deviation of returns calculated using the IPD index will be understated because the return series has high levels of serial correlation. Appendix 6B examines this problem in relation to both the IPD and Richard Ellis monthly indices. From this analysis it will be seen that the standard deviation of returns calculated using the raw index figures understate the true standard deviation by a factor of about three. This correction is therefore made in estimating the total risk of the market.

With regard to estimating the total risk of individual properties it will be evident that this could be acheived by simulating the risk using some form of Monte Carlo or multi-factor model. (Multi-factor models for predicting the risk of individual properties are in their infancy. They nevertheless have much to offer and it is probable that significant advances will be seen in this area.) This would require a considerable number of calculations particularly if the portfolio consisted of a large number of properties.

An alternative approach is to assume that each property is similar to the average for its sector and to use this as the starting point for estimating total risk. Appendix 4B showed that an estimate of the average standard deviation could be calculated from knowledge of the level of risk reduction for each sector. This figure can then be adjusted by taking account of the latest observation expressed as a deviation from its average value.

The rationale for doing this is to assume that the latest observation is as likely as any other observation. In other words there is no prior knowledge which would attach any greater weight to the realized return. The adjusted estimate for the total risk is therefore calculated merely by averaging the average standard deviation with the observed deviation.

Another way at looking at this is to say that if we had a model which was capable of forecasting the return in the next period it would have predicted the actual return achieved. This return is merely a random drawing from a distribution of returns for the property being analysed.

Although this system can be criticized for being too simplistic it should be borne in mind that the low correlation of returns between individual properties is such that a portfolio can achieve high levels of risk reduction very quickly. The benefits to be gained by using a complex simulation are likely to be diversified away after a few properties have been added into the portfolio. This is not to say that simulation models should be ignored. They have a useful rôle to play and could produce insights into the way property behaves.

It should be recalled that portfolio theory is drafted in terms of expectations. The standard deviation of returns for each property should therefore be an estimate of expected risk at the beginning of the analysis period because it is on the basis of this knowledge that the portfolio is managed. In the absence of other information this approach probably represents a reasonable approximation of an ex-ante standard deviation.

The riskless rate of return

The riskless rate of return has been taken as the return that would have been earned on government securities with a maturity period of one year. The figure can be calculated by compounding Treasury Bill rates to the required period.

The market rate of return

The reference portfolio is taken as the returns on IPD monthly index. Any other property index could have been used although this has been chosen to maintain consistency with the calculation of market risk.

One of the principal issues in the choice of a reference index is to ensure that it is representative of the market in which the portfolio is operating.

The target position

The targets for the portfolio should be clearly defined as part of the analysis. These should be set by the trustees in discussion with the portfolio manager as a means of guiding the long-term strategy of the portfolio. For example one portfolio might be constructed on the basis of being income producing whereas another might be aimed at producing capital growth. Each of these implies a different level of market risk, or beta, which sets the target for comparison. Not all trustees are content with the desire to out-perform an index.

The target beta should therefore represent a long-term optimal position. With this information it should be possible to establish whether management skill was successful in controlling portfolio risk in line with expectations.

For the purposes of this analysis it will be assumed that the long-term optimal position for the portfolio is to maintain a beta of 1.00. This is a neutral position and is probably similar to a policy adopted by funds.

Portfolio analysis

Using the above information Table 6A.1 analyses the portfolio in terms of its market risk and provides the following information:

1. property reference;
2. the capital weight of each property in the portfolio;
3. the market risk of each property assuming upward only rent reviews;
4. the expected return for each property;
5. the actual return achieved for each property;
6. the abnormal return for each property;
7. the net present value for each property.

Although the retail sector has the highest market risk many properties have negative or low abnormal returns. The net present value of this sector is −£2 418 001 even though its total return is making a positive contribution of 1.73% to the total return of the portfolio. The poor performance of the retail sector could not be reversed by the office or retail sector even though they achieved positive net present values of £1 276 801 and £270 801. The average returns of these sectors are similar at 24.44% and 24.76%. After adjusting for risk, however, their abnormal returns are 8.87% and 10.47%. On a value-weighted basis their contributions to the performance of the portfolio are only 1.46% and 0.33%.

It will be seen that there is considerable variation in the total returns over the one-year period. They range from −3.30% to +67.30% and illustrate how risky investment in property can be. The variation in abnormal returns measured relative to the security market line is also wide and ranges from −21.30% to +53.99%. By contrast the range of expected returns is very low. At the bottom end it is the same as the riskless return of +13.31% but only rises to +18.23% reflecting the

Table 6A.1 Portfolio analysis

Analysis date: 1988–89
Portfolio name: Sample portfolio
Assuming upward only rent reviews

Portfolio value 1988: £98 348 000

Sector	Reference	Weight	Risk beta	Expected % return	Property % return	Abnormal return	Net present (£) value
Industrial	005	0.16	0.13	13.75	22.50	8.75	10 671
	031	0.71	0.00	13.31	32.00	18.69	106 190
	002	0.73	0.00	13.31	25.80	12.49	70 091
	006	2.80	0.58	15.32	30.80	15.48	351 258
	014	11.18	0.70	15.74	12.70	−3.04	−267 409
	Sector averages		0.28	14.29	24.76	10.47	
	Standard deviation		0.30	1.04	6.94	7.51	
	Contribution	15.38	0.09	2.40	2.73	0.33	270 801
Office	008	0.51	0.00	13.31	23.50	10.19	41 870
	009	0.53	0.00	13.31	32.00	18.69	79 971
	025	0.61	0.00	13.31	67.30	53.99	285 205
	001	0.64	1.08	17.09	10.50	−6.59	−33 867
	012	0.69	0.52	15.12	31.30	16.18	90 950
	027	1.23	1.19	17.47	20.50	3.03	30 249
	030	1.31	0.87	16.35	25.90	9.55	99 726
	004	2.02	0.94	16.58	22.10	5.52	89 275
	023	2.11	0.31	14.38	23.40	9.02	152 800
	026	2.54	0.37	14.60	37.30	22.70	476 048
	029	2.91	0.68	15.69	21.10	5.41	124 800
	019	3.15	0.81	16.15	15.00	−1.15	−29 372
	036	3.79	0.17	13.90	21.00	7.10	218 842
	007	3.86	0.67	15.65	9.30	−6.35	−190 852
	028	3.97	1.20	17.49	27.40	9.91	318 744
	011	4.32	0.61	15.42	43.30	27.88	985 560
	024	4.73	1.09	17.10	7.30	−9.80	−374 231
	020	6.61	0.42	14.78	29.40	14.62	787 512
	033	11.18	1.34	18.00	−3.30	−21.30	−1 876 429
	Sector averages		0.65	15.56	24.44	8.87	
	Standard deviation		0.42	1.47	14.72	15.67	
	Contribution	56.71	0.45	9.13	10.58	1.46	1 276 801
Retail	003	0.45	0.81	16.14	7.70	−8.44	−30 030
	010	0.46	1.05	16.98	−2.00	−18.98	−68 680
	013	0.46	1.09	17.13	5.00	−12.13	−45 354
	016	0.66	1.23	17.59	24.90	7.31	38 051
	034	0.71	1.09	17.11	8.80	−8.31	−46 969
	017	1.15	1.12	17.23	29.20	11.97	110 586
	035	1.68	0.20	14.02	15.90	1.88	25 627
	018	1.78	1.26	17.69	2.00	−15.69	−222 124
	022	3.89	1.34	17.98	7.80	−10.18	−322 276
	032	3.89	1.34	17.98	7.80	−10.18	−322 276
	015	4.20	1.41	18.23	7.70	−10.53	−357 599
	021	8.39	0.85	16.29	−1.30	−17.59	−1 176 957
	Sector averages		1.07	17.03	9.46	−7.57	
	Standard deviation		0.32	1.10	9.15	9.28	
	Contribution	27.72	0.30	4.75	1.73	−3.01	−2 418 001
	Value-weighted totals		0.85	16.28	15.05	−1.23	−870 402
	Equal-weighted totals		0.74	15.88	19.49	3.61	

fact that during the analysis period the security market line was relatively flat.

Figure 6A.1 plots the total return of each property relative to its market risk and also provides an illustration of the spread of market risk for each sector within the portfolio. Various aspects of performance shown in this illustration are discussed below.

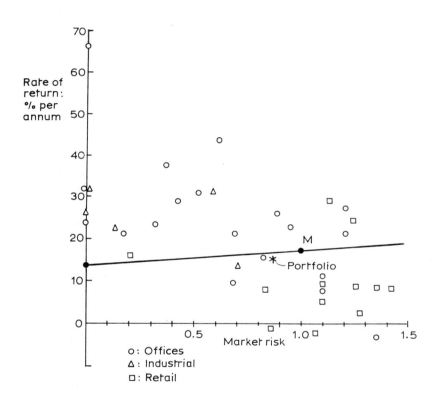

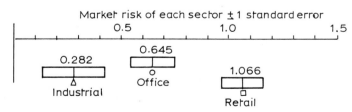

Figure 6A.1 Portfolio analysis 1988–9.

The net present value

The capital value of the portfolio at the beginning of the period has been calculated as £98 348 000. The net present value of the portfolio however is negative (−£870 402).

Even though the capital value of the portfolio increased over the year, after taking into consideration the income received and discounting back to the beginning of the year at the risk-adjusted expected return, the portfolio has a value less than the original capital value. This implies that over the year the management of the portfolio was insufficient to compensate for the risk of the portfolio.

Clearly any increase in capital value is important to the fund. However, bearing in mind that it is unlikely that the increase could be distributed, the negative net present value indicates that the portfolio has not contributed any added value. If this trend is maintained over a number of years it could have a serious impact on the performance of the portfolio.

The portfolio market risk

A further aspect revealed in these figures is the fact that the portfolio beta on a value-weighted basis is only 0.85. The long-term optimal position has been decided as 1.00 and so the risk class of the portfolio is considerably below expectations. Again if this is maintained over a number of years the long-term return on the portfolio will under-perform the target position.

The equally-weighted beta at 0.74 indicates that the portfolio is being influenced by some large-valued properties. In fact over 22% of the value of the portfolio is contained in two properties. This is not unusual for property portfolios and the influence of sub-optimal weights can often impair performance. The two properties concerned, i.e. 014 and 033, have returns of 12.70% and −3.30% respectively. After adjusting for the differences in risk class, which for property 033 ($\beta_{033} = 1.34$) is almost twice that of property 014 ($\beta_{014} = 0.70$), their abnormal returns are −3.04% and −21.30%. It is this aspect which has severely affected performance.

In terms of future strategy the fund should aim to select properties or manage the portfolio in such a way that the market risk is increased up to the target level. Figure 6A.2 plots the changes in market risk of the portfolio assuming that the acquisition policy followed the sequence shown in Table 6A.1 and the market conditions during the

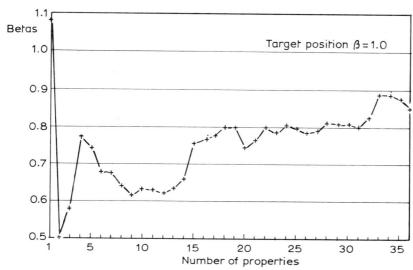

Figure 6A.2 Changes in portfolio market risk.

analysis period have remained constant. This is shown merely for illustrative purposes. The sequence of acquisition will have no effect on the final figure which will remain the same irrespective of when the properties were included. It is nevertheless a useful guide to show how the risk of the portfolio can change when the next property is acquired.

Comparison between the market and portfolio

Table 6A.2 provides a comparison between the market index and the portfolio during the analysis period.

Analysis of abnormal return

From Table 6A.2 it will be seen that the abnormal return on the portfolio is −1.23% (i.e. 15.05% − 16.28%) during 1988–9. On its own this figure does not mean a great deal because it has to be related to the residual risk of the portfolio. The abnormal return results from the the fact that the portfolio is poorly diversified and so the fund manager is in effect placing bets on individual properties to produce better than expected returns.

Table 6A.2 Comparison between the market and the portfolio (1988–9)

		IPD	Portfolio
Total return	(% per annum)	16.80	15.05
Capital growth	(% per annum)	11.20	9.27
Income yield	(% per annum)	5.60	5.92
Equivalent yield	(% per annum)	7.77	8.17
Rental value yield	(% per annum)	8.22	9.28
Expected growth	(% per annum)	6.24	5.15
Expected return	(% per annum)		16.28
Total risk	(standard deviation % per annum)	8.80	8.66
Market risk	(standard deviation % per annum)	8.80	7.48
Residual risk	(standard deviation % per annum)	0.00	4.38
Diversification	(R^2)	100.00	74.47
Reduction in risk	(%)	68.00	56.71

Although the IPD index contains some residual risk for the purposes of this analysis it is assumed to have an R^2 value of 100%.

Figure 6A.1 shows that the portfolio has considerable upside potential since most of the abnormal returns lie above the security market line during the analysis period. The effect of differences in capital value on performance is illustrated in Table 6A.3 which compares the abnormal performance by number with the value-weighted returns. Although there were more properties on the upside of performance the effect of value-weighting was more marked on the downside.

This aspect of performance results from the portfolio being poorly diversified. Even though the portfolio holds 36 properties its R^2 value is only 74.47%. The fund manager, if he has skill, should be able to exploit this position by managing or selecting those properties which contribute to positive abnormal returns. The figure of −1.23% is merely one observation in a time series of abnormal returns which will fluctuate around some average value. The fact that it is negative in one year cannot be taken as confirmation of consistent poor management. If however we are trying to evaluate the skill of the portfolio manager,

Table 6A.3 Comparison of abnormal performance

Abnormal performance by number of properties	Value-weighted returns
23 properties > 0%	+5.51%
15 properties < 0%	−6.74%
Aggregate abnormal performance:	−1.23%

we need to know the target value of the abnormal return needed to justify taking on the additional risk arising from the portfolio not being efficiently diversified.

Fortunately this can be established quite simply using the principles of portfolio theory and assuming that the investor maintains the same level of indifference to both the systematic and residual components of the portfolio (Rudd and Clasing, 1982). On this basis the required abnormal return can be found by equating the mean/variance ratio for the active part of the portfolio to the same ratio for the passive or target position. This is shown in equations (6A.1) and (6A.2).

$$\frac{\alpha_p}{\sigma_e^2} = \frac{\beta_p[E(r_m) - r_f]}{\beta_p^2 \sigma_m^2}. \tag{6A.1}$$

$$\alpha_p = \frac{[E(r_m) - r_f]\sigma_e^2}{\beta_p \sigma_m^2}. \tag{6A.2}$$

In these equations the abnormal return (α_p) represents the required position and is based on the long-term market premium, $[E(r_m - r_f]$, the average market variance, σ_m^2 and the target position for the portfolio, β_p.

We have already established that the portfolio beta should be 1.00. If we also assume that the market premium is expected to be about 2%, all that remains to be established is an estimate of the long-term market variance. At the present time this is the most difficult figure to calculate accurately. Further research is needed in this area but it is probable that the average standard deviation is in the region of 8% per annum, giving a variance of 64%.

From Table 6A.2 the residual standard deviation for the portfolio has been estimated at 4.38% per annum. Substituting these figures into equation (6A.2) gives the following required abnormal return.

$$\alpha_p = \frac{(2\%)(4.38\%)^2}{(8\%)^2}$$

$$= 0.60\%$$

This is the compensation required to justify taking on the extra risk in the portfolio, and assuming constant conditions it is the figure around which the observed abnormal return will fluctuate from year to year. The figure is low in relation to the residual risk so the portfolio has an information ratio of only 0.14 (0.60/4.38). As this figure is analogous to a t-value it will be evident that it is not statistically significant and cannot be regarded therefore as being any different from zero. In fact in any year there will a 95% chance that the abnormal return will lie within the range of −8.16% to +9.30% (i.e. 0.60% ± [2 × 4.38%]).

If however portfolio returns are measured over increasingly long periods the residual standard deviation will decrease inversely with the square root of the time. For example over 1988−9 the residual risk was estimated to be 4.38% per annum. If returns are measured over a period of, say, 25 years the residual standard deviation, assuming that it has not changed on an annual basis, will now be $4.38\%/\sqrt{25}$, i.e. 0.876% per annum. Using the same target abnormal return the information ratio will increase to 0.68 and the abnormal return will now have a 95% chance of lying within the range −1.15% to +2.35%.

The question which needs to be asked is how long will it take before the portfolio manager can be 95% sure that his investment actions are providing significant positive abnormal returns? This can be found by using a one-tailed *t*-test at the 95% level of significance, comparing this with the information ratio, and solving for the holding period. For a one-tailed test the appropriate *t*-value is 1.64 and the required period can be calculated as follows.

$$\frac{\alpha_p}{\alpha_e/\sqrt{T}} = 1.64 \qquad (6A.3)$$

$$T = \left(\frac{1.64\sigma_e}{\alpha_p}\right)^2 \qquad (6A.4)$$

Again using the figures from the above analysis the value for T can be found as follows.

$$T = \left(\frac{1.64 \times 4.38}{0.75}\right)^2$$

$$= 143.3 \text{ years.}$$

On this evidence it will take over 140 years before the portfolio manager can be 95% certain that his management strategy is profitable!

It is difficult to read a lot into this other than the fact that it may be difficult to be absolutely certain that professional investment advice will lead to positive abnormal performance. The reason the period is so long is because the residual risk represents a high proportion of the total risk of the portfolio and as discussed in Chapter 4 it requires very large property holdings to show significant reductions in residual risk. For an equity portfolio with the same number of assets the residual risk would be relatively small. When combined with appropriate estimates for the market premium and risk the investment strategy can be usually be justified in about 25 years.

For property the estimates given above are very sensitive to the figure used for the long-term market variance. (If for example the consensus view was that the long-term standard deviation of returns for the market was 6% (i.e. 2% less than used in this example) then the period required to justify the strategy would drop to 45 years. Similar adjustments to other estimates can also have a dramatic effect on the estimated period.)

This analysis clearly indicates that the emphasis should be on maintaining positive abnormal returns. This in turn points to the need to be able to utilize information in such a way that the manager can influence added value.

Further information about the abnormal return can be gleaned by undertaking the decomposition shown in Chapter 6. Given estimates of the portfolio risk it is possible to split this as follows.

1. Abnormal return due to diversification: 0.47%. This is the extra return that could have been earned had the portfolio consisted only

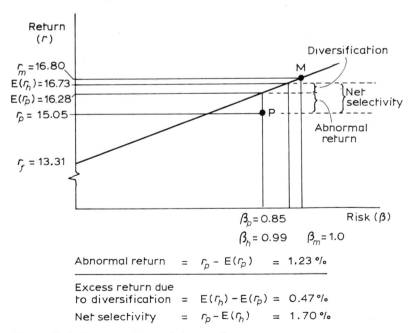

Figure 6A.3 Decomposition of abnormal returns.

of systematic risk. The fact that there is an excess return indicates that the portfolio is poorly diversified.

2. Abnormal return due to selection: -1.70%. Because the abnormal return measures the total selectivity, the net selectivity effect can be found by taking out the excess return due to diversification. In this case it has resulted in a negative figure implying that the investor has not been adequately compensated for taking on the excess risk.

In this example not only is the portfolio poorly diversified but the ability to select properties or manage the portfolio is also poor.

The fact that the portfolio is poorly diversified should not be considered as a problem. Only by taking on additional risk is it possible to out-perform the market. Over the year however the selection/management skill has not been good. This should alert the manager to the fact that portfolio should be looked at more closely in the future to ensure that the effects of net selectivity are not repeated.

The decomposition of abnormal returns are shown in Figure 6A.3.

Analysis of timing

In Chapter 6 it was shown that comparison of the time-weighted rate of return with the money-weighted rate of return enables an evaluation of the success of the timing decision to be made. To do this successfully however requires data on the cash flows from the portfolio over long periods.

Over a single period the analysis of timing can be evaluated by comparing the target position for the portfolio with the observed position. The difference in betas between the two positions will therefore be due to timing decisions concerning the management of the portfolio. This can quantified as follows.

The target position for the portfolio has been established with a beta of 1.00, while the observed beta is only 0.85. The difference in beta represents the return earned during the year due to timing.

$$\mathrm{E}(r_p) - \mathrm{E}(r_t) = (\beta_p - \beta_t)(r_m - r_f) \qquad (6\mathrm{A}.5)$$

where

$\mathrm{E}(r_p)$ = expected return based on observed beta, β_p;
$\mathrm{E}(r_t)$ = expected return based on target beta, β_t.

Using the figures from the portfolio gives the following return due to timing.

$$E(r_p) - E(r_t) = (0.85 - 1.00)(16.80\% - 13.31\%)$$
$$= -0.52\%.$$

This loss of 0.52% during the year was due the timing decisions which prevented the observed beta from matching the target position. In other words the manager's bets were placed on those properties which on a value-weighted basis contributed to negative abnormal return. In a well-managed portfolio it should have been possible to avoid this if the manager had access to good information concerning the prospects for each property.

Analysis of total risk

A major part of the above analysis has revolved around the partitioning of the variance into its component parts, i.e. market risk and residual risk.

The total risk of the portfolio has been computed by taking the estimates of total risk and market risk for each property and using this information to estimate all the variance and covariance terms for each property. These are then weighted by their respective property values and combined to form the total portfolio risk. This is a straightforward application of the Markowitz model where the weights of the individual properties are fixed.

Using this approach, the total risk can be split into its market and residual components and compared with the market as shown in Table 6A.4. The risk reduction profile for the portfolio is shown in Figure 6A.4 using the same assumptions as given in Figure 6A.2. This merely shows how the risk profile changes in response to adding properties to the portfolio. It also shows that it is possible for the risk of the portfolio to increase when new properties are added. It cannot be assumed therefore that the addition of properties will always show a reduction in risk.

Table 6A.4 Comparison of total risk for the portfolio and the market

	Total risk	Market risk	Residual risk	R^2
Variance	75.13	55.95	19.18	74.47
Standard deviation	8.66	7.48	4.38	
Market standard deviation	8.80	8.80	0.00	100.00

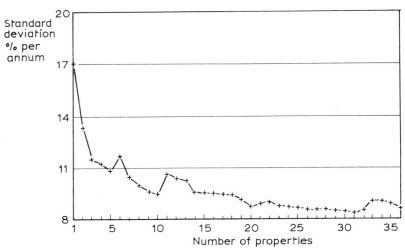

Figure 6A.4 Reduction in total risk.

Table 6A.4 shows that the residual risk is still very high even though the portfolio consists of 36 properties. This means there will be a considerable variation in realized returns from year to year relative to the market because this additional risk has not been diversified away. The reduction in risk relative to the average is only 56.71% whereas the limit for a well-diversified portfolio is likely to be about 68%.

It should be noted that the residual risk is a function of the correlation of returns between the individual properties. This is what causes the wide spread of returns in the portfolio. Residual risk will therefore exist even though a performance analysis system may not take risk into consideration.

Table 6A.4 also shows that the market explains about 74% of the variation in returns of the portfolio. The remaining 25.5% is therefore due to the effect of the individual properties.

Conclusion

This analysis has confirmed our belief that the portfolio has exhibited little management skill. It is way below its target in terms of market risk and although it has good upside potential, poor control of the value-weighting of the properties has contributed to a negative abnormal return. The lack of management skill during the period has failed to add value to the portfolio. The analysis also revealed that it would take many years to prove conclusively that the strategy being pursued by the portfolio manager was correct.

In terms of using this information for strategic purposes it must be borne in mind that it is not always possible to readjust a portfolio in response to the findings due to the relatively long time it takes to buy or sell a property. The system described should be used to develop a picture of the performance of individual properties over a number of years. This will help to identify those properties which are potential candidates for disposal.

A further development would be to examine the optimal weights for each of the properties in order to maximize the return for the level of risk achieved. This would help to identify whether the portfolio was over- or under-weighted in any sector or region.

This appendix has gone beyond the simple performance analysis of property portfolios and has shown that by incorporating risk it is possible to gain better insights into the way a portfolio is performing. In the long run this type of analysis will provide a better basis for developing portfolio strategy and monitoring performance.

This simple application has shown that it is probably very difficult to achieve abnormal returns on a consistent basis even though the opportunities for doing this may well be present. The opportunities for improving performance will only come about by exploiting inefficiencies in the market. This in turn relies upon a good information network which will alert the investor to opportunities which can give rise to returns which have not fully discounted the information subset. It is in these areas that the application and understanding of risk analysis will become more important.

Appendix 6B: Comparison of property indices

The measurement of performance requires the use of an index which is intended to be representative of the market. With so many property indices available it is difficult to know whether they are each telling the same story.

Although it is only within the last several years that total returns have been published on an annual basis it is interesting to note that the development of indices has undergone a rapid transformation and with the recent publication of monthly indices they are beginning to achieve the status of other financial index numbers.

Apart from the fact that monthly indices provide a more up to date indication of property movements they are extremely valuable because they can provide the basis for undertaking a performance analysis over any period.

The two indices of monthly figures are published by the Investment Property Databank (IPD) and Richard Ellis Investment (RE). This appendix makes a comparison between the total returns series of each of these indices to see whether they are tracking the same market.

Other indices

Before proceeding with this analysis however it is useful to consider some of the other indices which are available to see how they compare. The principal concern is with average total returns, standard deviations and serial correlation. Table 6B.1 summarizes these figures for a group of common indices. Because of the wide variation in the dates of the indices it is difficult to make a direct comparison between the figures produced. However one or two interesting points do emerge. For example where the periods analysed are comparable, the average returns are in the same order although there is a significant difference in magnitude in the annual standard deviation of returns between those indices which have been computed on an annual basis and those which are quarterly or monthly. This difference is highlighted in the serial correlation figures which show a greater dependence between total returns when the index number is calculated over shorter periods.

It will be recalled from Chapter 2 that if the market is reasonably efficient then the serial correlation coefficients should be close to zero. This would indicate that pricing of properties was responding to new information. The fact that there is such a difference between the serial correlation coefficients and that this increases significantly as the index

Table 6B.1 Comparison of property indices

Index	Frequency	Dates	Returns % per annum	Annual standard deviation	Serial correlation–lags							
					1	2	3	4	5	6	7	8
WGS-Total returns	Annual	Dec 79–Dec 88	14.72	8.83	0.30	-0.20	-0.17	-0.19	-0.36	-0.23	0.18	0.18
The property index	Annual	Mar 81–Mar 89	13.79	10.02	0.54	-0.04	-0.20	-0.24	-0.31	-0.23	-0.03	0.01
MGL-CIG index	Annual	Dec 78–Dec 88	16.04	7.14	0.55	-0.02	-0.22	-0.34	-0.46	-0.38	-0.08	0.13
Jones Lang Wooton	Annual	Jun 67–Jun 68	15.23	10.13	0.09	-0.04	-0.28	-0.20	-0.21	0.01	-0.07	0.02
Hiller Parker	Annual	May 73–May 88	20.01	17.78	-0.03	-0.06	0.11	-0.31	-0.23	-0.03	-0.08	0.02
Jones Lang Wooton	Quarterly	Mar 82–Dec 88	12.07	4.15	0.70	0.62	0.48	0.31	0.20	0.12	0.00	0.00
Investment Property Databank	Monthly	Dec 86–Dec 89	21.54	2.37	0.74	0.58	0.42	0.33	0.21	0.10	0.04	0.00
Richard Ellis	Monthly	Jan 88–Apr 90	20.28	4.23	0.74	0.60	0.42	0.19	0.11	0.02	-0.01	-0.01

period gets shorter seems to indicate statistical problems associated with the index numbers, obscuring the true underlying performance.

The following analysis shows how this affects the IPD index and makes a comparison with the RE monthly index.

The IPD index

The IPD index consists of 894 properties spread over each sector of the market. From the analyses carried out in earlier chapters it will be evident that there will be some residual variance although this is unlikely to be great. As long as the properties used in the index are representative of the market the index should provide a good indication of market movements.

The problem with property indices is that they rely solely on valuations as the input data. If valuations are a good proxy for prices then this should not cause too great a problem. The principal difficulty comes in the dating of the valuations and how market information is taken into consideration in forming the value. With annual data, for example, it would not be uncommon to incorporate valuations which occur around the valuation date. As it is impossible to value all properties on exactly the same date, the reported index figure will be an average of valuations on either side of the publication date. An index reporting the market in, say, March may well contain valuations which have been prepared in February or April.

When the interval between valuations shortens the problem is exacerbated. With monthly indices it would not be unusual to find the reported figure picking up information from a previous period. Alternatively it is possible that some valuations may have been prepared on a sampling basis. For example a portfolio which is valued monthly may well have only a sample of the properties formally valued. The percentage change estimated for the sample is then applied to all other properties in the portfolio. This process will introduce serial correlation. It is also possible that valuers may find it difficult to respond accurately to small changes in the market.

The combination of these factors, because they are occurring over a relatively short period, are likely to induce higher levels of serial correlation in the return series for monthly data than exhibited in the annual data. This can be illustrated by plotting the serial correlation coefficients for the IPD monthly returns series over a three-year period. As shown in Figure 6B.1, the correlation coefficients take a long time to die away. The first-order coefficient is 0.739 indicating a high level

		-1.0 -0.8 -0.6 -0.4 -0.2 0.0 0.2 0.4 0.6 0.8 1.0
1	0.739	xxxxxxxxxxxxxxxxxx
2	0.575	xxxxxxxxxxxxxx
3	0.423	xxxxxxxxxxx
4	0.330	xxxxxxxx
5	0.213	xxxxx
6	0.097	xxx
7	0.039	xx
8	-0.003	x
9	0.023	xx
10	-0.043	xx
11	-0.167	xxxxx
12	-0.265	xxxxxxx
13	-0.362	xxxxxxxxx
14	-0.414	xxxxxxxxxx
15	-0.468	xxxxxxxxxxxx
16	-0.520	xxxxxxxxxxxxx

Figure 6B.1 Serial correlation coefficients for the IPD monthly returns index (1987–90).

of dependence on the returns in the previous period. Squaring this figure gives an R^2 value of 0.55 which implies that 55% of the return in one month can be explained by the return in the previous month!

Because the serial correlation coefficients shown in Figure 6B.1 die away slowly they imply that the underlying series is non-stationary. This is one in which the underlying returns-generating process does not have a constant mean and/or a constant variance. This finding is important because non-stationary series are difficult to model in a simple algebraic form and consequently difficult to forecast. (An example of a non-stationary series which can be modelled is a random walk with drift. However it has been shown that the returns-generating process for property does not conform to a random walk but follows a fair game.)

As far as performance measurement is concerned, the principal difficulty serial correlation creates is that the standard deviation of returns will be understated. Table 6B.1 shows this to be the case and the following analysis uses the technique described in Appendix 5A to re-estimate the standard deviation.

Using continuous returns it will be recalled that the time series of returns can be transformed into a stationary series by lagging the returns by one period. The parameters of equation (5A.16) can be found by regression analysis, the results of which are given in equation (6B.1).

$$r_t = (1 - A)B + A(r_{t-1}) + (1 - A)e_t \qquad (6B.1)$$
$$= 0.247 + 0.865(r_{t-1}).$$

The standard deviation of returns computed for the returns series over the three-year period has been estimated as 0.683% per month. Given that the value of A from equation (6B.1) has been estimated as 0.865 this enables the adjusted standard deviation to be computed from equation (5A.16) as follows.

$$\text{Var}\,(rm) = \text{Var}\,(r)\,\frac{1 - A^2}{(1 - A)^2}$$

$$= (0.683)^2\,\frac{1 - 0.865^2}{(1 - 0.865)^2}$$

$$= 6.44\%\ \text{per month.}$$

This can be converted to an annual standard deviation as follows:

$$\sigma_{rm} = \sqrt{(12 \times 6.44)}$$

$$= 8.80\%\ \text{per annum.}$$

A comparison between the unadjusted and adjusted standard deviation figures is given in Table 6B.2, from which it will be seen that after taking account of the effects of serial correlation there is a factor difference between the unadjusted and adjusted figures of over 3.4. In other words the standard deviation of returns calculated from the raw index numbers are likely to be over three times too small in relation to their true value.

Table 6B.2 Comparison between unadjusted and adjusted standard deviation figures for the IPD total returns index (1987–90)

Period	Unadjusted	Adjusted
Monthly (% per month)	0.68	2.34
Annual (% per annum)	2.54	8.80

Proof that by using this transformation the smoothing has been removed from the series can be seen by plotting the serial correlation for the adjusted returns, as shown in Figure 6B.2. The impact on the original returns series, by plotting the unadjusted returns in relation to the adjusted return, can be seen in Figure 6B.3.

Clearly this shows that there are considerable changes in return from month to month which are being obscured. It is useful to note however that although there is an increase in the variance the mean return over the period being analysed will not change (see Appendix 5A).

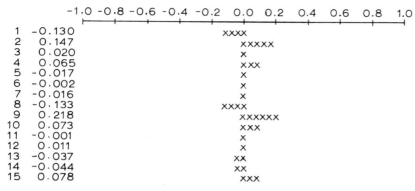

Figure 6B.2 Serial correlation coefficients after taking out effects of smoothing.

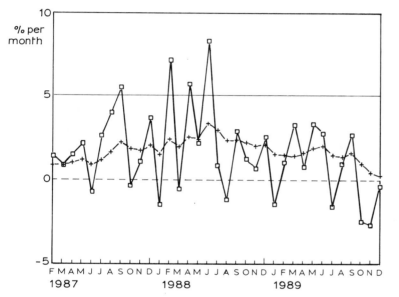

Figure 6B.3 Comparison of adjusted and unadjusted returns for the IPD monthly returns index.

The IPD index compared with the RE index

The only other monthly index currently published is prepared by Richard Ellis and based on a smaller sample of about 200 properties. Because it is smaller than the IPD index it is likely to carry more residual risk. If however both indices have been drawn from samples of properties which are representative of the market then both should be telling the same story.

One way of examining this is to plot the index of total return over comparable periods, as illustrated in Figure 6B.4. The coefficient of correlation between the two sets of index numbers is 0.99 implying a close relationship between the two indices. This however does not give a true relationship between the underlying return series and can be revealed by plotting the monthly returns for each index, as shown in Figure 6B.5.

The difference between the two indices is now more marked although there is a general tendency for the two indices to move in the same general direction. The coefficient of correlation between the two returns series drops to 0.83 with an R^2 value of 0.69 (i.e. 0.83^2) implying that one index explains only about 69% of the variation in returns of the other.

Bearing in mind they are both tracking the same market this figure is very low. One of the reasons for this is the fact that both indices are built from different properties and the diversification of the two indices differs. This factor is then compounded by the smoothing that occurs in both returns series.

Table 6B.3 compares the average return and standard deviation of both indices. The average returns are approximately the same but there is a considerable difference in the standard deviations with the RE index having greater variation in returns on a monthly basis than IPD.

Table 6B.3 Comparison of average monthly returns and standard deviations for RE and IPD

Index	Average return	Standard deviation	Numbers
IPD	1.64%	0.913%	894
RE	1.69%	1.218%	200

Despite these differences the two indices should still be reasonably good substitutes for each other if they are tracking the same market. This can be tested by regressing the returns from the RE index against the IPD index. The hypothesis being tested is that the intercept term should be zero and the slope coefficient should be statistically indistinguishable from 1.0.

The results of this analysis, given in Table 6B.4, confirm our hypothesis. Over the period analysed the slope coefficient was slightly greater than 1.0 so there was a tendency for the RE index to

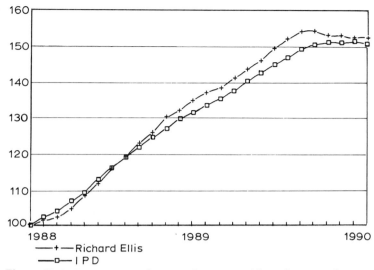

Figure 6B.4 Comparison of IPD and RE (monthly indices) total return indexes.

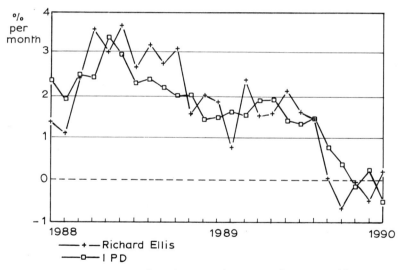

Figure 6B.5 Comparison of total returns for IPD and RE (monthly returns).

out-perform IPD. This is clearly seen in Figure 6B.4 although this trend is not statistically significant.

It would appear therefore that the two indices are tracking the same market.

Table 6B.4 Regression analysis of RE versus IPD (1988–90)

$RE = \alpha + \beta \, (IPD)$

α	β	$\bar{R}^2$
−0.259	1.18	0.698
(0.291)	(0.156)	

Standard errors are shown in brackets.

Like the IPD index the RE index also suffers from high levels of serial correlation, as shown in Figure 6B.6.

Using the same technique as described above it is possible to show that by taking out the serial correlation, the unadjusted standard deviation of returns increases by a factor of 2.9 from 1.218% to 3.54% per month. A comparison of the unadjusted and adjusted figures is given in Table 6B.5.

We have already shown that the average returns for both series is the same. If our belief is that the true variance of the two series is the same

Table 6B.5
Comparison between unadjusted and adjusted standard deviation figures for the RE total returns index (1988–90)

Period	Unadjusted	Adjusted
Monthly (% per month)	1.22	3.54
Annual (% per annum)	4.23	12.26

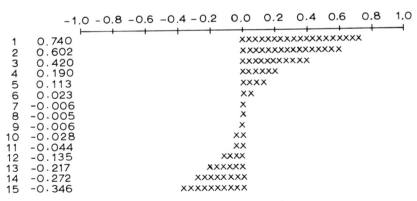

Figure 6B.6 Serial correlation coefficients for the RE monthly total returns index (1988–90).

it should be possible to infer the value of A for the IPD index given the adjusted standard deviation estimated above. It will be recalled that the value of A was used in equation (5A.16) and is taken from the slope coefficient of the regression of current returns versus lagged returns.

As we know that on a monthly basis the adjusted standard deviation of returns for the RE index is 3.54% and that the unadjusted figure for the IPD index over the same period is 0.913%, it is possible to substitute these figures into equation (5A.16) in order to solve for the value of A. This is shown below.

$$\text{Var}\,(r_{RE})_{\text{(ADJUSTED)}} = \text{Var}\,(r_{IPD})_{\text{(UNADJUSTED)}} \frac{1 - A^2}{(1 - A)^2}$$

$$(3.54)^2 = (0.92)^2 \frac{1 - A^2}{(1 - A)^2}$$

If this is rearranged it can be transformed into the form of the following quadratic equation.

$$15.81A^2 - 29.62A + 13.81 = 0$$

$$A = 1.0 \text{ or } 0.875$$

The empirical version of A can be tested by regressing current returns on the IPD index over the period from January 1988 to February 1990 against values lagged by one month. If both indices have the same standard deviation of returns our prior belief is that the slope coefficient should be 1.00 or 0.875. The results are shown in Table 6B.6.

Table 6B.6 Regression for IPD returns against lagged values (1988–90)

$\text{IPD}_t = \alpha + \beta(\text{IPD}_{t-1})$

α	β	$\bar{R}^2$
−0.124	1.00	0.78
(0.21)	(0.11)	

Standard errors are shown in brackets.

The regression analysis shows a slope coefficient of 1.0 which is statistically significant. In fact the alternative figure of 0.875 calculated above is within 1.14 standard errors of this solution.

Bearing in mind the small sample size used (i.e. 24 observations) this result shows that the true standard deviation of returns for the IPD and Richard Ellis monthly indices is probably the same but the observed values are masked by statistical problems.

Conclusion

The existence of monthly property indices is a positive move which helps to integrate property into the financial markets. The problems which are associated with the indices should not, however, be overlooked. For example, if a fund manager decides to adjust the value of some of his properties in line with changes in an index he will induce serial correlation into the time series of returns for his properties if the index has significant levels of correlation. If those properties then form part of another index that too will have its serial correlation compounded.

The method used for computing property indices is to rely solely on valuations. Although this is intuitively attractive it is not the only way of dealing with the problem. Explanatory multi-factor methods based on known transactions may also provide a valid approach which may well be more sensitive to changes in the market. This area has yet to be explored in any detail in the UK commercial property market.

The principal problem caused by serial correlation however is for the standard deviation of returns to be understated. This has an effect on the analysis of risk in the context of performance measurement. If this is ignored then the relationship between risk and return could appear to be far more favourable for property than is actually the case. Comparisons with other investment assets without making appropriate adjustments could be totally misleading and in the context of mixed-asset allocation could produce biased results.

References

Bank Administration Institute (1968) *Measuring the investment performance of pension funds*, Park Ridge, Illinois.

Dimson, E. (1978) *Risk measurement when shares are subject to infrequent trading*, Institute of Finance and Accounting, London Business School, IFA–30–78.

Fama, E. (1965) The behaviour of stock-market prices. *Journal of Business*, 38, 34–105.

Franks, J. and Broyles, J. (1979) *Modern managerial finance*, John Wiley & Sons, New York.

Hager D. P. and Lord, D. J. (1985) *The property market, property valuations and property performance measurement*, Institute of Actuaries.

Hall, P. (1985) The measurement of property investment performance: Some considerations, *Journal of Valuation*, 3, (4), 376–84.

Roll, R. (1977) A critique of the asset pricing theory's tests: Part 1, On past and potential testability of the theory, *Journal of Financial Economics*, March, 4, (2), 129–76.

Rudd, A. and Clasing, H. K. (1982) *Modern Portfolio Theory: the principles of investment management*, Dow Jones-Irwin, Homewood, Illinois.

Sykes, S. (1983) The uncertainties in property valuation and performance measurement, *The Investment Analysts*, (67), January, 25–35.

7
Conclusions

The main message of this book is that property is risky and that understanding the value of information is vital in terms of achieving positive abnormal returns.

Any technique used to analyse property investments which fails to take this into consideration is likely to lead to sub-optimal decisions. Similarly measuring the performance of investment decisions after the event without acknowledging the importance of risk is also likely to result in the true position being misinterpreted.

If property investors operated in a world where risk did not matter these issues would not be important. However, institutional investment is becoming increasingly more complex and professional advisors are having to compete with the growing sophistication of other markets. It is probably competition from other markets that is to have the greatest impact on the way property advisors behave in the future.

It is interesting to note that following deregulation and the subsequent collapse of the stock market there has been a greater interest in risk models derived from portfolio theory. Most if not all the major pension funds now tend to use some form of risk-based model as the means of developing investment strategy. The current downturn in the property market may well kindle a similar level of interest.

This book has tried to show that property has a number of favourable characteristics which encourages its inclusion within mixed-asset portfolios. For example property is one of the few assets which can be regarded as a complete hedge against inflation. It is also extremely valuable for diversifying mixed-asset portfolios because its returns have low correlation with other assets. There are opportunities too for capitalizing on information and turning it to the advantage of the investor. On the negative side we know that property is lumpy and can be difficult to sell at times. It also depreciates and can become technically obsolete. With skilful management, however, these aspects can be turned to advantage.

Property therefore offers many challenges to the institutional investor. However to aim for positive abnormal returns on a consistent basis requires a clear understanding of the underlying investment principles. This in turn provides clear messages about the way the research function should develop.

It has been shown that the principal aim of investment is to achieve added value through the generation of positive net present value. As discussed in Chapter 1 this is a sensible criterion to pursue. The main feature of this approach is that properties and locations should be sought which have the potential for offering positive abnormal returns. The research function should therefore be concerned with two things. The first is being able to forecast what the market is going to do over defined periods and the second is to identify those properties which are under-priced relative to the forecasts. This must of course be done on a risk-adjusted basis. Although the process is very straightforward in practice it is difficult to achieve. Because there is much noise and poor information affecting property returns it is difficult to make clear decisions.

It is also difficult to know whether observed information has real value in determining whether a property is under- or over-priced. It is here that the development of comprehensive databases of property will begin to reap rewards. Multi-factor models can be developed which will help to explain those factors which have an impact on value. Knowing the sensitivity of property to certain explanatory variables it is then possible to use this information to help in the search for under-priced properties. This approach has a long pedigree in the equity field but as yet is still in its infancy as far as property is concerned. Nevertheless it is likely that this could be one of the main thrusts that will develop over the next several years.

It is clear that considerable amounts of money are being committed to the development of equity risk models in an attempt to identify under-priced stocks with a view to out-performing the index. The margins for making such gains in equities are very narrow. However in the property field we know that there are likely to be more opportunitites for identifying under-priced assets. This is particularly the case where information is localized and access to information may be restricted. The fact that the search for such properties is not done in a way which is related to the compensation required for different levels of risk is evidenced by the difficulty in achieving superior returns on a consistent basis. If all properties were being acquired on the assumption that they were under-priced it should be possible to show empirically that property companies always have positive abnormal returns. This however is not the case.

Part of the problem is education: building up awareness of the type of models which should be developed. Fortunately the position is changing. There are now a number of courses which consider property in a broader context and introduce the student to the implications of modern portfolio theory. Successful graduates with MBAs and MScs are better equipped to make judgements concerning the expected return characteristics of property investments and in the future will demand the use of risk models. This is particularly true of the fund managers with a finance and investment background whose principal interest is in managing mixed-asset portfolios and who currently has access to equity optimization models.

The professional response to these trends has been gradual. Managing the change has been slow but most of the larger firms of chartered surveyors now have research departments, as do some of the institutions. The growth of independent research organizations is also seen as an important part of this trend and the collection and analysis of data is now seen to be vital to property organizations in the quest for competitive advantage. Similarly the need to forecast future market movements is also seen as a major part of understanding property.

What should not be overlooked is that quantitative models of investment behaviour can only provide insights to what is happening in the market. They cannot provide definitive answers. There is bound to be a complex interaction between people which is always difficult to quantify. There is considerable danger in believing that if a model produces an answer it is bound to be correct because it has been run through a computer. Financial models cannot produce all the answers without careful interpretation. If poor information is fed in then the answers that are produced will be poor. The message from this is that the output from computer-generated analyses need careful study if they are to have value and be used in guiding the future strategy of the portfolio.

One of the most useful spin-offs of developing the types of model described in this book is that they are able to question long-held beliefs concerning the market. Common beliefs concerning diversification for example have been shown to be invalid. This can give rise to the search for different types of property or of constructing portfolios in different ways.

But what of the future? The analysis of property based on past history has its place but it is probably more interesting to speculate on future directions. One of the most significant aspects affecting all the investment markets is the growing acceptance of computers in investment management. Not only is the cost of hardware dropping rapidly, it is being accompanied by a significant increase in computing power. Complex portfolio models which, twenty years ago, took several hours to run can now be processed in a matter of minutes. This exponential growth in power is likely to continue for some time and have a profound effect on all our lives.

As far as property is concerned what was considered impossible or unrealistic will become common. For example it is quite conceivable that in the near future screen-based systems will be providing all the vital information and projections required to make a sound investment decision related to various scenarios of future market movements with databases of property being scanned and analysed to find inefficiencies in the market.

Portfolio strategy and performance measurement is also likely to take on new dimensions by incorporating risk. This in turn will lead to the development of new property-based investment products aimed at improving the trade-off between risk and return. A good example of this has been the work undertaken by Richard Ellis in the development of unitized property. Apart from the original reason for developing this new market, it represents a significant move towards investors being able to take variable positions in property. This goes a long way towards overcoming many of the problems associated with creating sub-optimal portfolios when the investor has little control over property weights. Although there have been a number of problems encountered in developing this market it is nevertheless one which should be encouraged. If sufficient properties could be unitized in different risk classes then there is considerable scope for using market models to optimize portfolios by recommending the acquisition of variable positions in different classes of property. This could have a beneficial effect on controlling the risk class of a portfolio.

In developing new ideas in property it is essential to base them on sound information derived from empirical research concerning the market. Despite the growing body of research there are still a great many areas where our knowledge is limited. The following list identifies the main areas, some of which have been covered in this book:

1. investment strategy;
2. performance measurement;
3. asset allocation;
4. multi-factor models;
5. forecasting models;
6. valuation models;
7. property-based financial products.

Each of these is important and needs to be researched in more depth in order to establish professional credibility in a changing market. The emphasis should be on a clear understanding of the underlying economics backed by sound empirical research developed from data-bases of property information. If this is not done then there is considerable danger that in the future the decision to invest will be made by non-property people who have analysed the property market in a completely different way bringing to bear those techniques which are commonplace in other markets. If this happens then the property profession will take on the rôle of providing information rather than advising.

The trend towards justifying property investment decisions in rela-tion to the risks being taken is already here. It is up to the property professionals to acquire the skills essential to develop the techniques needed for developing innovative solutions.

It is my belief that approaching these problems through an under-standing of the capital markets will result in solutions which are economically defensible and which will provide greater insights of one of the major investment markets.

Bibliography

The following bibliography includes a number of books and papers from both the property and investment fields. The intention has been to give the reader with little knowledge of finance some indication of the main sources of information. To this end the bibliography has been categorized under headings relating to main issues.

The list is not comprehensive but should provide a useful source of information for further reading.

Arbitrage pricing model

Ross, S. (1976) The arbitrage theory of capital asset pricing. *Journal of Economic Theory*, **13**, 341–60.

Capital asset pricing model

Brown, K. C. and Brown, G. D. (1987) Does the composition of the market portfolio really matter? *Journal of Portfolio Management*.
Draper, D. W. and Findlay, M. C. (1982) Capital asset pricing and real estate valuation. *AREUEA Journal*.
Hamada, R. S. (1972) The effect of the firm's capital structure on the systematic risk of common stocks. *Journal of Finance*.
Roll, R. (1977) A critique of the asset pricing theory's tests. *Journal of Financial Economics*.

Capital market theory

Brennan, M. (1973) An approach to the valuation of uncertain income streams. *Journal of Finance*.
Brown, G. R. (1982) Making property investment decisions via capital market theory. *Journal of Valuation*.

Jensen, M. (1972) *Studies in the Theory of Capital Markets*, Praeger, New York.

Jensen, M. (1972) Capital markets: theory and evidence. *Bell Journal*.

Levy, H. and Sarnat, M. (1984) *Portfolio and Investment Selection*, Prentice Hall, New Jersey.

Sharpe, W. (1964) Capital asset prices: a theory of market equilibrium under conditions of risk. *Journal of Finance*.

Wofford, L. E. and Moses, E. A. (1978) Relationship between capital markets and real estate investment yields. *Real Estate Appraiser & Analyst*.

Corporate finance and investment

Brealey, R. and Myers, S. (1984) *Principles of Corporate Finance*, McGraw Hill, New York.

Brigham, E. (1985) *Financial Management*, Dryden, Chicago.

Copeland, T. E. and Weston, J. F. (1983) *Financial Theory and Corporate Policy*, Addison Wesley, Massachusetts.

Fama, E. and Miller, M. H. (1972) *The Theory of Finance*, Dryden Press, Hinsdale, Illinois.

Fisher, I. (1930) *The Theory of Interest*, Macmillan, London.

Francis, J. C. (1986) *Investments: Analysis and Management*, McGraw Hill.

Franks, J., Broyles, J. and Carleton, W. T. (1985) *Corporate Finance: Concepts and Applications*, Kent Publishing Co., Boston.

Jackson, A. S. and Townsend, E. C. (1970) *Financial Management*, George Harrap & Co Ltd.

Levy, H. and Sarnat, M. (1977) *Financial Decision-making Under Uncertainty*, Academic Press.

Lorie, J. H. and Hamilton, M. T. (1973) *The Stock Market: Theories and Evidence*, Richard D. Irwin, Homewood, Illinois.

McIntosh, A. P. J. and Sykes, S. G. (1984) *A Guide to Institutional Property Investment*, Macmillan, London.

Robichek, A. A. and Myers, S. C. (1965) *Optimal Financing Decisions*, Prentice Hall, New Jersey.

Rutterford, J. (1983) *Introduction to Stock Exchange Investment*, Macmillan, London.

Sharpe, W. (1985) *Investments*, Prentice Hall, New Jersey.

Smith, K. V. (1968) Alternative procedures for revising investment portfolios. *Journal of Financial & Quantitative Analysis*.

Van Horne, J. C. (1970) *Function and Analysis of Capital Market Rates*, Prentice Hall, New Jersey.

Van Horne, J. C. (1984) *Financial Markets and Flows*, Prentice Hall, New Jersey.

Efficient markets

Brown, G. R. (1984) The importance of information in assessing value. *Journal of Valuation*.

Brown, G. R. (1985) The information content of property valuations. *Journal of Valuation*.

Cootner, P. (1964) *The Random Character of Stock Market Prices*, MIT Cambridge.

Fama, E. (1970) Efficient capital markets: a review of theory and empirical work. *Journal of Finance*.

Fama, E., Fisher, L., Jensen, M. and Roll, R. (1969) The adjustment of stock prices to new information. *International Economic Review*.

Gau, G. (1984) Weak form tests of the efficiency of real estate investment markets. *The Financial Review*.

Jaffe, J. (1974) Special information and insider trading. *Journal of Business*.

Samuelson, P. (1965) Proof that properly anticipated prices fluctuate randomly. *Industrial Management Review*.

Forecasting

Box, G. E. P. and Jenkins, G. M. (1976) *Time Series Analysis, Forecasting and Control*, Holden Day, San Fransisco.

Maddala, G. S. (1977) *Econometrics*, McGraw Hill, New York.

Makridakis, S., Wheelwright, S. and McGee, V. (1983) *Forecasting: Methods and Applications*, John Wiley & Sons, New York.

Nelson, C. R. (1973) *Applied Time Series for Managerial Forecasting*, Holden Day, San Francisco.

Indices

Cootner, P. (1966) Stock market Indexes: Fallacies and Illusions, *Commercial & Financial Chronicle*.

Crowe, W. R. (1965) *Index Numbers*, MacDonald & Evans.

Fisher, L. (1966) Some new stock market indices. *Journal of Business*.

Hoag, J. W. (1980) Towards indices of real estate value and return. *Journal of Finance*.

Lorie, H. and Hamilton, M. T. (1978) Stock market indexes, in *Modern Developments in Investment Management*, Dryden Press, Illinois.

Inflation

Bodie, Z. (1976) Common stocks as a hedge against inflation. *Journal of Finance*.

Fama, E. and Schwert, G. W. (1977) Asset returns and inflation. *Journal of Financial Economics*.

Fraser, W. D. (1977) The valuation and analysis of leasehold investments in times of inflation. *Estates Gazette*.

Hartzell, D., Hekman, J. and Miles, M. (1986) Real estate returns and inflation, University of Texas Working Paper.

Hess, P. J. and Bicksler, J. L. (1975) Capital asset prices versus time series models as predictors of inflation. *Journal of Financial Economics*.

Limmack, R. J. and Ward, C. W. R. (1988) *Property Returns and Inflation*, Land Development Studies.

Performance measurement

Brown, G. R. (1985) Property investment and performance measurement: a reply. *Journal of Valuation*.

Brown, G. R. (1987) The performance of property bonds. *The Estates Gazette*.

Burns, W. L. and Epley, D. R. (1982) The performance of portfolios of REITS and stocks. *Journal of Portfolio Management*.

Cullen, T. F. and Blake, B. (1980) How does real estate as an investment compare with stocks and bonds? *Trusts and Estates*.

Dimson, E. (1978) Measuring investment performance. *The Investment Analyst*.

Dimson, E. and Marsh, P. (1981) New approaches to measuring share selection skills. *The Investment Analyst*.

Fama, E. (1972) Components of investment performance. *Journal of Finance*.

Friend, I. and Blume, M. (1970) Measurement of portfolio performance under uncertainty. *American Economic Review*.

Jensen, M. (1968) The performance of mutual funds in the period 1945–64. *Journal of Finance*.

Lehmann, B. and Modest, D. M. (1987) Mutual fund performance evaluation: a comparison of benchmarks and benchmark comparisons. *Journal of Finance*.

Moses, E. A., Cheyney, J. M. and Veit, E. T. (1987) A new and more complete performance measure. *Journal of Portfolio Management*.

Prodano, S. (1987) *Pension Funds: Investment and Performance*, Gower Publishing Company.

Roulac, S. E. (1976) Can real estate outperform common stock? *Journal of Portfolio Management*.

Sharpe, W. (1966) Mutual fund performance. *Journal of Business*.

Wendt, P. F. and Wong, S. N. (1965) Investment performance of common stocks versus apartment houses. *Journal of Finance*.

Portfolio theory

Black, F. (1972) Capital market equilibrium with restricted borrowing. *Journal of Business*.

Brown, G. R. (1985) Explaining portfolio performance. *The Estates Gazette*.

Brown, G. R. (1988) Reducing the dispersion of returns in real estate portfolios. *Journal of Valuation*, **6**, (2).

Chen, S. N. (1987) Simple optimal asset allocation under uncertainty. *Journal of Portfolio Management*.

Cohen, K. J. and Pogue, J. A. (1967) An empirical evaluation of alternative portfolio selection models. *Journal of Business*.

Elton, E. and Gruber, M. J. (1981) *Modern Portfolio Theory and Investment Analysis*, John Wiley & Sons.

Elton, E. J. and Gruber, M. J. (1977) Risk reduction and portfolio size: an empirical analysis. *Journal of Business*.

Elton, E. J., Gruber, M. J. and Padberg, M. W. (1978) Optimal portfolios from simple ranking devices. *Journal of Portfolio Management*.

Evans, E. J. and Archer, S. H. (1968) Diversification and the reduction of dispersion: an empirical analysis. *Journal of Finance*.

Fama, E. (1968) Risk, return and equilibrium: some clarifying comments. *Journal of Finance*.

Fama, E. (1976) *Foundations of Finance*, Basil Blackwell, Oxford.

Findlay, M., Hamilton, C. W., Messner, S. D. and Yormark, J. S. (1979) Optimal real estate portfolios. *AREUEA Journal*.

Findlay, M. *et al.* (1983) *Real Estate Portfolio Analysis*, Lexington Books, Massachusetts.

Firstenberg, P. B., Ross, S. A. and Zisler, R. C. (1987) Managing real estate portfolios. *Real Estate Research*.

Fogler, R. H. (1984) 20% in real estate: can theory justify it? *Journal of Portfolio Management*.

Francis, J. C. and Archer, S. H. (1979) *Portfolio Analysis*, Prentice Hall, New Jersey.

Friedman, H. C. (1970) Real-estate investment and portfolio theory. *Journal of Financial and Quantitative Analysis*.

Grissom, T. V., Kuhle, J. L. and Walther, C. H. (1987) Diversification works in real estate, too. *Journal of Portfolio Management*.

Hartzell, D., Hekman, J. and Miles, M. (1986) Diversification categories in investment real estate. *AREUEA Journal* **14**, (2).

Markowitz, H. (1956) The optimization of a quadratic function subject to linear constraints. *Naval Research Logistics Quarterly*.

Markowitz, H. (1959) *Portfolio Selection: Efficient Diversification of Investments*, Yale University Press.

Roulac, S. E. (1978) Influence of capital market theory on real estate returns and the value of economic analysis. *Real Estate Appraiser and Analyst*.

Rubinstein, M. (1973) A mean-variance synthesis of corporate financial theory. *Journal of Finance*.

Rudd, A. and Clasing, H. K. (1982) *Modern Portfolio Theory: The Principles of Investment Management*, Dow Jones Irwin.

Samuelson, P. (1967) General proof that diversification pays. *Journal of Financial and Quantitative Analysis*.

Sharpe, W. (1970) *Portfolio Theory and Capital Markets*, McGraw Hill.

Webb, J. R. and Sirmans, C. F. (1980) Yields and risk measures for real estate. *Journal of Portfolio Management*.

Risk analysis

Hertz, D. B. and Thomas, H. (1983) *Risk Analysis and its Applications*, John Wiley & Sons.
Hillier, F. S. (1963) The derivation of probabilistic information for the evaluation of risky investments. *Management Science*, 9.
Hull, J. C. (1980) *The Evaluation of Risk in Business Investment*, Pergamon Press.
Sykes, S. (1983) The assessment of property risk. *Journal of Valuation*.

Term structure

Michaelson, J. B. (1973) *The Term Structure of Interest Rates*, Intext Inc.
Nelson, C. R. (1972) *The Term Structure of Interest Rates*, Basic Books, New York.

Valuation

Baum, A. (1982) The enigma of the short leasehold. *Journal of Valuation*.
Baum, A. (1984) The valuation of reversionary freeholds: a review. *Journal of Valuation*.
Baum, A. (1984) The all risks yield: exposing the implicit. *Journal of Valuation*.
Baum, A. and Butler, D. (1986) The valuation of short leasehold investments. *Journal of Valuation*.
Baum, A. and Crosby, N. (1988) *Property Investment Appraisal*, Routledge, London.
Baum, A. and Yu, S. M. (1985) The valuation leaseholds: a review. *Journal of Valuation*.
Bierman, H. (1982) *The Lease versus Buy Decision*, Prentice Hall, New Jersey.
Bowcock, P. (1983) The valuation of varying incomes. *Journal of Valuation*.
Brown, G. R. (1984) Assessing an all-risks yield. *The Estates Gazette*.
Brown, G. R. (1986) A certainty equivalent expectations model for estimating the systematic risk of property investments. *Journal of Valuation*.
Crosby, N. (1983) The investment method of valuation. *Journal of Valuation*.
Crosby, N. (1986) The application of equated yield and real value approaches to market valuation. *Journal of Valuation*.
Crosby, N. (1987) A critical examination of the rational model, University of Reading.
Enever, N. (1981) The valuation of property investments. *Estates Gazette*.
Fraser, W. D. (1984) *Principles of Property Investment and Pricing*, Macmillan, London.
Fraser, W. D. (1985) Rational models or practical methods. *Journal of Valuation*.
Froland, C. (1987) What determines cap rates on real estate? *Journal of Portfolio Management*.
Marshall, P. (1976) Equated yield analysis. *Estates Gazette*.
Miles, M. and McCue, T. (1984) Commercial real estate returns. *AREUEA Journal*.

Ratcliff, R. (1965) *Modern Real Estate Valuation*, Democrat Press, Madison.
Shenkel, W. M. (1978) *Modern Real Estate Appraisal,* McGraw Hill, New York.
Sykes, S. (1981) Property valuation: a rational model. *The Investment Analyst*.
Williams, J. B. (1938) *Evaluation by the Rule of Present Worth*, Harvard University Press.
Zerbst, R. H. and Cambon, B. R. (1984) Historical returns on real estate investments. *Journal of Portfolio Management*.

Index

312   *Index*